best wishes

FROM EMS to EMU

Cover:
The cover graph shows GDP growth (white line) and inflation (private consumption deflator) (grey line) in the Eurozone, using outturn data for 1979 to 1997 from the OECD's December 1998 *Economic Outlook* and forecasts for 1998 to 2001 from the 'World Economy' report in the January 1999 *National Institute Economic Review*.

From EMS to EMU:
1979 to 1999 and Beyond

Edited by
David Cobham and George Zis

on behalf of the Money, Macro and Finance Research Group

First published in Great Britain 1999 by
MACMILLAN PRESS LTD
Houndmills, Basingstoke, Hampshire RG21 6XS and London
Companies and representatives throughout the world

A catalogue record for this book is available from the British Library.

ISBN 0–333–77091–9

 First published in the United States of America 1999 by
ST. MARTIN'S PRESS, INC.,
Scholarly and Reference Division,
175 Fifth Avenue, New York, N.Y. 10010

ISBN 0–312–22799–X

Library of Congress Cataloging-in-Publication Data
From EMS to EMU—1979 to 1999 and beyond / edited by David Cobham and
George Zis on behalf of the Money, Macro and Finance Research
Group.
     p.   cm.
"Papers presented at a conference held under the auspices of the
Money, Macro and Finance Research Group on 30 January 1999 at the
London Business School, a date nearly thirty years from the start of
the European Monetary System and one month after the inauguration of
Economic and Monetary Union in Europe"—Introd.
Includes bibliographical references and index.
ISBN 0–312–22799–X (cloth)
     1. Monetary unions—European Union countries—Congresses.
     2. European Monetary System (Organization)—Congresses.   3. European
Monetary Union—Congresses.   I. Cobham, David P.   II. Zis, George.
III. Money, Macro, and Finance Research Group.
HG925.F76   1999
332.4'94—dc21   99–36944
                                                                                  CIP

Contents

List of Figures

List of Tables

List of Tables

Contributors

Christopher Allsopp, Oxford University

Yunus Aksoy, Catholic University of Leuven

Ignazio Angeloni, European Central Bank

Michael Artis, European University Institute and CEPR

Stephen Bazen, Université Montesquieu-Bordeaux IV

Joe Bisignano, Bank for International Settlements

Vincenzo Chiorazzo, Crediop and Centro Europa Ricerche

David Cobham, University of St Andrews

John Curtice, University of Strathclyde

Hans Dewachter, Catholic University of Leuven

Paul De Grauwe, Catholic University of Leuven

John Driffill, University of Southampton

Vítor Gaspar, European Central Bank

Eric Girardin, Université Montesquieu-Bordeaux IV

Charles Goodhart, London School of Economics and Bank of England Monetary Policy Committee

Andrew Haldane, Bank of England

Paul Mizen, University of Nottingham and CEPR

Robert Pringle, Central Banking Publications

Luigi Spaventa, University of Rome La Sapienza (on leave), CONSOB and CEPR

Philip Stephens, *Financial Times*

Rolf Strauch, ZEI, University of Bonn

Alan Sutherland, University of York

Oreste Tristani, European Central Bank

Matthew Turner, Central Banking Publications

Jürgen von Hagen, ZEI, University of Bonn, Indiana University and CEPR

Martin Weale, National Institute of Economic and Social Research

George Zis, Manchester Metropolitan University

1 Introduction

David Cobham and George Zis

This book contains the papers presented at a conference held under the auspices of the Money, Macro and Finance Research Group on 30 January 1999 at the London Business School, a date nearly thirty years from the start of the European Monetary System (EMS) and one month after the inauguration of Economic and Monetary Union (EMU) in Europe.

Chapter 2 is the keynote paper presented at the conference by Vítor Gaspar, Director General of Research at the European Central Bank (ECB), on the monetary policy strategy of the ECB. The paper explains the reasons why the ECB had to adopt a new type of strategy, and sets out the various elements of that strategy, from the definition of price stability and the role of monetary aggregates through the ECB's 'broad assessment' of the prospects for price stability to the operational framework.

In Chapter 3 George Zis looks back to the start of the EMS, underlining the importance of political factors in the creation of the system and contrasting the relatively successful outcome with the gloomy predictions and critiques made by many observers at the beginning. Zis attributes to the EMS an 'unexpected success', but one which should have been anticipated.

Chapters 4, 5 and 6 explore the experiences of the three largest countries in EMU in trying to satisfy the Maastricht criteria in the period before the decision was taken on which countries were qualified to join. Jürgen von Hagen and Rolf Strauch analyse the development of German fiscal deficits and debt over the 1990s, and Germany's difficulties in meeting the criteria, in terms of the way in which the government chose to respond to German unification. They argue that, while externally the German government argued for tight fiscal constraints for EMU, domestically it allowed a significant weakening of Germany's budgetary institutions which will have continuing adverse implications for German fiscal discipline.

Stephen Bazen and Eric Girardin assess both the nature of the fiscal retrenchment undertaken in France in its effort to meet the criteria and the extent of adjustment in the labour market. They find that the fiscal retrenchment was unconvincing and that, while the labour market is more flexible than sometimes assumed, the changes in it have not been deep enough to allow an easy solution to the problem of high unemployment.

Vincenzo Chiorazzo and Luigi Spaventa explain how Italy managed to qualify for EMU despite widespread scepticism and even political hostility. Their conclusion is that Italy did indeed play a 'confidence trick' (through the effect of growing credibility on the government's debt service costs), but this was possible only because Italy had in fact managed to achieve a substantial, although messy, fiscal adjustment in the first half of the 1990s.

Chapters 7 and 8 explore the economics and the politics, respectively, of possible UK entry into EMU. Michael Artis reviews the findings of optimum currency area analyses on whether the UK should or should not be a member of EMU. His conclusion is that the economic case in favour of entry is uncompelling, but he also considers the limitations of such analyses and argues that possible political benefits might tip the balance in favour of membership, in which case the UK should enter 'later' but soon. John Curtice assesses the opinion poll evidence on UK attitudes to entry, which suggests continuing hostility. However, there are some signs that these attitudes could change, and Curtice advises the government, if it wishes to win a referendum, to declare its support for entry sooner rather than later.

The last three chapters consider the likely functioning of EMU. In Chapter 9 Paul De Grauwe, Hans Dewachter and Yunus Aksoy analyse the potential for conflict within the Governing Council of the ESCB (European System of Central Banks) resulting from asymmetric shocks and different transmission mechanisms, under alternative voting procedures. They find that the views of the ECB Board (if it is cohesive) are likely to prevail, and that member countries stand to benefit from decisions made on the basis of a Euroland-wide rather than of a purely nationalistic perspective.

In Chapter 10 Robert Pringle and Matthew Turner assess the likely relationships under EMU between the national central banks and the ECB. They play down concerns about the effect of the governance structure of the ESCB on monetary policy decisions, on the lack of clarity regarding the exercise of the function of lender of last resort, and about the location of responsibility for banking supervision, arguing that the challenges involved can be, and are likely to be, met by good policy and management.

In Chapter 11 Paul Mizen investigates whether the euro is likely to become not just a major currency but also an international currency. In his view it will become an important international currency, but it is unlikely to overtake the dollar.

Finally, the Epilogue by David Cobham makes some further comments on the prospects for EMU under three headings: the process of monetary integration, the strategy of the ECB, and the question of UK membership.

2 The Monetary Policy Strategy of the ECB*

Ignazio Angeloni, Vítor Gaspar and Oreste Tristani

> The man of system... is often so enamoured with the supposed beauty of his own ideal plan of government, that he cannot suffer the smallest deviation from any part of it... He seems to imagine that he can arrange the elements of a great society with as much ease as the hand arranges different pieces upon a chessboard. He does not consider that the pieces upon the chessboard have no other principle of motion besides that which the hand impresses upon them; but that, in the great chessboard of human society, every single piece has a principle of motion of its own, altogether different from that which the legislature may choose to impress upon it. (Smith, 1759)

1 INTRODUCTION

Monetary policy is an ongoing process, whose implications can only be understood in conjunction with the broad economic context and with the goals that policy itself is trying to achieve. Just as chess moves acquire meaning in succession, as part of the player's overall game plan, so sequences of policy actions are linked together with the underlying circumstances and goals by a rigorous, although flexible, logical thread. From Lucas' early contributions we learned that specific monetary policy actions have different impacts on economic agents depending on the overall policy framework according to which they are conducted. It is the *monetary policy strategy* – in short, the framework that a central bank uses to translate relevant information into actions and to publicly explain such actions – that really matters when it comes to affecting market expectations and, indirectly, economic behaviour and outcomes.

From this perspective, the European Central Bank (ECB) actually started 'making policy' (specifically, explaining the strategy it intended to adopt) well before 4 January 1999. As early as in 1997, the European Monetary

---

* The opinions expressed are personal and do not necessarily reflect the views of the European Central Bank.

Institute (EMI) published substantive anticipations of the broad lines of the ECB operational framework and of other aspects of the strategy.[1] After its creation, in mid-1998, the ECB proceeded to gradually unveil further details, alongside the process of internal elaboration: key press releases and statements by the ECB president on this subject bear the dates of 13 October, 1 December, 22 December, 1998.[2]

The ECB strategy is, like the sections of the EU Treaty that deal with monetary policy, the result of a collective intellectual effort, combining many diverse experiences and influences into a consistent overall set. As for its antecedents, at least three sources of influence come to mind. First, the strategy reflects, and contributes to promote, the fundamental principles that have guided the process of European economic integration. Second, the strategy clearly bears the mark of recent monetary and economic history and the policy experience of the last decades, in particular the high levels of inflation recorded since the late 1960s. Third, the strategy also draws intellectual inspiration from the developments of economic theory in the same period, which in turn are closely connected with that economic history. The rest of the paper will deal mostly with the latter aspect, while presenting the ECB's monetary policy strategy. It is thus perhaps not pointless to make a brief reference here to the first two.

From the spirit of European integration, the ECB monetary policy strategy embodies the notion of *one* money as a component of a *single* market – for goods, labour, capital – operating under open and free competition. The link is most evident if we consider the strategy in a broad sense, to include the operational framework of monetary policy and the architecture of the payment system. Many aspects of this overall framework are intended to preserve or enhance the efficiency of the area-wide money and financial market. For example, the structure of the TARGET system is designed to ensure that uniform monetary conditions prevail in the Euro-area. This is a requirement equally essential for monetary policy and for facilitating a level playing field in the single financial market. All key features of the payments system and of the eligible collateral reflect a constant attention to avoiding market segmentation and promoting a high degree of capital mobility in the area. More broadly, all monetary policy instruments are intended to operate indirectly, in a market-friendly way. The overall result is at least as consistent with free and competitive markets as the overall framework formerly used by any participating central bank. Moreover, in accordance with the principle of subsidiarity, all operational tasks in the conduct of monetary policy are, wherever possible, delegated to National Central Banks (NCBs).

An even stronger link exists between the ECB strategy and our recent economic and monetary history. The birth of the ECB coincides, not by chance, with the end of a 30-year period of global monetary instability characterised by high inflation. The 'era of instability' started with excessive expansion of nominal demand in the US in the 1960s, associated with the Vietnam war build-up and government spending in general. From 1968 until the final break up in 1973 the 'Bretton Woods' system was clearly under strain. The impact on inflation was exacerbated by the first oil shock,[3] which occurred against the background of an already over-heated aggregate demand. In the subsequent propagation process, a prominent role was played by domestic factors, notably, the structural characteristics of goods and labour markets and the stance of monetary and fiscal policies. The outcome took the forms of economic recession, high inflation and unemployment, currency instability and misalignments, persistent public deficits, high and volatile interest rates. Europe still bears in its high level of unemployment a painful mark of that period.[4] Through this phase, the old monetary order, built on fixed exchange rates and anchored to gold via the dollar, was transformed into a multipolar system of purely fiat monies, where the credibility of central banks in the maintenance of price stability is the only anchor. It thus seems natural that the ECB strategy was designed in such a way as to incorporate all elements that, in light of this experience, could contribute to preserve the newly regained monetary stability.

The ECB strategy includes elements drawn from the strategies of the most successful central banks. First, and most fundamentally, the commitment to price stability as a primary policy goal. Second, the emphasis on monetary aggregates, that reflects the role that quantitative targets played in curbing inflation both in the US and Europe. Third, an awareness of the potential for instability in money demand, which suggests a role for money as a reference value rather than a target. Finally, the role assigned to a transparent, broadly based assessment of the outlook for, and the risks to, price stability, an element that has recently become central to the inflation targeting strategies adopted by some central banks. In the ECB strategy, these elements coexist and are intended to operate synergetically, in a flexible and forward looking manner.

The last, but not least important, reference point in the design of the strategy is represented by the macroeconomic and monetary literature, and especially the advances of the last three decades. These advances were closely related to the aforementioned period of monetary instability and can be seen as attempts to find ways to overcome the inflationary phase and to build the monetary policy credibility which is necessary to achieve a more orderly monetary system. Specifically, we refer to the following: in the earlier years, rational expectations, the critique of the inflation–unemployment trade-off, the analyses of the costs of inflation, the time inconsistency literature, the debate on rules versus discretion; more recently, the role assigned to institutional design with a view to enhancing central bank independence, the theory and practice of inflation targeting, the literature on monetary policy rules and on the conduct of policy under uncertainty. In the ECB monetary policy strategy, the elements produced by these debates are purposefully reflected and summarised, as will be discussed in the remainder of the paper.

Before starting our review of the analytical underpinnings of the ECB strategy, a caveat is in order: we have deliberately chosen not to discuss here the relationship between monetary policy and financial stability. This important question has attracted considerable attention in recent times, often from critics of the EU Treaty and of the strategy itself.[5] However, given that the focus of this chapter is mainly on the links between the ECB strategy and the macro-monetary literature, a thorough consideration of the financial stability issues would take us a long way from our line of argument. More importantly, contrary to the views recently expressed by some observers, we are convinced that the 'monetary framework' we discuss here – taken to include, again, the operational side – in no way constrains the 'financial stability framework' of the Euro-area, or its future evolution. There are four key elements in that framework: the information exchange between national supervisory agencies and the ECB; the effectiveness of the emergency liquidity-providing instruments; the cross-country sharing of the related costs; the international (that is, extra Euro-area) dimension of supervisory co-ordination. The single monetary policy has no implications for any of these elements. It does not enhance, nor prevent, the effective flow of supervisory information in the system. It allows for a multiplicity of instruments to be used to assist illiquid financial institutions. It imposes no constraint on cost sharing. Finally, it has no implications whatsoever for cross-border supervisory co-ordination.

The chapter is organised as follows. In Section 2, we discuss the reasons for adopting a new and original strategy. Each following section covers one building block of the overall framework for the stability-orientated monetary policy strategy. Section 3 deals with the definition of price stability, which is crucial for a precise understanding of the final goal of monetary policy. Section 4 describes the role of money in the strategy. Section 5 presents the broadly based assessment of the outlook for price developments and risks to price stability. Section 6 briefly presents the operational framework and section 7 concludes with a concise summary of money market developments during the first month of operation of the single monetary policy.

2 WHY A *NEW* STRATEGY?

As a key component of communication policy, the explanation of the monetary policy strategy is, for every central bank, an ongoing process. New elements are occasionally added, which modify, at the margin, the existing set of public knowledge about the central bank framework. The recent monetary history shows relatively few occasions where central banks have felt the need to announce, at one single point in time, radical changes in their strategies, to quickly affect market expectations or, more often in recent times, to adjust to changes in the institutional position of the central bank itself. Examples are the change of operational targets by the Fed (Federal Reserve System) in October 1979 or the approach taken by the Bank of England and other central banks adopting inflation targeting.

The announcement of the strategy of the ECB clearly represents another example of these relatively infrequent changes decided by central banks. As such, however, it differs markedly from previous examples in two key respects: the circumstances of the change and its intrinsic nature.

The circumstances – that is the external conditions prevailing when the change takes place – are much more favourable than the ones faced by other central banks in the recent past. While the latter were sometimes 'forced' to modify their monetary policy strategy in order to curb rising inflation expectations, for example after the abandonment of an exchange rate targeting regime, the ECB has been established in a period of current and expected price stability. Consequently, the ECB finds itself in a position in which there is no urgency to give a signal of a renewed anti-inflationary determination with respect to the behaviour of the participating NCBs. On the contrary, the ECB is quite content to provide a signal of *continuity* with respect to the past, in order to inherit the anti-inflationary credibility earned by the participating NCB with the best track record. Thus, there is no need to underline the adoption of the new strategy through a communication device suitable for financial market audiences and for the general public. The discussion of policy decisions and the analysis of current macroeconomic conditions can continue to take place in official publications, such as periodic bulletins, that have traditionally been used by central banks to these ends.

This decision is in contrast with that taken by other central banks that have recently changed strategy. These banks have felt the need to distance themselves from the past and, consequently, to mark the change of the strategy with the creation of new means of communication: for example, the so-called 'inflation reports'. Since this decision was, in many instances, accompanied by a renewed emphasis on transparency, it has been argued that the inflation report constitutes in itself a means to enhance transparency. However, no economic reason appears to be involved in the choice of the name of the publication in which the central bank explains its policy choices. Hence, we would argue that the emphasis often put in the academic literature on the need to publish a separate report on inflation is misplaced.

In spite of the more favourable circumstances discussed above, the nature of the strategy change undertaken by the ECB has, in other respects, been more extreme. For the strategy has not simply been changed, but it has been built entirely 'from scratch', for a newly created monetary area.

While the example of existing central banks has always been a key element in the preparation of the ECB strategy, from the very beginning it has been clear that no existing monetary policy frameworks could work if transferred, without modification, into the very specific circumstances likely to prevail at the beginning of Stage Three.[6] The switch to a common currency entails changes in at least two areas. First, the new policy environment can have potentially profound effects on private agents' behaviour, for the reasons made popular by Lucas (1976) in his famous 'critique'. Changes can take place in a variety of economic areas, from private savings to fixed and inventory investment, from financial to pricing decisions of firms, from banks' behaviour to households' portfolio allocation. Through expectations, the entire process of monetary transmission could be affected. Second, another facet of the regime shift is the discontinuity it induces in statistical information. Some Euro-area data series have only recently been constructed or harmonised according to newly adopted definitions. Some of the new series were simply non-existent before, and there is sometimes relatively little knowledge of their economic characteristics due to the lack of sufficiently long data series to conduct reliable econometric estimates. Until the concept and methodologies underlying the new aggregates are fine tuned by the statistical offices, newly defined series can be subject to more frequent or marked revisions, which can make the newly released figures temporarily less reliable relative to past, country-specific data. To summarise, the ECB does not just face the problem that few economic relationships could be considered well known for the euro data *before* the changeover to the single currency, but also that these relationships could change *after* the establishment of the EMU.

The presence of uncertainty about the impact of the regime shift on economic behaviour and on statistical information would have made particularly problematic a straightforward application to the ECB of any existing monetary policy strategy. This holds also, and in particular, for the two strategies most commonly proposed, and the ones that the EMI (1997b) singled out as potentially applicable to the ECB: the pure version of monetary targeting and direct inflation targeting. While both strategies present attractive features, neither of the two could be applied directly to the single monetary policy. Before discussing the reasons in more detail, it is perhaps worth emphasising what exactly we mean when using these two definitions. A clarification is in order because in the academic literature this distinction becomes blurred once so-called 'pure' strategies are ruled out.

Following the literature on 'targets, instruments and indicators',[7] we define monetary targeting (MT) as a rule in which the central bank announces a growth path for a chosen monetary aggregate and acts, within a given (not too short) period of time (the 'targeting period') as if that growth path was actually its final target (the 'intermediate target' is 'final' in the interim period). Such a strict version of MT has been shown, on theoretical grounds, to be optimal only under very restrictive and unrealistic circumstances.[8] In practice, however, some central banks, notably the Bundesbank, have successfully used a monetary targeting framework to present their behaviour in a systematic and time consistent way, while using the information conveyed by monetary aggregates flexibly and pragmatically.[9] Such a 'practical' version requires that information on money can be exploited to pre-empt movements in prices, a milder requirement than that implied by the strict version of MT. The central bank treats unexpected developments in monetary aggregates as signals of future price changes, leading to changes of the policy instrument in such a way as to offset these developments.

By direct inflation targeting (DIT) we mean a strategy in which the central bank announces a desired profile for future inflation and pursues it by adjusting its monetary policy instruments to all available information.[10] Relevant indicators are chosen and weighted depending on the information that, according to empirical evidence, they possess about the final goal. Proponents of DIT normally associate this strategy with a high degree of transparency: the central bank is typically asked to disclose all details concerning its own subjective distribution of future inflation and its own policy reaction rule. Such a rule may take the form of an 'inflation forecast targeting rule',[11] as the central bank attempts to set policy in a way to make its own conditional forecast equal to the target. The first key element of DIT is thus an 'informational approach' to the interpretation of economic indicators;[12] monetary aggregates, as other potential leading variables, are relevant if they contain information on future inflation. The second, normally associated with it but logically separate, is full transparency, applied to all information available to the central bank.

A number of reasons connected to the peculiarity of the 'regime change' discouraged the adoption of either strategy by the ECB.

A strict version of MT requires a high degree of confidence in the leading indicator properties of the selected monetary aggregate over prices at the short- to medium-term horizon. A large amount of existing empirical tests suggests that broad area-wide monetary aggregates have enjoyed these properties until now,[13] but it is not certain that they will continue to do so after the adoption of the single currency. When related to the properties of monetary aggregates, the general 'structural break problem' is sometimes expressed in the form of the Arnold critique. Arnold (1994) argued that the good performance of area-wide aggregates, sometimes superior to that of national aggregates, is a normal statistical result of the aggregation procedure, which tends to average out national idiosyncratic shocks. According to this view, the satisfactory properties of EMU-wide aggregates will disappear as monetary union enhances the integration of monetary and financial markets and the synchronisation of shocks.

The risks prefigured in the Arnold critique may turn out to be of limited quantitative relevance. Fagan and Henry (1998) have carried out simulations showing that a larger incidence of common shocks would not have disruptive effects on the behaviour of area-wide monetary aggregates. Nonetheless, their potentially greater instability in the EMU represents an important drawback for the adoption of strict MT by the Eurosystem.[14]

Inflation targeting, in particular in its *operational* version of inflation-forecast targeting, is argued by its proponents to be capable of taking into account all the information available to the central bank. It would therefore allow the central bank to continuously adapt its implicit interest-setting rule as new information on the functioning of the economy is released or learnt. Its advocates would therefore argue that it is also suitable for especially uncertain conditions such as those currently faced by the ECB.

Inflation targeting, however, is based on the assumption that a few basic properties of the monetary policy transmission process are well known, so that the *true* (even if possibly complex) model of the functioning of monetary economies can be specified in order to find the optimal policy rule. As argued by McCallum (1997b), however:

such an argument fails entirely to recognise one basic and fundamental difficulty that underlies a large fraction of the issues concerning monetary policy
rules. This difficulty stems from the lack of professional agreement concerning
the appropriate specification of a model suitable for the analysis of monetary
policy issues.

In making monetary policy for the real world, the ECB must take this
lack of agreement into account, thereby avoiding a strategy based entirely
on any one view of the functioning of monetary economies. The need to
adopt such a 'conservative' approach is obviously reinforced by the lack of
conclusive empirical evidence on the monetary transmission process in the
Euro-area, which could in principle help to discriminate among different
theoretical models.

Another argument against the adoption of inflation targeting by the
Eurosystem is that this choice would amount to dismissing the previous
experience of the Bundesbank. In this respect, EMI (1997b) suggests that
monetary targeting

> would offer the advantage of ensuring continuity with the strategy of the EU
> central bank which has performed an anchor function in the ERM [exchange
> rate mechanism], in view of its long-term track record of fighting inflation.
> Following a monetary targeting strategy might therefore help the Eurosystem to
> inherit credibility from the start of its operations.

To summarise, the single monetary policy faces very special problems
that tend to discourage the straightforward adoption of any of the currently
employed monetary policy strategies. The uncertainties involved in the
adoption of a common currency in the participating member states creates
the need for a strategy capable of communicating both the long-term
commitment to price stability and the special conditions faced at the start
of the EMU.

Accordingly, the 'stability-orientated monetary policy strategy'
announced by the ECB constitutes a new framework for monetary policy,
drawing elements from previously used strategies in a way that aims at
ensuring the best combination of effectiveness, transparency, accountability, forward-looking orientation, clarity, and continuity with past and
successful strategies.[15] It is characterised by a number of distinct elements,
that will be reviewed in detail in the coming sections. The central feature is
the announcement of a precise, quantitative definition of price stability. In
order to achieve the objective of price stability, a strategy based on two

'pillars' is adopted. The first pillar attributes a special role to money among the monitored variables. Money announcements take the form of reference values, not of strict targets, meaning that significant deviations from announced paths will only normally, but not invariably, warrant changes in the monetary policy stance. In this way, the ECB recognises economists' imprecise knowledge of the true model describing the functioning of monetary economies. The second, complementary pillar is a broad-based assessment of the prospects for price stability, in which all potentially useful indicators are taken into account. As in the 'informational approach' to monetary policy, available indicators are weighted in relation to the informational value they possess with respect to future price developments.

The stability-orientated strategy is a framework, rather than an ironclad rule (see Bernanke and Mishkin, 1997, and Bernanke *et al.*, 1999). In terms of the recent distinction made in the theory between target and instrument rules (Svensson, especially 1998c), the full information approach adopted by the ECB can be interpreted as a target rule. Thus, the ECB will base all its decisions on the scrutiny, at each moment in time, of all the variables relevant for the evaluation of prospective price developments and for the assessment of the risks to price stability. In this respect, the kind of indicators monitored by the ECB is likely to change over time as the understanding of the functioning of the area-wide economy is improved and as enough observations allowing for more reliable statistical inference become available. The ensuing potential change of the information variables, however, will not modify the fundamental characteristic of the rule – the policy instrument will always be set in such a way as to avoid deviations from price stability over the medium term.[16]

The starting point of the full information analysis of the risks to price stability is an assessment of the signals arising from the reference value for money. This indicator provides a reference point for the evaluation of the prospects for price stability, through a simple framework which is robust across virtually all the existing models of monetary economies. In this respect, the role of money in the strategy presents a number of similarities with the role advocated for instrument rules (such as those put forward, most notably, by McCallum, 1988, and by Taylor, 1993).[17] Proponents of instrument rules, while aware of their sub-optimality within any single model, argue in their favour on the grounds of their robustness, that is of their capacity to deliver reasonably good outcomes irrespective of the interpretation scheme adopted. However, the reference value for money obviously differs from simple instrument rules because it does not directly express a rule for setting the monetary policy instrument – the interest rate.

3 DEFINING PRICE STABILITY

Although the EU Treaty prescribes price stability as the ESCB's primary goal, it does not provide any definition of price stability. The lack of a precise definition has been interpreted by some authors as leading to an insufficient degree of commitment to the final objective (see, for example, Romer and Romer, 1997), since the central bank could always define *ex post* price stability as the inflation rate it has effectively managed to achieve. The ECB's announcement of an operational, precise definition of price stability had already been recognised by the EMI as a necessary element of the future strategy. It was also acknowledged that a definition such as the one proposed by Alan Greenspan (1989) for the US ('price levels sufficiently stable so that expectations of change do not become major factors in key economic decisions') would not be sufficiently precise.

Accordingly, it was decided that 'price stability shall be defined as a year-on-year increase in the Harmonised Index of Consumer Prices (HICP) for the Euro-area of below 2 per cent'. Price stability 'is to be maintained over the medium term' (ECB, 1998b).

A number of characteristics of this definition must be emphasised (see also ECB, 1999a).

First, price stability is to be pursued 'over the medium term'. This emphasis reflects the acknowledgement that the timing of the effects of monetary policy is uncertain. Hence, the medium term is the relevant period over which monetary policy is responsible for price developments and over which its performance should be judged. The medium-term orientation is also compatible with a gradualist response to unforeseen exogenous shocks, which is typically necessary under model uncertainty (for example, Smets, 1998) and helpful to avoid the risk of introducing unnecessary variability in the interest rates.

The medium-term orientation is re-emphasised by the decision to refer to annual ('year-on-year') price increases. Seasonal movements or short term volatility of prices are of no direct interest for the conduct of the single monetary policy.

The definition of the objective in terms of 'price increases of less than two per cent' aims, through the use of the word 'increases', to exclude deflation from the definition of price stability. The definition of price stability is therefore symmetric, according to the wording used in Buiter (1998). Unlike the maximum, the minimum rate of increase of prices considered compatible with price stability is not made explicit simply because of the absence of reliable evidence on the measurement bias that may be associated with the HICP. This price index has only recently been developed, in connection with the need to evaluate price convergence during Stage II of the Economic and Monetary Union. It is therefore based on a relatively new methodology and extended time series are still not available, thus preventing the application of standard econometric methods to ascertain the likely measurement bias in the HICP.

It was also felt that the announcement of a definition of price stability in the form of a target range, with precise maximum and minimum levels, would easily lead to the interpretation that any possible price development outside the range would automatically entail a policy response. This risk is clearly perceived for example by Bernanke *et al.* (1999, p. 294): 'with target ranges in place, politicians, financial markets and the public often focus on whatever inflation is just outside or just inside the edge of the range, rather than on the magnitude of the deviation from the midpoint of the range'. Such an interpretation would be incorrect because, even if deviations from price stability would generally be met by a policy response, this response would not be mechanical. Thus, for example, a deviation from price stability in a given month, well known as being of a temporary nature, would not trigger a policy response: this is a direct consequence of the forward looking, medium-term orientation of monetary policy.

It was, however, deemed necessary to state a precise figure for the ceiling of price increases compatible with price stability. The choice of 2 per cent can be justified mainly on grounds of continuity. It is a value that has been used in the past by the Bundesbank, the central bank with the best record in terms of price stability, and has also appeared in the text of the European Union's Broad Economic Guidelines. Other reasons to allow for small, but non-zero inflation rates have been put forward in the literature. It is argued that keeping inflation 'too' low may be costly in terms of output volatility, for example due to the existence of nominal and real rigidities in relative prices and wages and the lower bound (at zero) to nominal interest rates. Recent estimates concerning the US economy (for example, Fuhrer and Madigan, 1997; Orphanides and Wieland, 1998) appear to indicate that the zero bound on nominal interest rates is unlikely to constitute a binding constraint for monetary policy when the inflation rate is just slightly higher than zero. Orphanides and Wieland (1998) conclude that 'the consequences of the zero bound are negligible for target inflation rates as low as 2 per cent. However, the effectiveness of the constraint becomes increasingly important to determine the effectiveness of policy with inflation targets between 0 and 1 per cent.' In spite of these results, the problem of determining a figure for the maximum rate of inflation compatible with price stability is far from settled. The aforementioned estimates are obviously sensitive to changes in a number of assumptions, for instance on the equilibrium level of the real interest rate. Moreover, it appears important to emphasise that most general equilibrium monetary models would provide no support for a positive *optimal* inflation rate. Whether a small, positive inflation rate can become optimal largely depends on the assumed price setting behaviour of private firms (Wolman, 1998).

Finally, it should be stressed that the mandate to maintain price stability refers to the Euro-area as a whole: no special attention will be paid to country- or sector-specific shocks, as long as they do not have a bearing on the HICP for the Euro-area. The HICP is the only available consumer price index that is sufficiently harmonised at the European Union level. EUROSTAT has devoted considerable attention to ensuring the widest possible coverage of the index. That process is still in progress, thus it is likely that the HICP will become an even better statistical product in the near future.

The announcement of precise figures for the rate of inflation to be considered consistent with price stability constitutes the most important step that has to be taken to achieve accountability. Accountability refers to the responsibility to be called to account, and such a responsibility hinges on the existence of an objective benchmark. It is in fact a necessary condition to allow a verification by independent third parties of the consistency of the central bank policy with its objective.

Some economists (most forcefully Svensson, 1997b, 1998c) argue, however, that such a condition is not sufficient and that the publication of the internal forecast of inflation should accompany the announcement of the objective. It must be acknowledged, however, that while the inflation objective is an unobservable variable which must be stated by the central bank, the same property does not apply to inflation forecasts. The emphasis on the need to publish the central bank's forecast would therefore seem to imply that the central bank retains some sort of asymmetric information on the outlook for price stability. On the contrary, the same proponents of the need to publish the forecast also find it 'unlikely that monetary authorities have much private information, relative to sophisticated outside observers, about the state of the economy and the behaviour of the economy' (Svensson, 1997b). We would then argue that, while certainly providing information on the central bank's ability as a professional forecaster, the publication of the forecast does not significantly matter as a means to increase accountability.

Nonetheless, the ECB is determined to publish its internal econometric models as soon as they have been sufficiently tested and found reliable. As concerns the publication of the forecast itself, however, it has been decided that a few conceptual problems still have to be solved before publication can be considered. Once it is assumed that central banks have virtually no private information as to the state of the economy, apart from on 'their own implicit goals and their corresponding plans for the future instruments' (Svensson, 1997b), then the information the forecast should primarily release is the planned future path for the policy rates. In its publications, the central bank should therefore consistently repeat that there are no risks to price stability in the medium term. It would also have to explain, however, that this constant forecast implies, over time, prolonged periods of increases or decreases of the interest rates, depending on the estimated impact of foreseeable exogenous shocks.

Such an explanation is likely to be hard to convey to the general public. This point of view appears to be implicitly shared by academics, whereby it is typically argued that the central bank should publish a *special kind of conditional forecast*, that is a forecast conditional not on the available information but on an unchanged-policy-rates hypothesis. This would obviously be a more suitable communication device, which would allow the central bank to argue for policy rates changes on the basis of a foreseeable worsening of the outlook for price stability. It would however be hardly transparent, in that it would not represent the *true* forecast of the central bank, but only an *ad hoc* communication device. Moreover, such a forecast would necessarily be internally inconsistent. For example, if a policy tightening were expected in the future, the term structure of interest rates would incorporate this expectation; an inflation forecast based on unchanged interest rates would obviously contradict this expectation and thus be the result of internally conflicting assumptions. Finally, and paradoxically, a forecast based on an unchanged path for the interest rates would effectively avoid disclosing the only piece of information – the projected path for policy rates – which is argued to be unobservable to private forecasters.

Once these caveats are borne in mind, the view that a central bank should disclose its assessment of the outlook for price stability and systematically explain the rationale behind all policy decisions is shared by the ECB. Accordingly, the stability-orientated strategy is characterised by a transparent approach to external communication: economic and inflationary prospects are extensively discussed in official publications, public speeches and parliamentary hearings by Executive Board and Governing Council members. More importantly, the reasoning behind monetary policy decisions is made public immediately after the Governing Council meeting by means of a press release and, at least once a month, a press conference.

4 THE ROLE OF MONEY

The role of money in the strategy is epitomised by the following two quotes from recent ECB President's statements:

First, money will be assigned a prominent role. This role will be signalled by the announcement of a quantitative reference value for the growth of a broad monetary aggregate. The reference value will be derived in a manner which is consistent with – and will serve to achieve – price stability.

Deviations of current monetary growth from the reference value would, under normal circumstances, signal risks to price stability. The ESCB will assess how best to counter these risks. However, the concept of a reference value does not imply a commitment on the part of the ESCB to mechanistically correct deviations of monetary growth from the reference value over the short term.

The relationship between actual monetary growth and the pre-announced reference value will be regularly and thoroughly analysed by the Governing Council of the ECB; the result of this analysis and its impact on monetary policy decisions will be explained to the public. The precise definition of the reference aggregate and the specific value of the quantitative reference value for monetary growth will be announced by the Governing Council of the ECB in December 1998.

However, while the monetary aggregates contain important and relevant information for monetary policy-making, monetary developments will not constitute a complete summary of all the information about the economy that needs to be known for an appropriate monetary policy to be set. (Introductory statement by the President, press conference of 13 October 1998)

The first reference value for monetary growth decided by the Governing Council, which plays a prominent role in the Governing Council's monetary policy assessment, will apply to the broad monetary aggregate M3 and has been set at an annual rate of $4\frac{1}{2}$%; it will be reviewed in December 1999. This rate is consistent with the maintenance of price stability according to the ESCB's published definition, while allowing for sustainable output growth. It has been derived by assuming that the trend growth rate of real GDP in the Euro-area is in the range of 2% to $2\frac{1}{2}$% per annum and the velocity of circulation of M3 declines at a trend rate of between $\frac{1}{2}$% and 1% each year. Further details related to the derivation of the reference rate and the definition of the broad aggregate M3 are described in a separate press statement to be released today. With regard to the reference value, let me stress two points very clearly.

First, the reference value for M3 growth has been derived in an explicit medium-term context, in line with the ESCB's monetary policy strategy. Analysis of monetary developments relative to the reference value will provide a firm anchor for the conduct of the stability-oriented single monetary policy.

Second, the ESCB's monetary policy strategy does not entail 'mechanistic' policy reactions to deviations of monetary growth from the announced reference value. In the first instance, deviations of monetary growth will be analysed thoroughly, in parallel with the broadly based assessment of the outlook for price developments. (Introductory statement by the President, press conference of 1 December, 1998)

The role of money that emerges from these quotes is quite different from that of money in 'textbook' versions of MT and DIT. As noted in section 4.1, the hallmark of MT is the existence of a 'targeting period' in which money is treated as a final target. That of DIT is the fact of viewing, somewhat agnostically, money as an information variable among all others, whose weight is determined empirically in relation to its information content on future price developments.

As already mentioned, the role of the reference value for money can be interpreted as that of a simple rule, selected for its robustness across economic models. It is based on the long-term unit-correlation between money and prices, which characterises virtually all economic models and which has been extensively found in empirical studies (see, most recently, McCandless and Weber, 1995). This correlation is a reminder of the fact that inflation is ultimately a monetary phenomenon and that significant deviations from price stability are always attributable to a certain degree of accommodation of exogenous shocks by the monetary authority.

The money stock is however not considered as a sufficient statistic of future inflation. Deviations of the rate of growth of money from an initially set value can easily take place simply as a result of velocity shocks, shocks that in a number of countries have proved to be quite persistent. Moreover, it has been demonstrated that a strict monetary policy rule whereby interest rates are set by the central bank solely on the basis of developments in the rate of growth of money would be sub-optimal, regardless of the occurrence of velocity shocks (Svensson, 1997).

However, these characteristics of the rate of growth of money do not suggest that it should not be considered as a key variable to be monitored. They simply highlight that such an analysis must be complemented by a wider, optimal assessment of the outlook for price stability. Thus, money is never, even temporarily, treated as a final objective. Deviations of money from the announcement are always considered for the information they are believed to convey about future price developments.

Three elements from the above quotes must be stressed (see also ECB, 1999a, b). First, the reference value is calculated in a way that is consistent with price stability. Monetary announcements must thus always correspond to the best (full information) conditional forecast of money in the medium term, given price stability. Second, the reference value has a medium-term connotation; this is the horizon over which a strong link between money and prices has been historically observed. This means that all information relevant for the calculation of the reference value – specifically, real growth and velocity changes – is related to medium-term trends, thus excluding short-term movements. In normal conditions, sizeable and persistent deviations of money from the reference value should be interpreted as signalling risks to price stability. Third, no mechanistic policy reaction to these deviations should be expected. Money developments will thus be analysed case by case, to identify the nature of the underlying shock; a marked departure from the 'intermediate target' approach inherent in MT.

The basis of the role of money in the strategy is supported by recent empirical analyses. Browne *et al.* (1997) and Fagan and Henry (1998) examined the cointegration properties of broad monetary aggregates in Europe; they found that cointegration exists with traditional money demand determinants. More recent and still unpublished research by the ECB, analysing the properties of EU-11 aggregates within a cointegrating model, found that:[18]

1. Cointegration among real money, real GDP, long- and short-term interest rates and inflation is confirmed at EU-11 level; cointegration is accepted more easily as one moves from narrow to broad monetary aggregates;
2. EU-11 monetary aggregates display good leading indicator properties with respect to prices; again, this holds increasingly as one moves from narrow to broad money definitions;
3. Short-run controllability of broad monetary aggregates – through the direct effect of interest rate changes – is, in general, weak or rejected altogether. Technically, this means that a monetary restriction does not bring about (for a given profile of prices and output) a significant decline of money growth relative to the baseline path. Controllability is, however, satisfied in the longer run, via the effect of interest rates on prices and output (see also Cabrero *et al.* 1998).

This evidence appears consistent with the three elements discussed above. The lack of short-run controllability, in particular, rules out the possibility of interpreting money as an intermediate target, but is fully consistent with an informational approach to the role of money in the strategy.

The above evidence also helps in settling a few more technical issues concerning the calculation of the reference value, to which we now turn.

First and foremost, on the definition of the monetary aggregate. The empirical evidence summarised above points to a clear stability versus controllability trade-off: when moving to broader monetary aggregates, gains in stability and leading indicator properties tend to be accompanied by a lower short-term control. The premises of the strategy clearly suggest that the preference should go to a broader definition. The chosen aggregate, labelled M3, is composed by all liabilities of monetary financial institutions with a maturity of less than two years, including repurchase agreements, bank issued securities and shares of money market funds.[19] Moreover, whereas M3 enjoys a special status as the basis for the reference value, narrower definitions (M1, M2) are also computed and published by the ECB.[20]

Several further technical issues arise in announcing the reference value. In particular: how the M3 path should be expressed; what time horizon it should refer to; whether a point value or a range should be used. Finally, in what form the analytical derivation of the reference value should be communicated to the public, so as to ensure a high degree of clarity and transparency.

On 1 December, 1999 the Governing Council issued the following announcements on the calculation of the reference value applicable at the start of Stage Three (see the above President's statement):

1. The underlying price assumption coincides with the price stability definition (that is, a year-on-year increase in the HICP for the Euro-area of less than 2 per cent).
2. Real GDP is assumed to grow at a trend rate between 2 and $2\frac{1}{2}$ per cent in the medium term.
3. The medium-term velocity of circulation of M3 is expected to decline by between $\frac{1}{2}$ and 1 per cent on an annual basis.
4. Taking all this into account, the reference value for M3 is set at $4\frac{1}{2}$ per cent. This value will be reviewed at the end of 1999.

Several remarks can be made concerning this announcement. First, no explicit time horizon is mentioned, but the intention is expressed to re-examine the reference value after the first year. This is consistent with the medium-term orientation of the strategy and also contributes to limit the so-called 'base drift'. Second, a point value rather than a range is announced. This avoids the risk that the Council may be wrongly expected to react automatically when M3 reaches the upper or lower end of a range. Most importantly from the viewpoint of external communication, the analytics of the reference value is expressed and explained by means of the simple 'quantity equation', that is the identity linking together money, its velocity, prices and output. This formulation is simple and transparent but at the same time does not rule out a structural interpretation of velocity and real growth. Considering the mid points of the ranges indicated for velocity and real growth, the 4½ per cent reference value for M3 is consistent with an annual increase of HICP equal to 1½ per cent, which is well within the definition of price stability.[21]

5 THE BROAD ASSESSMENT OF THE PROSPECTS FOR PRICE STABILITY

Whereas money is the central determinant of the inflation process in the long run, and therefore a key pillar in the ECB monetary policy strategy, a more comprehensive and broad based assessment of economic conditions is necessary. In this assessment, which constitutes the second pillar of the ECB strategy, a broad set of indicators is taken into account within a full information framework. Such a framework aims at ensuring that price stability is attained in a way that best contributes to collective welfare.

At first sight, the reference to a broad set of indicators in addition to money could appear contradictory with the premise that inflation is ultimately a monetary phenomenon. A hasty and simple minded syllogism could lead to the conclusion that money alone is relevant, but such a conclusion would reflect an excessively simplified view of the inflation process.

In the medium run (a time horizon that we view as intermediate between the short run – in which 'money does not matter' for prices – and the long run – in which 'only money matters') price developments are influenced by monetary policy as well as by a combination of non-monetary factors. In order to maintain price stability over the medium term, monetary policy must thus consider a broad range of indicators of price stability prospects. More importantly, medium-term deviations from price stability could also change the costs for monetary policy of restoring price stability over a longer term. For example, changes in inflationary expectations or in the market perception of central bank credibility, stemming from whatever source, can, if they become entrenched, increase the cost of stability-orientated monetary policies. So can other factors, such as fiscal policies or labour market developments. The central bank can, acting in a pre-emptive and forward-looking way, prevent or limit the worsening in the cost/benefit balance of stability-orientated monetary policy and contribute, in the longer run, to enhance its effectiveness.

In practice the choice and the interpretation of the relevant range of indicators is a complex task, which requires a flexible combination of theory, empirical evidence and statistical expertise. There are two relevant issues: *what* indicators should be looked at and *how* they should be combined in a coherent overall assessment. 'Looking at everything' in an unsystematic fashion comes close to 'looking at nothing'. The selection of indicators is obviously an ongoing process, that will proceed hand in hand with the development of area wide statistics and analytical tools. Due to space constraints, we limit ourselves here to a few preliminary remarks on what indicators may be relevant for a broad based assessment of inflationary prospects for the Euro-area, and what 'models' may prove most useful to support such analysis. Both issues are made particularly complex by the potential change in expectation formation mechanisms and economic relationships that the transition to Stage Three might bring about. For the purpose of presentation we can group potential indicators into five broad classes: 'gap' measures; labour cost measures; exchange rates and international prices; asset prices; direct (survey-based) measures of expectations.

As shown by a wide body of empirical literature,[22] *gap measures* (including output gaps, capacity utilisation and measures of labour market gaps such as unemployment[23]) are key elements in predicting inflationary pressures and in guiding central banks' actions. Their relevance tends to be higher the lower the degree of external opening of the economy, which determines the extent to which domestic prices are driven by domestic market conditions. As a consequence, gap measures will be more relevant for the Euro-area than they have been in the past monetary policy experience in each individual country. The main difficulty with gap measures is that they are often 'latent' variables, whose estimation is particularly difficult.[24] Obtaining reliable empirical measures of output and labour market gaps is a priority item in the present research agenda on the Euro-area economy, but not an easy one.

Labour cost measures (wage dynamics, unit labour costs) are easier to compute, since they are widely available at the individual country level. They have been empirically shown to be good short-term predictors of price dynamics. The main drawback is that they focus only on the very proximate determinants of inflation, overlooking the more fundamental underlying factors; focusing excessively on wage and labour cost measures may therefore entail the risk of an excessively shortsighted approach to anti-inflationary policy. It may also induce excessive emphasis on administrative income and wage policies as instruments for inflation control, overlooking the fact that these policies are often the result, not the cause, of more fundamental elements, including the credibility and social acceptance of price-stability orientated central bank policies.

Despite the fact that the degree of openness of the Euro-area is much lower than that of any of the participating countries, the *exchange rate* (and, by extension, *international prices*) remain a key element of a broad-based assessment of price stability prospects.[25] Prolonged exchange rate swings, even if originally inconsistent with developments in economic fundamentals, can become themselves causes of imbalances and inflationary or deflationary pressures. In the ECB strategy, exchange rates are considered not for their own sake, but for the effect they may have on the Euro-area price developments.

Finally, a key role will necessarily be assigned to *asset prices* other than exchange rates. The size and the role of asset markets in the monetary policy transmission process suggest that they should be assigned a high weight among relevant indicators. In particular, the yield curve has proved to be an invaluable tool for price stability orientated monetary policy strategies in Europe in the last decade, often providing a yardstick for inflation and fiscal convergence among potential EMU participants.[26] However, interpreting the yield curve and other asset prices is a particularly complex task, not only in light of the behavioural changes deriving from the transition to Stage Three. Particular caution must be exercised since asset prices are not only a link in the transmission process, but also a measure of market expectations of broad economic developments, including central bank actions. Multiple equilibria and policy-induced instability could result, if asset prices were used mechanically in monetary policy decision making.[27] From this point of view, *survey measures of expectations* may be subject to a similar criticism, although their relatively slower response to news reduces considerably the ensuing risk of policy instability.

This very short and necessarily incomplete review of relevant indicators cannot be concluded without a reference to the analytical framework that the ECB will use to filter the available information and translate it into input for policy action. Yet again, the need for a consistent and comprehensive 'model' must be weighed against the wide range of existing information and the potential behavioural changes stemming from the adoption of a single currency. Despite these and other complexities, we believe that the policy-making experience of most central banks in recent decades suggests that in-house structural econometric models are an invaluable tool for ensuring consistency in the internal debate, the current analysis and the external communication of a central bank. Hence, the ECB will devote significant resources to developing, maintaining and using econometric models for the Euro-area.

At this moment, the ECB relies on a quarterly macro-econometric model for the Euro-area and (in conjunction with the NCBs) a quarterly multi-country model. The Eurosystem performs broad forecasting exercises focusing on a broad range of economic variables allowing for a fair degree of detail and covering a number of years. These exercises use models but allow the exercise of judgement following a detailed analysis of the information available on the short-term developments and prospects in the Euro-area. The expertise and the wealth of information available in the various NCBs are precious in this context. The Eurosystem also performs narrow fore-casting exercises focusing on high time frequency developments in prices.

Macroeconomic models will not exhaust the range of tools that are used for monetary policy. In particular the Eurosystem does and will make use of more detailed as well as sectoral analyses to evaluate additional infor-mation that does not easily feed directly into the economy-wide models. In all cases, consistency should be ensured in the specification of models and the interpretation of different analytical results. The reconciliation of conflicting results often becomes, in itself, a source of insight and a stim-ulus for further research.

6 IMPLEMENTING THE STRATEGY: THE OPERATIONAL FRAMEWORK

As for all central banks, the operational framework of the Eurosystem is intended to comprise the set of instruments, and procedures, through which the system itself intervenes in the market to achieve its objectives, as defined by its monetary policy strategy.

Recent international experience of central banking practices has shown that a successful operational framework must satisfy at least three broad requirements. First, it must be consistent with the strategy, that is specifi-cally with the intermediate and final targets of monetary policy. In accor-dance with the EU Treaty, the framework must therefore be efficient in

Table 2.1 Eurosystem monetary policy operations

Monetary policy operations	Types of transactions		Maturity	Frequency	Procedure	Conditions applicable (period)
	Provision of liquidity	*Absorption of liquidity*				
Open market operations						
Main refinancing operations	Reverse transactions	–	Two weeks	Weekly	Standard tenders	3.0 per cent fixed rate tenders
Longer-term refinancing operations	Reverse transactions	–	Three months	Monthly	Standard tenders	Variable rate tenders
Fine-tuning operations	Reverse transactions; Foreign exchange swaps	Foreign exchange swaps; Collection of fixed-term deposits; Reverse transactions	Non-standardised	Non-regular	Quick tenders; Bilateral procedures	na
	Outright purchase	Outright sales	–	Non-regular	Bilateral procedures	
Structural operations	Reverse transactions	Issuance of debt certificates	Standardised/non-standardised	Regular and non-regular	Standard tenders	na
	Outright purchases	Outright sales	–	Non-regular	Bilateral procedures	
Standing facilities						
The marginal lending facility	Reverse transactions		Overnight	Access at the discretion of counterparties		2 per cent (from 1–3 Jan); 2.75 per cent (from 4–21 Jan); 2 per cent (from 22 Jan)
The deposit facility	–	Deposits	Overnight	Access at the discretion of counterparties		4.5 per cent (from 1–3 Jan); 3.25 per cent (from 1–3 Jan); 4.5 per cent (from 22 Jan)

attaining the price stability objective. This is ensured, in the context of the stability-orientated monetary policy strategy, by responding in an adequate and timely way to information coming from monetary aggregates (measured against the announced reference value) and the broad based assessment of the future price stability prospects. Second, it must ensure an effective communication between the central bank and the market. This means that through the operational framework the central bank must influence expectations in a way consistent with the attainment of the final goal; this implies, *inter alia*, that the framework should be simple and transparent. Third, the framework must be in line with the principles of a market economy, favouring the efficient allocation of financial resources. These three criteria – *goal efficiency, signalling capability, market compatibility* – have in fact guided the evolution of the operational framework of all main European central banks in recent years.[28]

A detailed description of the framework adopted by the Eurosystem can be found in the preparatory works published by the EMI before the end of Stage Two. More recently a complete summing up has been made available by the ECB.[29] What follows in this section is a brief outline of these documents, focusing only on the key monetary policy instruments, in light of the operational decisions adopted by the Governing Council in late December 1998 and confirmed by the first council meeting(s) of 1999. Money market developments in the first month of operation of the single monetary policy will also be briefly summarised.

The operational framework of the Eurosystem includes three main instruments: open market operations; standing facilities; reserve requirements. Table 2.1 (based on ECB, 1998a) provides an overview of the Eurosystem's open market operations and standing facilities.

Open market operations mainly take the form of repurchase agreements, that is operations in which the system – operating through the NCBs – provides or withdraws liquidity in exchange for pre-selected collateral assets.[30] Allocation of funds through this channel always takes place through auctions, in order to ensure an efficient distribution of base money among 'eligible' counterparties.[31] Different types of auctions – fixed or flexible rate; with discriminatory or uniform prices; and so on – can be used, according to the needs identified by the ECB governing bodies in each specific case. The choice of repurchase operations, as opposed to outright transactions, as the main monetary policy instrument is dictated by the wish to transmit impulses to the interest rate structure *indirectly*, through the market at the short end of the term structure. Long-term rates are expected to react to monetary policy changes through expectations. For the beginning of Stage Three, the Governing Council has decided that 'regular' repurchase operations would be executed using fixed rate tenders, while longer-term refinancing operations would be carried out through variable rate tenders.[32] This is consistent with the determination of the term structure by the market. Repo operations will constitute the main instrument for controlling market liquidity and for steering short-term rates.

The operational framework also includes two standing facilities. Standing facilities are not activated by initiative of the Eurosystem, and are not addressed to the market as a whole, but are directed to, and activated by, individual counterparties. There are two standing facilities. The *marginal lending facility* is used to provide overnight credit at penalty cost. Credit is conditional only on the presentation of sufficient assets. The *deposit facility* allows counterparties to place overnight funds with the Eurosystem, at rates below the market level. Since the two facilities are constantly available ('standing'), the official interest rates applied to them define a range, or corridor, within which the oscillation of overnight market rates is bounded as a result of money market arbitrage.[33]

The third main instrument is the minimum reserve requirement. The ECB imposes minimum reserves on all credit institutions in the proportion of 2 per cent of a reserve base. The latter includes all liabilities by credit institutions *vis-à-vis* the (non-bank) public with maturity up to 2 years. The reserve requirement operates with an averaging mechanism calculated over a period of one month. It is intended mainly to provide flexibility to day-by-day operations of the payment system. All institutions subject to the reserve obligation are allowed to deposit or withdraw funds freely, on a daily basis, provided the requirement is fulfilled on average over the monthly maintenance period. The reserve deposits are remunerated at the money market rate determined in the main refinancing operations.

It is interesting to look at the instruments described above in the light of the three guiding criteria indicated at the beginning of this sub-section. In accordance with the principle of *goal efficiency*, the instruments used by the Eurosystem are designed to ensure an effective control over money market rates, and, indirectly, to influence the whole-term structure, through the management of liquidity conditions in the money market. The reserve requirement system is used to give flexibility to the money market, but being fully remunerated contains no penalty element. Therefore, no artificial wedge is introduced between bank deposit and lending rates. Reserve requirements are not intended as an instrument for short-run control of the money stock.

The function of *signalling* is performed mainly by the interaction of the repurchase operations and the corridor between the two rates applied on standing facilities. The width of the corridor gives the market an indication of the potential range of variation of money market rates in the very short run. The alternative auction mechanisms for repo allocation also contribute to the signalling function: in particular, the fixed rate auction makes it possible to convey to the market a stronger – relative to the variable rate one – signal of the level of short-term rates deemed appropriate by the central bank. The position of market rates inside the corridor, defined by the standing facilities, may signal market perceptions about the likely future course of the repo rate.

Finally, all the main aspects of the operational framework are designed in a way compatible with the *efficient working of the market mechanism*. The reserve requirement system and its averaging mechanism provide an incentive to credit institutions to optimise their liquidity flows during the monthly computation period, based on their expectations of future market conditions and their attitude towards risk. Not least, the whole structure of the payments system supporting the operation of the single monetary policy, as well as the regulations governing the use of collateral – two aspects that for brevity we do not describe here – are designed to permit an efficient flow of central bank money and securities throughout the entire Euro-area.

At its meeting of 21 December 1998, the Governing Council adopted the following decisions regarding the setting of interest rates at the beginning of Stage Three:

1. The rate in the marginal standing facility was set at 4.5 per cent, while that in the deposit facility was set at 2 per cent (effective from 1 January 1999).
2. The rate on the first main refinancing (repurchase) operation, to take place on 4 January 1999, through a fixed-rate tender and a maturity of 2 weeks, was fixed at 3 per cent.
3. The corridor between the rate in the marginal lending and the deposit facility was temporarily (from 4 January to 21 January) narrowed to 50 basis points, from 2.75 to 3.25 per cent. This avoided, in the first operational days of Stage Three, excessive fluctuations or spreads in interest rates that might derive from the transition to the new regime.

The adoption of a temporarily narrow corridor (point 3) highlights the willingness by the Governing Council to flexibly adjust the strategy to enhance its signalling function and to face contingent operational needs.

7 THE SINGLE MONETARY POLICY IN OPERATION: THE FIRST MONTH

A short message, reaching all Reuters screens at 3:36 pm CET (central European time) on 4 January 1999, announced that the Eurosystem was launching its first open market operation, a 2-week fixed rate repo tender at an interest rate of 3 per cent. This announcement was the first operational act of the new monetary policy institution and marked the beginning of the implementation of the new strategy.

In this paper, we have argued that the stability-orientated monetary policy strategy of the ECB, which draws inspiration from economic history and from the general principles of European economic integration, is also firmly grounded in the macroeconomic and monetary literature. Specifically, it is consistent with recent theoretical and empirical advances aimed at finding ways to overcome the monetary instability which has characterised the world in the past 30 years. In our view, the stability-orientated strategy is appropriate, given the objectives of the ECB and our current economic knowledge. Time will have to pass, however, before its performance can be assessed in practice.

Nevertheless, a few encouraging signs can be observed from the experience of the first month of operation of the single monetary policy.

Money market developments, in January, were consistent with what can be defined as a smooth start of the single monetary policy. In the first days of the month, money market conditions were tight and there was some volatility and dispersion in money market interest rates (see Figure 2.1, taken from ECB, 1999b). The average money market interest rate (measured by EONIA[34]) was close to the rate of the marginal lending facility. Therefore the average recourse to the marginal lending facility during the first week of January was EUR 15.6 billion. At the same time there was also significant recourse to the deposit facility (EUR 6.3 billion during the same period). The intense recourse to both standing facilities during the first week vindicated their role in limiting money market interest rate fluctuations while individual credit institutions worked to adapt to the functioning of the Euro-area money market payments systems. The situation improved rapidly and, during the second week of January, the recourse to the standing facilities declined to, respectively, EUR 6.3 billion and EUR 1.3 billion.

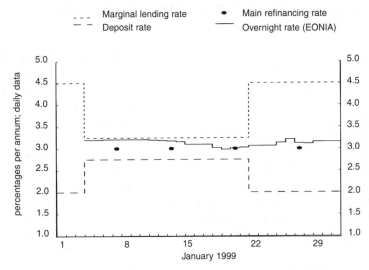

Figure 2.1   ECB interest rates and the overnight market interest rate

The TARGET (**T**rans-European **A**utomated **R**eal-time **G**ross settlement **E**xpress **T**ransfer) performed in a broadly satisfactory way during the first month of operation. It processed about EUR 1000 billion every day. This value constitutes a substantial increase over the value processed, on average, by the national RTGS (Real Time Gross Settlements Systems) in 1998 and is comparable to the amounts processed through the US Fedwire system. The only incident worth mentioning was a technical failure in one national interlinking component on 29 January. Given this performance TARGET rapidly fulfilled the aims of providing a safe, rapid and reliable means for the settlement of cross border payments and promoting the efficient functioning of the Euro-area money market.

On 21 January, given the clear improvement in the functioning of the Euro-area money market, the Council decided to discontinue the temporary narrow corridor for overnight interest rates. The conditions for the standing facilities reverted to the levels fixed for the period from 1 January to 3 January: 4.5 per cent for the marginal lending facility and 2 per cent for the deposit facility.

ACKNOWLEDGEMENTS

We wish to thank Benjamin Friedman, Marvin Goodfriend, Charles Goodhart, Ron McKinnon, Lars Svensson, Gabriel Talmain, Mike Wickens, the participants in conferences held at the London Business School and the University of York, and a number of colleagues at the ECB, especially Frank Browne, Philipp Hartmann, Huw Pill, Frank Smets and Bernhard Winkler for their helpful comments and suggestions. Remaining errors are, of course, our responsibility.

NOTES

1. See EMI (1997a, 1997b, 1997c).
2. On 13 October, the Governing Council released the broad outlines of the monetary policy strategy; on 1 December, the reference value for money after the start of Stage Three was announced and further details on the strategy were given; finally, on 22 December, the Governing Council provided complete information on the interest rates that would be applied by the Eurosystem at the beginning of Stage Three. All press releases and the related President's statements can be accessed from the ECB website.
3. For an excellent presentation of the nature of the shocks and the subsequent propagation mechanisms see Bruno and Sachs (1985).
4. The combination of policy and institutions in explaining the European unemployment problem is emphasised by Blanchard (1998).
5. Folkerts-Landau and Garber (1994); International Monetary Fund (1998); Centre for Economic Policy Research (1998); Gros and Tabellini (1998).
6. A number of authors have written essays discussing the choices available to the ECB, sometimes providing helpful contributions to the internal decision-making process (see for example Artis and Kontolemis, 1998; Bernanke *et al.* 1999, Ch. 12; Buiter, 1998; Neumann, 1997; Svensson, 1999; von Hagen, 1995).
7. See for example Friedman (1990).
8. See for example Friedman (1975, 1990, 1996). In summary, money demand must be a stable function of the final goal only, with no role played by interest rates or any other factors.
9. See Bernanke and Mihov (1997), Bernanke and Mishkin (1997), Laubach and Posen (1997), Mishkin and Posen (1997). For accounts of the monetary targeting experience by the Bundesbank, see Issing (1997) and König (1996).
10. See Bernanke and Mishkin (1997), Goodhart and Viñals (1994), Leiderman and Svensson (1995).
11. See, for example, Svensson (1997b, 1998c).
12. The use of 'information variables' for monetary policy was first formalised by Kareken, Muench and Wallace (1973) and Friedman (1975).

13. See Fagan and Henry (1998), Monticelli and Papi (1996). Angeloni *et al.* (1994) analyse the aggregation of money demand functions across the main EU countries.
14. The Eurosystem includes the ECB and the 11 NCBs adopting the euro as of 1 January 1999. The ESCB (European System of Central Banks) includes, in addition, the four non-participating NCBs. According to article 8 of the Statute of the ESCB and the ECB, the Eurosystem is governed by the ECB's decision-making bodies, which are the Governing Council and the Executive Board.
15. EMI (1997a), Chapter 2.
16. The time inconsistency problem faced in monetary policy making (whose *facets* have recently been articulated in an inflationary – possibly also state contingent – bias and a stabilisation bias; Svensson, 1997a) is therefore implicitly solved through a commitment to avoid policies aimed at pushing unemployment below the natural level and through the institutional assignment of an overriding weight to the objective of price stability.
17. These rules have been explored empirically in a burgeoning literature. See, for example, Bryant *et al.* (1993); Clarida *et al.* (1997); Fuhrer and Moore (1995); Peersman and Smets (1998); Taylor (1998).
18. See Coenen and Vega (1999) and Coenen (1999). See also Vlaar and Schuberth (1999).
19. The maturity threshold and the composition of M3 are also dictated, to some extent, by statistical considerations, linked to the features of the existing bank reporting system. In particular, the econometric evidence does not provide clear-cut indications for or against the inclusion of money market funds.
20 Preliminary information on the characteristics of the three monetary aggregates can be found in ECB (1999a); detailed information in ECB (1999b).
21. The calculation is based, for simplicity, on logarithmic approximations. A 1.5% growth rate of HICP obviously rules out both inflation and deflation, for any plausible values of statistical bias present in the harmonised index.
22. See, for example, the papers presented at the conference on 'The return of the Phillips curve', Frankfurt, 7–10 October 1998, and the recent work on Taylor rules (Clarida *et al.*, 1998; Bernanke and Mihov, 1997).
23. We include in this category all the variables that convey information about the current state of the business cycle relative to its trend, or potential.
24. Recent work on estimating output gaps with latent variable techniques is contained in Smets (1998) and Gerlach and Smets (1999).
25. The role of the exchange rate in the transmission process is investigated in BIS (1995).
26. See Angeloni and Rovelli (1998).
27. See Woodford (1994) and Bernanke and Woodford (1997).
28. See, for example, Escrivá and Fagan (1996) and Aspetsberger (1996) and the references therein.
29. EMI (1997a, 1997b, 1997c) and ECB (1998a).

30. According to the Treaty (Art. 18.1 of ECB/ESCB Statute), all credit operations by the Eurosystem must be backed by adequate collateral.
31. The range of counterparties is broad to facilitate a smooth distribution of funds. The list of financial institutions allowed to operate with the Eurosystem is published by the ECB.
32. All repo operations are expected to take these two standard forms. In case of specific needs, the Eurosystem may decide to use 'fine tuning' operations, with quicker and simplified procedures. The possibility is also foreseen, in special cases, of intervening through outright operations or by issuing central bank debt certificates (see Table 2.1).
33. This result holds in normal circumstances. The most important qualification is that access to the marginal lending facility is conditional on the availability of adequate collateral.
34. EONIA: 'euro overnight index average' refers to the weighted average of overnight (unsecured) rates reported by a panel of large banks in the Euro-area.

REFERENCES

Akerlof, G., Dickens, W. and Perry, G. (1996) 'The macroeconomics of low inflation', *Brookings Papers on Economic Activity*, **1**: 1–59.

Alesina, A. and Roubini, N. (1998) *Political Cycles and the Macroeconomy*, Cambridge, MA: MIT Press.

Angeloni, I., Cottarelli, C. and Levy, A. (1994) 'Cross-border deposits, aggregation, and money demand in the transition to EMU', *Journal of Policy Modeling*, **16**: 27–54.

Angeloni, I. and Rovelli, R. (eds) (1998) *Monetary Policy and Interest Rates*, London: Macmillan.

Arnold, I. J. M. (1994) 'The myth of a stable European money demand', *Open Economies Review*, **5**: 245–59.

Artis, M. J. and Kontolemis, Z. G. (1998) 'Inflation targeting and the European Central Bank', paper presented at the Conference on 'Monetary policy of the ESCB: Strategic and Implementation Issues', Milan, July.

Aspetsberger, A. (1996) 'Open market operations in EU countries', EMI Staff Paper No. 3.

Barro, R. J. and Gordon, D. B. (1983) 'Rules, discretion and reputation in a model of monetary policy', *Journal of Monetary Economics*, **12**: 101–21.

Bernanke, B. S. and Mihov, I. (1997) 'What does the Bundesbank target?', *European Economic Review*, **41**: 1025–53.

Bernanke, B. S. and Mishkin, F. S. (1997) 'Inflation targeting: a new framework for monetary policy?', *Journal of Economic Perspectives*, **11**: 97–116.

Bernanke, B. S., Laubach, T., Mishkin, F. S. and Posen, A. S. (1999) *Inflation Targeting: Lessons from the International Experience*, Princeton: Princeton University Press.

34 *From EMS to EMU*

Bernanke, B. and Woodford, M. (1997) 'Inflation forecasts and monetary policy', *Journal of Money, Credit and Banking*, **29**: 653–84.

BIS (1995) *Financial Structure and the Monetary Policy Transmission Mechanism*, Basle.

Blanchard, O. J. (1998) 'European Unemployment: Shocks and institutions', Baffi Lecture, Banca d'Italia.

Boskin, M. (1996) (chairman) 'Toward a more accurate measure of the cost of living', final report to the US Senate Finance Committee from the Advisory Commission to study the consumer price index.

Browne, F. X., Fagan, G. and Henry, J. (1997) 'Money demand in EU countries: a survey', EMI Staff Paper No. 7, Frankfurt am Main.

Bruno, M. and Sachs, J. (1985) *The Economics of World-wide Stagflation*, Oxford: Basil Blackwell.

Bryant, R., Hooper, P. and Mann, C. (1993) *Evaluating Policy Regimes: New Empirical Research in Empirical Macroeconomics*, Washington: Brookings Institution.

Buiter, W. H. (1998) 'Central banks and the joy of accountability', *Sunday Telegraph*, 18 October.

Cabrero, A., Escrivá, J. L., Muñoz, E. and J. Peñalosa (1998) 'The controllability of a monetary aggregate in the EMU', Banco de España, Servicio de Estudios, Documento de Trabajo No. 9817.

Cecchetti, S. G. (1997) 'Central bank policy rules: conceptual issues and practical considerations', NBER working paper No. 6306.

Centre for Economic Policy Research (1998) *The ECB: Safe at any Speed? Monitoring the European Central Bank*, 1.

Clarida, R., Galí, J. and Gertler, M. (1997) 'Monetary policy rules and macroeconomic stability: evidence and some theory', mimeo, May.

Clarida, R., Galí, J. and Gertler, M. (1997) 'The science of monetary policy', mimeo, September.

Clarida, R., Galí, J. and Gertler, M. (1998) 'Monetary policy rules in practice: some international evidence', *European Economic Review*, **42**: 1033–68.

Coenen, G. (1999) 'Comments to Vlaar and Schuberth', forthcoming in the Research Memorandum series of De Netherlandsche Bank.

Coenen, G. and Vega, J. L. (1999) 'Money demand relationship for the Euro-area', work in progress, ECB.

ECB (1998a) 'The Single Monetary Policy in Stage Three: general documentation on ESCB monetary policy instruments and procedures', September.

ECB (1998b) 'A stability-oriented monetary policy strategy for the ESCB', press release, available on the Internet: 13 October.

ECB (1998c) 'The quantitative reference value for monetary growth', press release, available on the Internet: 1 December.

ECB (1998d) 'The ECB interest rates to be applied at the start of Stage Three', Press release, available on the Internet: 22 December.

ECB (1999a) 'The stability-oriented monetary policy strategy of the Eurosystem', *Monthly Bulletin*, January, 39–50.

ECB (1999b) 'Euro-area monetary aggregates and their role in the Eurosystem's monetary policy strategy', *Monthly Bulletin*, February.

Eijffinger, S., Hoeberichts, M. and Schaling, E. (1998) 'A theory of central bank accountability', mimeo, September.

EMI (1997a) *The Single Monetary Policy in Stage Three: Specification of the Operational Framework*, available on the Internet: January.

EMI (1997b) *The Single Monetary Policy in Stage Three: Elements of the Monetary Policy Strategy of the ESCB*, available on the Internet: February.

EMI (1997c) *The Single Monetary Policy in Stage Three: General Documentation on ESCB Monetary Policy Instruments and Procedures*, available on the Internet: September.

Escrivá, J. L. and Fagan, G. (1996) 'Empirical assessment of monetary policy instruments and procedures in EU countries', EMI Staff Paper No. 2.

Estrella A. and Mishkin, F. S. (1997) 'Is there a role for monetary aggregates in the conduct of monetary policy?' *Journal of Monetary Economics*, **40**: 279–304.

Fagan, G. and Henry, J. (1998) 'Long run money demand in the EU: evidence for area-wide aggregates', *Empirical Economics*, **23**: 483–506.

Fischer, S. (1983) 'A framework for monetary and banking analysis', *Economic Journal*, **93**: 1–16.

Fischer, S. (1995) 'Modern approaches to central banking', NBER working paper No. 5064.

Folkerts-Landau, D. and Garber, P. (1994) 'What role for the ECB in Europe's financial markets?', in Alfred Steinherr (ed.) *30 Years of European Monetary Integration from the Werner Plan to EMU*, London: Longman.

Friedman, B. M. (1975) 'Targets, instruments, and indicators of monetary policy', *Journal of Monetary Economics*, **1**: 443–73.

Friedman, B. M. (1990) 'Targets and instruments of monetary policy', in Friedman, B. M and Hahn, F. H. (eds) *Handbook of Monetary Economics, 2*: Ch. 22, Amsterdam: North Holland.

Friedman, B. M. (1996) 'The rise and fall of money growth targets as guidelines for US monetary policy', NBER working paper No. 5465.

Friedman, B. M. and Kuttner, K. N. (1996) 'A price target for US monetary policy? Lessons from the experience with money growth targets', *Brookings Papers on Economic Activity*, **1**: 77–125.

Fuhrer, J. and Madigan, B. (1997) 'Monetary policy when interest rates are bounded at zero', *Review of Economics and Statistics*, **79**: 573–85.

Fuhrer, J. and Moore, G. (1995) 'Inflation persistence', *Quarterly Journal of Economics*, **110**: 127–59.

Gerlach, S. and Smets, F. (1999) 'Output gaps and monetary policy in the EMU area', *European Economic Review*, forthcoming.

Goodhart, C. A. E. and Viñals, J. (1994) 'Strategy and tactics of monetary policy: examples from Europe and the Antipodes', in Fuhrer, J. (ed.) *Goals, Guidelines and Constraints facing Monetary Policymakers*, Federal Reserve Bank of Boston Conference Series, **38**: 139–87.

Greenspan, A. (1989) 'Statement before House Committee on Banking, Finance and Urban Affairs', 24 January.

Gros, D. and Tabellini, G. (1998) 'The institutional framework for monetary policy in Europe', CEPS Working Document No. 126.

International Monetary Fund (1998) *International Capital Markets, Developments and Prospects and Key Policy Issues*, Washington.

Issing, O. (1995) 'Stability of monetary policy, stability of the monetary system. experience with monetary targeting in Germany', Deutsche Bundesbank.

Issing, O. (1997) 'Monetary targeting in Germany: The stability of monetary policy and of the monetary system', *Journal of Monetary Economics*, **39**: 67–79.

Kareken, J. H., Muench, T. and Wallace, N. (1973) 'Optimal open market strategy: the use of information variables', *American Economic Review*, **63**: 156–72.

King, M. (1997) 'Changes in UK monetary policy: rules and discretion in practice', *Journal of Monetary Economics*, **39**: 81–97.

König, R. (1996) 'The Bundesbank's experience of monetary targeting', in *Monetary Policy Strategies in Europe*, Munich: Verlag Vahlen.

Kuttner, K. and Posen, A. (1998) 'Does talk matter after all? Identifying the effects of inflation targeting', paper presented at the conference on 'Monetary policy of the ESCB: strategic and implementation issues', Bocconi University.

Kydland, F. E. and Prescott, E. C. (1977) 'Rules rather than discretion: the inconsistency of optimal plans', *Journal of Political Economy*, **85**: 473–91.

Laubach T. and Posen, A. S. (1997) 'Disciplined discretion: monetary targeting in Germany and Switzerland', *Essays in International Finance,* **206**, Princeton University.

Leiderman, L. and Svensson, L. E. O. (eds) (1995) *Inflation Targets*, Centre for Economic Policy Research, London.

Lucas, R. E. (1976) 'Econometric policy evaluation: a critique', *Carnegie-Rochester Conference Series on Public Policy*, **1**: 19–46.

McCallum, B. T. (1988) 'Robustness properties of a rule for monetary policy', *Carnegie-Rochester Conference Series on Public Policy*, **29**: 173–204.

McCallum, B. T. (1995) 'Two fallacies concerning central bank independence', *American Economic Review Papers and Proceedings*, **85**: 207–11.

McCallum, B. T. (1996) 'Inflation targeting in Canada, New Zealand, Sweden, the United Kingdom, and in general', NBER working paper No. 5579.

McCallum, B. T. (1997a) 'Crucial issues concerning central bank independence', *Journal of Monetary Economics*, **39**: 99–112.

McCallum, B. T. (1997b) 'Issues in the design of monetary policy rules', NBER working paper No. 6016.

McCandless, G. T. and Weber, W. E. (1995) 'Some monetary facts', *Federal Reserve Bank of Minneapolis Quarterly Review*, **19**: 2–11.

Mishkin, F. S. (1996) 'What monetary policy can and cannot do', *Proceedings of the conference: monetary policy in transition in east and west: strategies, instruments and transmission mechanisms*, Österreichische Nationalbank, Vienna.

Mishkin, F. S. (1998) 'International experiences with different monetary policy regimes', Stockholm University, Institute for International Economics Studies Seminar Paper No. 648.

Mishkin, F. S. and Posen, A. S. (1997) 'Inflation targeting: lessons from four countries', NBER working paper No. 6126.

Monticelli, C. and Papi, L. (1996) *European integration, monetary co-ordination, and the demand for money*, Oxford: Clarendon Press.

Mueller, D. (1989) *Public Choice II, A Revised Edition of Public Choice*, Cambridge: Cambridge University Press.

Neumann, M. (1997) 'Monetary targeting in Germany', in I. Kuroda (ed.) *Towards a More Effective Monetary Policy*, New York: St Martin's Press.

Orphanides, A. and Wieland, V. (1998) 'Price stability and monetary policy effectiveness when nominal interest rates are bound at zero', Finance and Economics Discussion Series Papers No. 1998–35, Federal Reserve Board.

Peersman, G. and Smets, F. (1998) 'The Taylor rule: a useful monetary policy guide for the ECB?', mimeo, September.

Persson, T. and Tabellini, G. (1993) 'Designing institutions for monetary stability', *Carnegie-Rochester Conference Series on Public Policy*, **39**: 53–84.

Persson, T. and Tabellini, G. (1995) 'Double edged incentives: Institutions and policy co-ordination' in Grossman, G. and Rogoff, K. (eds) *Handbook of International Economics*, **3**: ch. 38, Amsterdam: North Holland.

Posen, A. and Laubach, T. (1997) 'Some comparative evidence on the effectiveness of inflation targets', Federal Reserve Bank of New York Research Paper No. 9714.

Rogoff, K. (1985) 'The optimal degree of commitment to an intermediate monetary target', *Quarterly Journal of Economics*, **100**: 1169–90.

Romer, C. D. and Romer, D. H. (1997) 'Institutions for monetary stability', in Romer, C. D. and Romer, D. H. (eds) *Reducing Inflation: Motivation and Strategy*, pp. 307–29, Chicago: University of Chicago Press.

Smets, F. (1998) 'Output gap uncertainty: does it matter for the Taylor rule?', paper presented at the Reserve Bank of New Zealand workshop on 'Monetary policy under uncertainty', 29–30 June.

Smith, A. (1759) *The theory of moral sentiment*.

Summers, L. (1991) 'How should long-term monetary policy be determined', *Journal of Money, Credit, and Banking*, **23**: 625–31.

Svensson, L. E. O. (1997a) 'Optimal inflation targets, 'Conservative' central banks, and linear inflation contracts', *American Economic Review*, **87**: 98–114.

Svensson, L. E. O. (1997b) 'Inflation forecast targeting: implementing and monitoring inflation targets', *European Economic Review*, **41**: 1111–46.

Svensson, L. E. O. (1998a) 'Inflation targeting: some extensions', *Scandinavian Journal of Economics*, forthcoming.

Svensson, L. E. O. (1998b) 'Price level targeting vs. inflation targeting', *Journal of Money, Credit and Banking*, forthcoming.

Svensson, L. E. O. (1998c) 'Inflation targeting as a monetary policy rule', mimeo, December.

Svensson, L. E. O. (1999) 'Monetary policy issues for the Eurosystem', mimeo, February.

Taylor, J. B. (1980) 'Aggregate dynamics and staggered contracts, *Journal of Political Economy*, **88**: 1–23.

Taylor, J. B. (1993) 'Discretion versus policy rules in practice', *Carnegie-Rochester Conference Series on Public Policy*, **39**: 195–214.

Taylor, J. B. (1996) 'Policy rules as a means to a more effective monetary policy', Bank of Japan, Institute for monetary and economic studies discussion paper 96-E-12.

Taylor, J. B. (1998) 'The robustness and efficiency of monetary policy rules as guidelines for interest rate setting by the European central bank', Stockholm University, Institute for International Economics Studies Seminar Paper No. 649.

Vlaar, P. J. G. and Schuberth, H. (1999) 'Monetary transmission and controllability of money in Europe: a structural vector error-correction approach', forthcoming in the Research Memorandum series of De Nederlandiche Bank.

von Hagen, J. (1995) 'Inflation and monetary targeting in Germany', in Leiderman, L. and Svensson, L. E. O. (eds).

von Hagen, J. (1998) 'Money growth targeting', Stockholm University, Institute for International Economics Studies Seminar Paper No. 643.

Walsh, C. (1995) 'Optimal contracts for independent central bankers', *American Economic Review*, **85**: 150–67.

Walsh, C. (1998) *Monetary Theory and Policy*, Cambridge (Mass.):, MIT Press.

Wolman, A. (1998) 'Real implications of the zero bound on nominal interest rates', mimeo, November.

Woodford, M. (1994) 'Non standard indicators of monetary policy: can their usefulness be judged from forecasting regressions?', in Mankiw, G. (ed.) *Monetary Policy*, Chicago: University of Chicago Press.

Discussion of Chapter 2

Charles Goodhart

Let me start by extending an extremely warm welcome both to Vítor Gaspar, the Director General of Research at the European Central Bank, and to his Research Group there. Although some of his group, like much of the rest of the staff at the ECB, will have metamorphosed from the preceding EMI, nevertheless the group is in an important sense newly born. It is good to have another Central Bank research department studying the crucial issues of the relationships between monetary and economic developments, and it is good that the ECB is giving so much importance and weight to such research.

They appear to be getting off to an excellent start with a sizeable number of new research papers dealing with subjects such as the demand for money and cointegration between monetary and other economic variables mentioned in the course of Vítor's paper.

One problem, which all in-house research departments invariably face, is the need to support the house line, but at the same time having to maintain objectivity. It is sometimes a fine and difficult line to sustain. And there was one point in this chapter, where I felt that the authors slightly transgressed that difficult line when they stated, and I quote:

> Accordingly, the 'stability-orientated monetary policy strategy' announced by the ECB, combines elements of previously used strategies in a way that aims at ensuring the maximum degree of effectiveness, transparency, accountability, forward-looking orientation, and continuity with past and successful strategies.

I find this somewhat over the top, as indeed is the common viewpoint in the UK. You know the British position on this; let me, for example, quote from a recent *Economist*, dated 16 January. In this, *The Economist* stated:

> Too little democracy and too much secrecy have long been the banes of the Union... Now Europe has a new central bank whose independence will not be matched by any ventilation of its workings or decision-making.

How can Vítor refer to 'maximum transparency and accountability', when we will not know the votes; when, at the moment anyhow, it seems unlikely that there will be published Minutes of Discussion, at least for many years; when the inflation forecast will not be reported, and when the internal discussions of the Governing Council of the ESCB are likely to remain opaque.

Let me turn to a more positive issue, which is the question of the appropriate time horizon for monetary analysis and policy. But, first, I just want to digress slightly to deal with an issue that Vítor raised in his chapter, which is whether a Central Bank might be too 'activist'. It is not clear to me exactly what this means. There are some suggestions, (and there have been some statements by the President, Wim Duisenberg), that what is meant by 'too activist' is the belief that the Central Bank should change interest rates only on rare occasions. An alternative interpretation is that a Central Bank should only try to adjust inflation into line with the target over some medium run. As I shall show later, I agree wholeheartedly with this second interpretation; but I have considerable difficulties with the first. If inflation appears, to the experts in the ECB, to be diverging from the target at the chosen horizon, then it is not clear what are the costs of moving rapidly to try to adjust such divergences.

Let me revert to the main issue, which is what is the appropriate horizon, at which monetary policy should try to make actual inflation close to the target level of inflation. Vítor and his co-authors refer in their chapter several times to the appropriate horizon, and they reaffirm that monetary policy should only seek to bring inflation into line with the target over the medium run, but they never specify exactly what that medium run might be. Is that medium run six months, or six years? They remain determinedly imprecise about the actual time lags.

The assessment of such time horizons are of the utmost importance, because, as Milton Friedman has told us, monetary policy works with long and variable lags. The one main exception to such long lags is that monetary policy can, but in an extremely uncertain way, affect exchange rates immediately and hence, to some extent, depending on import price pass-through, rapidly affect domestic price levels more generally. But to control inflation in the short-run would require such a change in interest rates and exchange rates, that it would surely destabilise the rate of growth of output.

The authors appear to claim at one point in their chapter that there is no trade-off between price stability and output stability. Thus they state, 'The monetary authority should not credibly commit to try to stablise unemployment below the natural rate. In such a case, again, price stability may be delivered at no cost of in terms of output volatility.' But that is surely wrong, at any rate in the short run. Let me quote from Lars Svensson's recent paper, 'Inflation targeting: some extensions', intended for *The Scandinavian Journal of Economics* (1999). There he writes:

> In a more elaborate model with shorter [quarterly] periods and empirically estimated coefficients, the first effect of the instrument [the short-term level of interest rates] on output and inflation may be quite small, with the effect growing to a maximum several periods later and then declining. For strict inflation targeting, the first effect is still the relevant one, and the task of monetary policy is then to fulfil the inflation target at the shortest possible horizon. That first effect being quite small, drastic adjustments of the instrument will be required, thus making strict inflation even less attractive. For flexible inflation targeting, the question arises which horizon should be emphasized by the central bank, both in its internal policy decisions and in its communications with the private sector. Some central banks have chosen to emphasize the horizon at which the effect is largest (this horizon is often assumed to be about two years). Generally, in a more elaborate model the whole time path of the inflation forecast is of relevance.

Again, Haldane *et al.*, in their 1997 Bank of England paper 'A forward-looking and probabilistic approach to monetary policy', found for the UK a relationship between output volatility and inflation volatility (as the horizon at which inflation was to be returned to the target varied, shown as J quarters ahead in Figure 2A.1), to have the somewhat rectangular shape in Figure 2A.1.

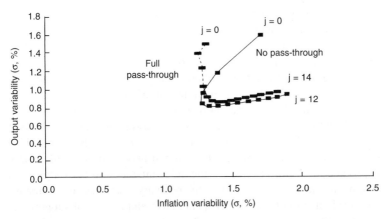

Figure 2A.1   j-loci: full and no pass-through cases (Bank of England)

The continuous line shows the trade-off if we suppress entirely the exchange rate-import pass-through channel. This approximates to what might happen in a closed economy. The dashed line shows the trade-off in an open economy, with a full pass-through. In either case, both output volatility and inflation volatility appear to be approximately minimised when a sensible horizon is chosen, about six to eight quarters from the current date. It is important that Vítor and his Research Group do similar work for the Eurozone economy, and that they should both quantify and publish the results.

Choosing the appropriate horizon, indeed over the 'medium term', for returning inflation to its target level after a shock, is of crucial importance. It is important that the issue is generally publicly understood, which can only be done if the results of such analytical work are put before the public.

The question of the appropriate horizon should also influence the relative weight put on the various information variables, such as monetary developments, at which the authorities look. Consider, for example, the following reduced-form equation, where i represents the number of quarters that the authorities are seeking to look ahead in order to return inflation to its desired target level.

$$\pi_{t+i} = f(\pi_{t-j},\ y\text{-}y^*_{t-j},\ e_{t-j},\ i_{t-j},\ dM_{t-j},\ dA_{t-j})$$

Here we show this future inflation, i quarters ahead, as a function of various possible information variables, current and past inflation, the current and past output gap, movements in the exchange rate, movements in asset prices (dA), changes in interest rates (the instrument variable), and monetary variables (dM). The question is exactly how much information do these movements in monetary variables add to the prediction of inflation over the forecast horizon? Certainly they add some information, and the longer the horizon, the more the relevant information that such monetary variables add. But, over an horizon of some six to eight quarters, the general belief is that such monetary variables add relatively little information, given the other variables which the authorities can also assess. In so far as this is true, monetary variables should play relatively little role in the prediction of inflation over the relevant medium-run target, and elevating the rate of growth of such monetary variables to a reference value would need to have greater quantitative and analytical support than it is often given.

3 The European Monetary System: an Unexpected Success?

*George Zis**

1 INTRODUCTION

An assessment of the actual relative to the expected performance of the European Monetary System (EMS) could be a useful input in the current debate on the desirability and viability of the recently created European Monetary Union (EMU). The contrast between the experience and the predictions articulated at the time of the establishment of the system in 1979 is pertinent for an evaluation not only of the case against EMU but also of the arguments in favour of the replacement of the European Union (EU) member countries' currencies by the euro. Just as firm supporters of EMU were among the most severe critics of the EMS back in 1979, today the introduction of the euro is welcomed by firm opponents of political union.

In what follows, first, the background to the establishment of the EMS will be outlined. Next, the reactions at the time of the creation of the system will be presented and assessed in terms of the perspectives prevailing at the end of the 1970s and the beginning of the 1980s. Third, the actual experience of the EMS will be contrasted with the predictions made immediately after the system became operational. Finally, some conclusions will be presented, the principal one being that the EMS was an unexpected success which, however, should have been anticipated.

2 EMS: BACKGROUND, OBJECTIVES AND FEATURES

The discussions which led to the negotiations and ultimately to the establishment of the EMS were initiated by Germany's Chancellor H. Schmidt.[1] This reflected the emergence of Germany as a major player in international

* I am indebted to D. Carline for useful comments on an earlier draft. I alone am responsible for views expressed.

economic relations during the 1970s and the country's newly developed self-confidence in responding to and initiating changes in the arena of world politics. The significance of Schmidt's decision to press ahead with the creation of a new European monetary system as an act of political independence is revealed by Jenkins (1989) in his recollections of the Copenhagen meeting of the European Council, April 1978. This is evident in how Schmidt presented his proposals and in Britain's reaction. According to Jenkins (1989) Schmidt spoke:

> in strongly anti-Carter terms, saying that the whole management of the dollar by the American administration was absolutely intolerable. At one point indeed he said no American President could lead the Alliance while presiding over such a degradation of the dollar as he had witnessed during his period as Federal Chancellor. (p. 247)

Jenkins (1989) also notes that Callaghan, Britain's Prime Minister, in reacting to Schmidt's ideas 'concentrated on his fear that what was proposed might appear as anti-dollar and might therefore be divisive from an Atlantic point of view' (p. 247).

After the Council's meeting Callaghan conceded that he was not sure that he had fully understood what was being proposed and invited Jenkins to a meeting in which some of the Prime Minister's principal advisers were present. One of the latter, Ken Cousins, looked, according to Jenkins (1989):

> pole-axed and kept on repeating: 'But it is very bold, Prime Minister. Did the Chancellor really go as far as that? It is very bold. It leaves the dollar on one side. I do not know what the Americans will say about it. It's very bold, Prime Minister.' (p. 248)

Of equal significance, however, is the fact that Schmidt proceeded to press for a new monetary system at Copenhagen only after he had previously secured the full support of the French President V. Giscard d'Estaing. This was not particularly difficult. At least since De Gaulle's ascent to power in 1958 a principal objective of France had been to assert its independence *vis-à-vis* the USA.[2]

How significantly economic and political relations in the Western alliance had changed between the second half of the 1960s and the late 1970s can be illustrated by contrasting the reactions of Germany and France to the symptoms of the terminal stage of the 'Bretton Woods' international monetary system and the political determination of these countries in 1978 to create a regional monetary system. In 1967 the UK could no longer resist the speculative pressures on sterling and was forced to devalue its currency. This was not sufficient to restore confidence in sterling. In 1968 the bizarre Basle Agreement on sterling balances was concluded. At the same time confidence in the dollar was collapsing. In March 1968 the two-tier gold market was introduced which implied that the world had effectively adopted a dollar standard. The 1967 decision to introduce the special drawing rights (SDR) scheme failed to restore confidence in the viability of the 'Bretton Woods' international monetary system. The Six, of course, were not insulated from these international monetary developments. Furthermore, the May 1968 events in France generated additional pressures for the Six. The turmoil gave rise to expectations that the French franc would be devalued and the German mark revalued. Germany and France could not agree to a common response to the turbulence in the foreign exchange markets. Thus, the former introduced export taxes and import rebates as well as restrictions on foreign deposits, while France resorted to severe exchange controls, subsidies on exports and highly deflationary policies. These measures were not sufficient to revive confidence and speculative pressures persisted. As a result, the franc was devalued in August 1969 and the German mark was revalued two months later after a month during which it was allowed to float.

The 1967–69 international monetary turmoil was perceived by Community member countries to be a threat to the process of European economic integration that had been set in motion by the creation of the customs union and the establishment of the Common Agricultural Policy. It was felt that neither, particularly the latter, could survive frequent intra-Community exchange rate changes. To preserve what had been achieved and maintain the momentum of integration, in December 1969 the Six announced their agreement that 'a plan in stages would be worked out during 1970 with a view to the creation of an economic and monetary union.' In March 1970 the Werner Committee was set up. In October of that year the Six adopted the Committee's plan for Europe's monetary unification by 1980. This was quite an extraordinary development. Throughout the 1967–69 period of international monetary turbulence the Six could not agree on a common response. Yet, less than a year later they were adopting the highly ambitious objective of monetary union.

The May 1971 foreign exchange market turmoil exposed how ill-founded was the adoption of the Werner Plan. Severe pressures on the dollar forced Germany, Holland and Belgium to close their foreign exchange markets in order to stem the large inflows of short-term capital.

The Six were once again unable to agree on a common approach to the developing crisis. France advocated the imposition of exchange controls and rejected exchange rate changes as a policy solution. Germany, on the other hand, argued that the currencies of the Six should float jointly against the dollar. As agreement proved impossible, the German mark and the Dutch guilder were allowed to float. Thus the start of the implementation of the Werner Plan, which involved the narrowing of the band within which intra-Community exchange rates would be allowed to fluctuate and had been scheduled to become operational in June 1970, was abandoned.

In August 1971 Germany and France were again unable to agree on a common response to the US decision to suspend the dollar's convertibility into gold. The latter introduced a two-tier foreign exchange market and further capital controls while the other five countries decided to allow their currencies to float and, therefore, revalue against the dollar. However, following the Smithsonian Agreement of December 1971, the Six sought to revive progress towards the implementation of the Werner Plan. This attempt was seriously undermined by the UK government when in June 1972 it decided to allow sterling to float, only weeks after it had opted to join the Six in narrowing the permitted band of fluctuation within the new band established by the Smithsonian Agreement. Britain's example was soon followed by Ireland and Denmark. The Six responded to the collapse of the international monetary system in March 1973 by attempting to maintain the narrow band while their currencies jointly floated against the dollar. In January 1974 France ceased to operate the European band. The Werner Plan had effectively been abandoned.

The international monetary disorder which followed the breakdown of the 'Bretton Woods' system was accentuated by the impact of the first oil price rise in the winter of 1973. Countries, no longer subject to a balance of payments constraint, determined their response to the oil price rise on a unilateral basis, motivated by narrowly defined national interests. This unco-ordinated reaction resulted in increasingly divergent monetary policies. National inflation rates rose and became ever more divergent. With the collapse of the international monetary system a greater divergence of national inflation rates, *ceteris paribus*, was inevitable. But the divergence that actually developed was beyond what could have been expected to follow the collapse of the 'Bretton Woods' system.

The conditions that emerged within Europe were described by the Commission, European Communities (1984), as follows:

During the 1970s, it became apparent that Community monitoring and co-ordination was in some ways a failure. That failure was, indeed, one of the main reasons why the first attempt to introduce a stable exchange rate system in the Community (The 'Snake') did not work out very well. Faced with a seriously disturbed international environment where fixed exchange relations had been abandoned and oil prices were soaring, *the member countries sometimes opted for economic policy choices which were fundamentally different; no one being really prepared to submit to an exchange rate constraint if that entailed sacrificing a domestic aim.* (italics added)

Thus, in October 1977 Jenkins (1978) observed that:

The concept and indeed the politics of monetary union stand immobilised in scepticism, following the demise of the Werner Plan, whose initial exchange rate mechanism was shattered by the turbulent monetary events of the past few years.

Consistent with the diagnosis that economic nationalism had emerged as a principal feature of the 1970s, Bilson (1979) interpreted the creation of the EMS as:

the first step back from the rugged individualism and national self-interest that lay behind the formal acceptance of flexible exchange rates at the Jamaica meetings of the International Monetary Fund in January 1976. (p. 36)

In March 1973 the world did not choose exchange rate flexibility in preference to the 'Bretton Woods' system. The latter simply collapsed leaving individual countries to react as they unilaterally deemed appropriate. In the period immediately after 1973, US attitudes prevented agreement on the creation of a new international monetary system. It is this failure to agree rather than a preference for flexible exchange rates which the Jamaica, 1976, Second Amendment to the IMF Articles of Agreement reflects. Williamson (1977) maintained that what the Second Amendment legitimised could not be:

described as an international monetary 'system', in so far as the word system implies a well-defined set of rights and obligations. *Countries are free to do in large measure as they please, with regard not only to their exchange rates* but also to the volume and composition of the reserves that they hold and the methods that they use to effect payments adjustment. *One country, at least,*

seems happy enough with a non-system in which the dollar is once again unri-
valled and the pretensions of the IMF to conduct a world monetary policy have
been brought to nought, leaving the Federal Reserve unchallenged. US
Secretary of the Treasury William Simon even compared the results of the
Jamaican meeting of the Interim Committee to those of the 'Bretton Woods'
Conference. (pp. 74–5, italics added)

Williamson (1977) described the agreement on the Second Amendment as 'a
complete victory for the United States' (p. 74) and went on to suggest that
although the rest of the world did not view Jamaica as the foundation on
which a new international monetary system could eventually be established:

> the advent of floating exchange rates has made acquiescence in a dollar-centred
> system markedly less irksome than a full dollar standard would have been, for
> the system no longer imposes obligations to follow US monetary policy, to
> finance US deficits involuntarily or to risk importing US inflation. (p. 75)

Williamson's observation in 1976 on how the world, other than the
USA, viewed the Second Amendment is not inconsistent with how flexible
exchange rates were expected to behave. However, these expectations
proved to be ill founded. Five years after the collapse of the 'Bretton
Woods' system, Mussa (1979) concluded:

> Looking at the totality of our experience with floating exchange rates, there is
> no sound basis for the belief that exchange rates will adjust slowly and smoothly
> to correct 'fundamental disequilibria' that would otherwise develop between
> national economies. Of course, the magnitude of fluctuations may increase or
> decrease with the magnitude of disturbances to the world economy, but *the*
> *smoothly adjusting exchange rate is, like the unicorn, a mythical beast.* (p. 9,
> italics added)

In other words, by 1978, when Schmidt presented his proposals, 'acquiescence' to the prevailing 'dollar-centred' international monetary relations
was no longer feasible, especially for the Community member countries.

To summarise, in the words of the Commission, European Communities
(1984):

> The EMS was set up as a result of a defensive reaction against the disorderly
> movements of the dollar and against the danger of economic deterioration in the
> Community if uncoordinated behaviour continued. (p. 2)

Finally, a significant dimension of the background to the establishment of the EMS related to domestic economic objectives and developments in the Community member countries. Since the mid-1970s the reduction of the rate of inflation had become the principal economic priority in these countries. The gyrations of intra-Community exchange rates and of the non-member countries' currencies had limited the ability of national authorities to pursue their anti-inflation objectives. Sumner (1980), for example, analysed how Germany and Switzerland were forced to revise their monetary targets in response to exchange rate changes while Ludlow (1982) emphasised that France's enthusiasm for Schmidt's proposals was largely motivated by the judgement that the EMS would facilitate the acceptance and success of the anti-inflation policies of the Barre government. By 1978, according to the Commission, European Communities (1984):

> Attitudes [had] converged on recognising that the main thrust of national economic policies should be directed towards achieving price stabilisation, and that the level to be desired was that of the most successful performer on this front. This was the approach that in fact prevailed in response to the second oil shock. (p. 3)

Notwithstanding the decision to adopt the Werner Plan in October 1970, Germany and France, although fully committed to the principle of European economic integration, throughout the era of the 'Bretton Woods' system and the years immediately after its collapse in 1973, could not agree on common responses to the disintegrating international monetary order. The balance of power within the Western Alliance and the relative positions of America, France and Germany were such that it was not politically feasible for the latter two to act independently of the USA until the end of the 1970s. During the 1960s America was less than happy with European Community member countries' reactions to the escalating international monetary crisis. But because these countries' reactions were essentially unilaterally determined, America did not perceive them to be a serious threat to its interests. However, by the end of the 1960s, the increasing efforts by the Six to act in unison, although not crowned with success, did concern the USA. For example, Senator Mansfield denounced the May 1971 foreign exchange market turmoil as an 'attack on the dollar' and introduced a legislative proposal for an immediate 50 per cent reduction in US troops in Europe. This proposal was narrowly defeated, by just eight votes, only after the Nixon administration engaged in what Bergsten (1973) has described as the most 'intensive lobbying... on any single issue' (p. 287).

It was generally accepted that in the conditions prevailing in the late 1960s and early 1970s the only retaliation available to America, in the event of an independently determined European monetary initiative deemed to be unacceptable, would be the withdrawal or significant reduction of its military involvement in Europe. If that were to happen, Germany would be the country that would suffer most, especially as it had by then embarked on a process of normalising its relations with the Soviet Union. Thus Germany was more sensitive to US anxieties than France. That is, Germany in order to secure America's acquiescence to its policies of rapprochement with the Socialist countries refrained from advocating or supporting measures aimed at easing the international monetary crisis but which were likely to provoke hostile reactions in the USA.

By 1978 the balance of power within the Western alliance had changed significantly. The US relative decline had continued while Germany had emerged as a major economic power, it had normalised its relations with the Socialist countries, and within the European Community its political weight was by then comparable to that of France. Germany had become increasingly inclined to assert its independence. But it could only do so through a closer alliance with France. This was facilitated by the developing convergence in the attitudes of both countries towards America. This convergence combined with the change of Germany's relative position within the Western alliance and the European Community to enable Schmidt in 1978 to press his proposals which resulted in the establishment of the EMS. But, as this would not have been possible without the active support of France, it is with justification that both critics and supporters of the EMS identified its creation not only with Schmidt but also with Giscard d'Estaing.

Schmidt's hostility to both the economic and foreign policies of the Carter administration is well documented.[3] However, this by itself would not have been sufficient either for Schmidt to take the initiative or for his proposals to be accepted by his European partners. Disenchantment with America's policies simply created an enabling environment within which Community member countries could agree on a common response, the establishment of the EMS, to developments judged to be incompatible with both the narrowly defined interests of these countries and of the Community as a whole.

The 'snake' in 1978 did not provide an adequate framework for the introduction of measures aimed at the revival of the process of European integration, the minimisation of the adverse effects of exchange rate volatility and American economic policies and the permanent reduction of inflation.

It was largely discredited. There was, therefore, a need for a new initiative in the monetary field. But the very nature of the objectives that such an initiative would have to serve determined that it would be political in character. Germany felt sufficiently politically confident, and Schmidt, by taking the lead and therefore asserting Germany's authority, demonstrated this political self-confidence. By the second half of the 1970s conditions were ripe for a European response to the deepening international politico-economic disorder. Germany, under the prevailing circumstances, was the only country that could take the lead. The timing of the initiative was determined by the policies of the Carter administration which antagonised France and Germany, particularly the latter.

3 REACTIONS

McMahon (1979) argued that:

> the emergence of the EMS in 1978 was both a symptom of and a broadly appropriate response to current economic and financial problems (p. 81)

while De Vries (1980) judged the EMS to be:

> quite an imaginative arrangement that exploits to the utmost the possibilities of the existing situation while staying within the bounds of realism. Moreover, it contains some starting points for further constructive progress. It is therefore a welcome step. (p. 14)

Dr Vries (1980) emphasised that:

> The establishment of the EMS was mainly political in character and part of a wider pattern of developments. Direct election of the members of the European Parliament, a new Lomé agreement, accession of new members to the Community, an economic agreement with Yugoslavia, a common political stand on the Middle East and on Soviet intervention in Afghanistan, all form part of the same picture. (pp. 43–4)

Similarly, Emerson (1979), who played a significant role in the design of the EMS, after noting that the establishment of the system 'confirm[ed] the Community in its integrationist course and underline[d] the need for convergence in economic performance' (p. 43), went on to observe that:

Enlargement of the Community to include Greece, Spain, and Portugal will
obviously not make the task of convergence easier. *But the EMS is also a sign of
political will to deepen as well as to enlarge the Community.* Enlargement in
these circumstances of course signals the political objectives of the Community.
This illustrates the contrast between the snake and the EMS, even if technically
there has been a smooth transition from one to the other; the former became a
limited special purpose club, *the latter aims to be central to the political structure of Europe.* (pp. 43–4, italics added)

For Emerson (1979), then, the establishment of the EMS was 'a strategic
catalyst in the Community's economic and political integration' (p. 25)
while Triffin (1979), an important contributor to the design of the EMS,
maintained that:

the adoption of a 'divergence indicator', which places on the country with the
divergent currency the presumptive burden for the readjustment of domestic
policies or exchange rates, or both, should help accelerate desirable readjustments. In contrast to the IMF Articles of Agreement as well as to the 'snake'
agreement consultations on such readjustments are no longer left exclusively to
the initiative of the country in question. The process can be triggered as well by
partner countries complaining of the impact of an undervalued or overvalued
exchange rate on their own economies. *This is an unprecedented breakthrough
in international monetary relations.* (p. 67, italics added)

These reactions are not representative of the sentiments with which the
establishment of the EMS was greeted. The system began its operations in
an atmosphere of deep scepticism, often verging on outright hostility. An
extreme example was provided by the reaction of *The Banker* (1979):

The problem with the EMS has always been to decide what the political leaders
who set it up would do when it failed. When mutual credits and patience began
to be exhausted in trying to keep members' exchange rates in line, would
governments of weaker countries tighten their monetary policies – in effect at
the behest of the Germans? If not, would the strong countries be ready to agree
to early and sufficient devaluations by deficit countries to prevent their industries from becoming increasingly uncompetitive?

It is because we have felt that the answer in present circumstances had to be
'no' to both questions that *The Banker* has not been ready to support the scheme
outlined at the Bremen summit. *Therefore, we are thankful that the scheme has
failed already, in the sense that the system that starts this month is a far cry from*

that which Helmut Schmidt and Giscard d'Estaing dreamt up in that moment of
common rapture last summer.

What both statesmen failed to understand is that no amount of political determination is sufficient to fix exchange rates. (p. 12, italics added)

Similarly dismissive of the prospects of the system's survival was
Congdon (1978)[4] who suggested that it was 'doubtful if the EMS could
work, but, even if it could, Britain should not join'. More confident was the
Centre for Banking and International Finance, The City University
(1978),[5] which in its evidence to the House of Commons Expenditure
Committee stated that it had 'no confidence in the ability of the proposed
European Monetary System to provide either short-term exchange rate
stability or longer-term monetary integration in Europe' and, therefore, its:

major conclusion [was] that the proposed EMS [was] by its very constitution an
unworkable system and will not solve the major problems of high unemployment, high inflation and low growth which European economies [were then]
experiencing. It [was] not that [they were] opposed to the idea of monetary integration in Europe or indeed even to the creation of a monetary union but *simply*
that the EMS is not a viable monetary system. From the British point of view,
therefore, the question of timing [was] irrelevant. The time to join the EMS
[was] never. (Appendix 5, italics added)

The most severe critics of the EMS included firm supporters of European monetary union. The publication of the All Saints Day Manifesto in
1975 had a significant impact on economists' perceptions of the relative
merits of alternative strategies aimed at Europe's monetary unification. An
increasing number of the proponents of monetary union was persuaded that
the strategy most likely to succeed in generating the emergence of a monetary union involved the introduction of a parallel currency. The attraction
of the proposal largely reflected intellectual developments. First, the
prescribed strategy by implying a process of monetary unification which
did not require the fixity of intra-Community exchange rates was consistent with the prevailing doubts as to whether governments were in fact able
to maintain fixed exchange rates. Disillusion with the post-1973 behaviour
of flexible exchange rates was not yet so severe as to motivate a re-
assessment of the case for fixed exchange rates allowing for the fact that
the 'Bretton Woods' system was only one of the many forms that an international monetary system of fixed exchange rates can potentially take.
Second, the parallel currency strategy by relying on market forces to

generate the emergence of Europe's monetary union echoed the rapidly growing economics literature in favour of market solutions and against governments intervening in the economy.

Vaubel (1978) had provided the most authoritative statement of the case for the parallel currency approach to European monetary union. Therefore, it is not surprising that his reaction to the establishment of the EMS was not one of enthusiasm. Vaubel (1979) belittled the system by suggesting that the 'cardinal feature of the new scheme [was] the return of France, Italy and Ireland to a snake-type adjustable-peg system' (p. 16), dismissed the pooling of reserves as a 'non-event' (p. 13), maintained that 'the considerable increase of easy credit facilities' introduced an 'inflationary bias' (p. 15) into the system, criticised the asymmetric nature of the EMS, inevitable in any adjustable-peg system, and, therefore, asserted that:

> Once it is realised that snake-type exchange-rate systems presuppose the hegemony of one currency, it becomes apparent that, however voluntarily such a scheme may be accepted by the smallest countries, there are strong political reasons for expecting that it will not prove operational for the Community of the Nine. (p. 17)

After predicting that intra-EMS exchange rate changes were inevitable and that they would increase in frequency and diminish in effectiveness Vaubel (1979) suggested that:

> What must worry all advocates of European integration is precisely that the choice of an unworkable strategy will – again, and this time fatally – discredit the whole idea of a united Western Europe. (p. 19)

In a more wide-ranging critique of the EMS, Vaubel (1980) strongly challenged the claims made for the divergence indicator by defenders of the system. First, he argued that 'a divergence indicator which assigns a "moral" responsibility for economic policy adjustment to the most deviant country, regardless of the direction in which it deviates, is inconsistent with the declared aim of reducing inflation rates in the Community' (pp. 182–3). Second, he maintained that the divergence indicator could not be relied upon 'to function as an early warning sign', (p. 185). Third, Vaubel (1980) suggested that:

> the divergence indicator does not only discriminate between member currencies because it is less likely to flash if the two extreme currencies have little weight

than if they have much weight; it will also drive the extreme currency with the smaller weight to its threshold before the extreme currency with the larger weight. (p. 186)

Fourth, Vaubel (1980) criticised the defenders of the divergence indicator for neglecting 'the fact that the obligations of member countries whose currencies reach an ECU-threshold are vague to the point of being meaningless' (p. 187). The final criticism of 'the divergence indicator scheme [was] that it [left] open the choice of currencies for intramarginal intervention, thus adding to market uncertainty and exchange rate instability' (p. 187).

Vaubel (1980) then turned his attention to the ECU. He dismissed 'the ECU as a means of settlement' on the grounds that it had 'virtually no effect' and declared it 'redundant' (p. 195). Next, he disputed whether the ECU could solve the nth-currency problem since it is not possible 'to gain an additional degree of freedom for exchange-rate policy by adding a currency unit which is merely composed of fixed amounts of the existing member currencies' (p. 197). Finally, Vaubel (1980) expressed severe doubts as to whether the ECU could develop into a European parallel currency.

Similar criticisms of the EMS were developed by De Grauwe and Peeters (1979), the latter being a signatory of the All Saints' Day Manifesto. They expressed strong reservations about the potential usefulness of the divergence indicator and asserted that the ECU was an unsatisfactory unit of account, an unsuitable means of payment and unlikely to emerge as an attractive store of value. In their view the ECU lacked the potential to develop into a European parallel currency and, consequently, they rejected it. In brief, they questioned the durability of the EMS.

Fratianni (1980), also a signatory of the All Saints' Day Manifesto, argued that 'the future of the ECU as a viable parallel money [was] not promising' (p. 151) and predicted that the 'EMS will work at best like the snake system with low-inflation countries revaluing periodically *vis-à-vis* high-inflation countries' with the German mark continuing 'to perform its *de facto* role of dominant money within a restricted group of Community countries' (pp. 155–6). He concluded that:

> The European Monetary System does not represent a forward step toward the achievement of monetary union in Europe. Behind the lofty ideals and the complex machinery of the December 1978 European Council resolution lies the desire of politicians to regain control over exchange rates without simultaneously

relinquishing control over domestic liquidity and, hence, the ability to determine national rates of inflation. The EMS is destined to become an adjustable-peg system. How well this system will fare depends on the disparity of inflation rates and the timeliness of parity adjustments. The current disparity of inflation rates and underlying policies among EEC countries suggests frequent realignments. Yet history teaches us that decision makers perceive parity changes as costly political decisions and, therefore, postpone taking action. (p. 165)

In contrast, in 1980 Emerson (1982) argued that 'the idea of a common, hard currency for Europe' had become 'a less controversial proposition' and maintained that 'the idea of progressing in monetary integration with the aid of parallel currency techniques [had] advanced, and could advance much more in the next few years on the basis of the ECU' (pp. 31–2).

The judgement that the Community member countries lacked the political will necessary for the successful operation of the EMS provided an alternative basis for the prediction that the system would not survive. Cohen (1979), after diagnosing the lack of 'political will' as the cause of the failure by the Community member countries to implement the Werner Plan and approvingly quoting Hirsch's conclusion 'that European monetary integration is not a serious issue' (p. 46), proceeded to assess the motivation of Community member countries in establishing the system in the following terms:

An EMS motivated by a sense of mutual confidence would pose few difficulties for the United States. *The problem, however, is that cooperation with the United States does not really seem to be what the Europeans have in mind.* Much more crucial to their thinking is the distrust of American policy that has become so endemic in recent years, symbolised by the system's stated purpose to create a 'zone of monetary stability' in Europe. The long decline of the dollar in 1977–78 wreaked havoc in European financial markets. The principal attraction of the EMS for most Community members is that it would help to shield them from similar instabilities in the future. *Isolation from America, not cooperation, seems to be the main purpose of the exercise. And this clearly will pose difficulties for the United States.* (p. 47, italics added)

Cohen (1979) proceeds then to argue that if the EMS were successful it would have undesirable consequences for the United States as 'the danger of further pressure on the dollar through continued switching by investors into European currencies (or into the ECU, if and when it becomes available)' (p. 47) would not be reduced. However, for Cohen (1979) Europe's 'isolationist' motivation suggested 'that the EMS may well never be successfully implemented' because it lacked the characteristic necessary for success, namely that it was a 'serious issue' (p. 47). As the EMS was not a 'serious issue' he argued that the 'most probable outcome' was that the system would 'simply fail' (p. 48). But such a failure would 'probably' result in 'even greater pressure on the dollar' (p. 48). Quite remarkably, then, the EMS was a threat to America whether it successfully survived or spectacularly failed.

In a more temperate assessment of the prospects of the EMS, Bryant (1979) suggested that if the establishment of the system simply reflected a disillusion with exchange rate flexibility or a preference for essentially fixed exchange rates, then the system was not likely to survive. On the other hand, if the creation of the EMS was motivated by a desire that in the pursuit of national macroeconomic objectives intra-EMS exchange rate changes would be 'orderly' and 'prompt', then the outlook for the system was more favourable. But if the objective of the EMS was to stimulate European integration, Bryant (1979) argued that the system seemed 'certain to be abortive' (p. 23). However, if the aim of the EMS was to revive the process of integration and its creation was followed by the introduction of 'a number of complementary direct measures to bring about a convergence of domestic economic policies' (pp. 23–4) and the required political will existed, then Bryant (1979) 'could reasonably foresee progress toward genuine integration... and good prospects for exchange rate stability' (p. 24).

Critical reactions to the establishment of the EMS also rested on perceptions that the system constituted a threat to the IMF and that the ECU would undermine the viability of the SDR. For example, D. Healey (1978)[6] in presenting the British Government's views to the House of Commons Expenditure Committee had outlined eight principles, which if the scheme under consideration were to embody them it 'would make sense for Britain to join a European monetary system', the seventh being that the system 'should not operate to the detriment either of currencies outside (like the dollar or the yen), or to the detriment of the international monetary organisation to which the Third World and Commonwealth countries belong (the IMF)'. Not surprisingly, then, defenders of the system sought to provide reassurances that the EMS presented no threat to America, the IMF or the SDR. Baquiast (1979) explained that the 'EMS respect[ed] the objectives and the Articles of Agreement of the International Monetary Fund' (p. 53) and how the system's 'operating rules [were] fully compatible with those of the IMF' (p. 53). Further, he declared that 'the ECU is not in competition with the SDR' (p. 55) which prompted Solomon (1979) to ask 'why it was necessary for the European countries to create a new reserve asset – the ECU – as a means of settlement' and why the Community could not 'have used the SDR for this purpose?' (p. 58). Still on the same theme Triffin (1979) argued that 'a sensible response to the EMS' by America required 'first of all, a determined attempt to "listen" before responding' (p. 60). He went on to maintain that 'the EMS should be viewed as an unprecedented opportunity to help the United States and the world resolve the awesome dollar problem' and to stress that 'Europeans share with Americans a deep desire to restore the dollar as a currency worthy of the richest and most powerful country in the world.' (p. 70). He suggested that the EMS could potentially contribute to the solution of the dollar problem as 'the adoption of the ECU as a parallel currency [could] soon enable the United States to denominate some official foreign borrowings in ECUs' (p. 71). Finally, he expressed the view 'that a successful functioning of the EMS and of the links to be established between it and the dollar area [could] provide invaluable guidelines for the reforms that will be negotiable and feasible on a global scale' (p. 73).

Schmidt's decision first to approach Giscard d'Estaing, and having secured his support to proceed to present his proposals to the Copenhagen summit, and the secrecy of the negotiations among the personal representatives of the French President, German Chancellor and British Prime Minister, who was after a few weeks left out, prior to the Bremen summit, provide a partial explanation of the reactions to the creation of the EMS. But even in the post-Bremen discussions that finally determined the principal features of the EMS van Ypersele (1979), who significantly influenced the design of the system, noted that with 'a few notable exceptions... the academic community [had] been largely absent' (p. 139). Similarly, Spaventa (1979) after asserting that 'the initiative to set up a European monetary system was suddenly and unexpectedly taken by a Prime Minister and a Head of State' (p. 144) goes on to observe:

> In almost all participating countries, the issue of the feasibility of the EMS caused a remarkable divorce between expert opinion, as expressed by officials, central bankers and academic circles, and political action. Arrangements of a very technical nature had to be almost improvised, in a great hurry, under political pressure. *It is perhaps an unprecedented fact that delicate options on highly technical matters were left to the decisions of a final meeting of unassisted (and often uninterested) Prime Ministers and Heads of State.* (p. 145, italics added)

The process through which the EMS was established and its main features determined was also denounced by Ken Cousins, the British representative in the secret discussions after the Copenhagen summit, in a press briefing soon after the Bremen meeting. *The Times* (1979) reported his views as follows:

> While still accepting the goal of greater monetary stability, *the Treasury remains sceptical to the point of contempt of most of the detailed content of the Franco-German scheme...* There is considerable anger at the way in which the proposal was 'sprung' on the rest of the Community... More substantial criticisms revolve around the vague and often confused terms in which the scheme is phrased, *coupled with deep suspicion that the system is little more than a means of holding down the mark and imposing restrictive policies on Germany's partners.* There is considerable resentment at what is seen as the success of the German government in presenting its national interest as being a move for the great good of Europe... *The fact that the whole thing is dealt with in just a few hundred words is generally felt to show the danger of allowing enthusiastic amateurs to dream up schemes for monetary reform.* (italics added)

4 ASSESSMENT

The decision to establish the system was perceived as running against the growing tide of opinion in favour of market forces and against governments' intervention in the economy. Assessments of the system were significantly influenced by the debate on fixed versus flexible exchange rates, with support for the latter being identified as consistent with the view that market solutions to economic ills are necessarily superior. But the debate on economic liberalism versus government interventionism was irrelevant for the debate on fixed versus flexible exchange rates and, therefore, when assessing the desirability of the EMS. As long as a decade earlier, Mundell (1969) had clarified that:

> The argument against fixed exchange rates is sometimes put as one of opposition to government price fixing: a liberal (or 'libertarian') is by tradition opposed to government price-fixing and therefore fixed exchange rates. But this is a false presentation of the case for liberty and should be scrapped. *The real choice is between price-fixing and quantity-fixing.* A country can fix the price of its currency to the international standard and allow the quantity to adapt, under a properly-run fixed exchange rate system; or it can fix the quantity of its

currency (or its rate of increase) and allow the price of it to adapt, as under a flexible exchange rate system. *Quantity-fixing is not necessarily more 'liberal' than price-fixing.* (p. 635, italics added)

The EMS did not reveal an 'inflationary bias' as it evolved during the 1980s. Nor did it reveal a relative deflationary bias. De Grauwe (1990) among others, was unable to detect any significant difference between countries which operated the Exchange Rate Mechanism (ERM) and countries which did not, in terms of the cost incurred in reducing their inflation rates. He noted, however, that the choice of anti-inflation strategies available to ERM countries had been limited by their EMS membership. Non-member countries could opt either for a gradualist or a rapid approach to the reduction of their inflation rates. But for member countries, because of their exchange rate commitments, the latter approach was not an available option. Thus, De Grauwe (1990) concluded that the EMS could be 'interpreted as a system which makes it hard for countries to gain reputation but makes it harder to lose their reputation once they have acquired it' (p. 171).

The supporters of the EMS turned out to be wrong when predicting that the divergence indicator would ensure the symmetry of the system. But the critics were just as wrong in their prediction that the EMS would be a highly asymmetric system dominated by Germany. Fratianni and von Hagen (1992) presented compelling evidence demonstrating that the German Dominance Hypothesis lacked empirical support while the statistical findings of Weber (1991) implied that the EMS during the 1980s operated as a bipolar system. In brief, empirical research has provided no support for the assertion that the EMS functioned as a German mark zone and would justify the description of Germany's position within the system as one of first among equals.

Nor were critics right when they predicted that intra-EMS exchange rate realignments would increase in frequency with the passage of time. What happened was exactly the opposite, with member countries' inflation and money supply growth rates becoming increasingly convergent.

Critics of the system accurately predicted that the ECU would not evolve into a European parallel currency and in this respect defenders of the EMS turned out to be wrong. Although it grew to be more attractive than the SDR and its private use substantially increased, it demonstrated no real potential to evolve into a genuine parallel currency. Therefore, the fact that the SDR did not develop to provide a momentum for international monetary reform can not be attributed to the presence of the ECU. But neither did the establishment of the ECU nor the actual operation of the

EMS provide the impetus for the creation of a new international monetary system. Triffin's expectations turned out to be ill founded.

The prediction that the EMS would not survive rested partly on assessments of the causes of the collapse of the 'Bretton Woods' system and partly on the fact that the system was somewhat ambiguous in that it did not embody a well defined set of rules and obligations to be adhered to by member countries. The EMS differed from the 'Bretton Woods' system in many respects. The difference, however, which implied that the experience of the latter was entirely irrelevant in any assessment of the viability of the EMS was that relating to the conditions of membership of the two systems. The international monetary system created at 'Bretton Woods' in 1944 was the outcome of a compromise between the White and Keynes Plans, with the former predominating. With the possible exception of Canada, no other country had a significant input. That in itself would eventually have generated friction in the post-1945 international monetary relations. However, even that system never became operational. The conditions attached to the Marshall Plan resulted in the system being still-born. The system that collapsed in 1973 was not that agreed upon at 'Bretton Woods' in 1944. It was a system created by the US for the US. Economic conditions after 1945 and the Cold War forced the rest of the world to acquiesce in an international monetary system over the design and development of which they had no influence. Withdrawal from the 'Bretton Woods' system was not an option available to any country. But with the relative economic decline of America the collapse of the system became inevitable. The process by which it came into being and its subsequent evolution implied that it could not be reformed while its replacement was not feasible as America continued to be the dominant country.

In contrast, the EMS reflected an informally agreed arrangement, in that its establishment did not become embodied in the Treaty of Rome. Countries were free to choose for or against membership. The UK decided against participation, then joined it and two years later dropped out of the system. Such behaviour was not possible under the 'Bretton Woods' system. This, of course, reflects that the position of America in the Western alliance in general and within the 'Bretton Woods' system in particular was significantly different from the position of Germany within the European Union (EU) even since the early 1980s. Schmidt was able to proceed with his proposals only after he had secured the unambiguous support of France. The difference between the two countries' relative positions in the respective systems may, perhaps, best be highlighted in terms of Mundell's

(1972) theory of monetary colonialism. While it provides an excellent explanation of the evolution of the 'Bretton Woods' system, it is entirely inadequate for an understanding of how the EMS functioned. In brief, the experience of the former was not an appropriate input in the assessments of the viability of the latter.

The establishment of the EMS was not accompanied by anything resembling the IMF Articles of Agreement. That is, Cousins was right when pointing out 'that the whole thing [was] dealt with in just a few hundred words' as Spaventa also was when complaining that 'unassisted' politicians made final decisions on highly technical matters. Therefore, it is true that the EMS did not rest on a set of well-defined rules and obligations and was shrouded in many ambiguities. This was perceived as a major weakness, and provided the basis for the judgement that the system was not viable. This perception involved a gross error of judgement. It rested on a total misjudgement of the nature of the Franco-German initiative. Ludlow (1982) convincingly argued that:

> The essence of the Bremen Annex is to be found not in its detailed provisions, but in the political determination that lay behind it and that it faithfully reflected. (p. 108)

Ludlow (1982) maintained that the British 'failed to grasp the significance of the determination of the French and the Germans to get something done, come what may' (p. 108). This was true not only of the British but also of the more general reaction to the establishment of the system. As it turned out, the EMS did generate a 'zone of monetary stability' in Europe through the monetary co-operation of member countries. It was not the features of the system or the world environment that secured this success. Ultimately, it was the unequivocal political commitment of the member countries, particularly of France and Germany, to the success of the system that ensured that monetary stability in Europe did emerge.

It may be objected that the above line of argument is ill founded as the 1992–93 crisis, which forced the widening of the permitted band of fluctuation, confirmed the prediction of those critics who back in 1978–79 had argued that the system would not survive. Such an objection is not sustainable as it ignores the fundamental change in the status of the EMS following the agreement on the Maastricht Treaty in December 1991. The EMS from being an informal arrangement, adherence to which involved no Treaty obligations for the EU member countries, was elevated to play a significant role in the implementation of the Maastricht Treaty. Its continuing existence became inextricably linked with the fate of the Treaty. Intra-ERM exchange rates came under pressure the day after the Danish referendum, the result of which generated severe doubts as to whether the EU could or would proceed with the implementation of the Maastricht Treaty. These doubts escalated as the date of the French referendum approached and its result became increasingly difficult to predict. Inevitably intra-ERM exchange rates came under pressure, as the new rationale for the EMS was severely questioned. These pressures re-emerged after the election of the new French government in March 1993, whose actions and policy measures gave rise to doubts as to the solidity of the Franco-German alliance which had so far propelled the process of European integration. Therefore, the 1992–93 crisis was a crisis of confidence in the political commitment of the EU member countries to proceed with the implementation of the Maastricht Treaty. The EMS of 1992 was not the EMS of 1978.

The EMS not only succeeded in establishing a 'zone of monetary stability' in Europe but in the process it also paved the way for Europe's monetary unification.

5 CONCLUSIONS

The success of the EMS was not anticipated at the time of its establishment. Assessments of the prospects of the system rested on essentially false premises. Had the political nature and implications of the Franco-German initiative been fully appreciated, then reactions to the creation of the system would have been radically different. It would have revealed that its collapse was not politically possible and, therefore, that it necessarily involved the first step towards Europe's monetary unification. In other words, the success of the EMS should have been anticipated.

Are similar errors of judgement currently being made by the participants in the debate on whether or not EU monetary union is desirable or viable? Can Germany and France afford the political cost of failure? Can monetary union survive without political union?

NOTES

1. See Ludlow (1982).
2. Giscard d'Estaing (1969).

3. See Ludlow (1982).
4. See House of Commons (1978).
5. See House of Commons (1978).
6. See House of Commons (1978).

REFERENCES

All Saints Day Manifesto for European Monetary Union, *The Economist*, 1 November 1975.

The Banker (1979) 'The problems of the EMS', January.

Baquiast, H. (1979) 'The European Monetary System and International Monetary Relations', in Trezise, P. H. (1979).

Bergsten, C. F. (1973) 'Comments', in Krause, L. B. and Salant, W. S. (eds) *European Monetary Unification and its Meaning for the United States*, Washington, DC: The Brookings Institution.

Bilson, G. F. O. (1979) 'Why the Deutschemark could trouble the EMS', *Euromoney*.

Bryant, C. R. (1979) 'Comments', in Trezise, P. H. (1979).

Cohen, B. J. (1979) 'Comments', in Trezise, P. H. (1979).

De Grauwe, P. (1990) 'The cost of disinflation and the European Monetary System', *Open Economies Review*, **1**: 147–73.

De Grauwe, P. and Peeters, T. (1979) 'The EMS, Europe and the Dollar', *Euromoney*.

De Vries, T. (1980) 'On the meaning and future of the European Monetary System', *Princeton Essays in International Finance*, No. 138.

Emerson, M. (1979) 'The European Monetary System in the Broader Setting of the Community's Economic and Political Development', in Trezise (1979).

Emerson, M. (1982) 'Experience under the EMS and prospects for further progress towards EMU', in Sumner, M. T. and Zis, G. (eds) *European Monetary Union: Progress and Prospects*, London: Macmillan.

European Communities (1984) 'Five Years of Monetary Cooperation in Europe', Communication from the Commission to the Council (Brussels, COM (84) 125 final).

Fratianni, M. (1980) 'The European Monetary System: a return to an adjustable-peg arrangement', *Carnegie-Rochester Conference Series on Public Policy*, **13**: 139–72.

Fratianni, M. and von Hagen, J. (1992) *The European Monetary System and Monetary Union*, Boulder: Westview.

Giscard d'Estaing, V. (1969) 'The international monetary order', in Mundell, R. A. and Swoboda, A. K. (eds) *Monetary Problems of the International Economy*, Chicago: Chicago University Press.

House of Commons (1978) *The European Monetary System: First Report from the Expenditure Committee Session 1978–79*, London: HMSO.

Jenkins, R. (1978) 'European Monetary Union', *Lloyds Bank Review*, (127): 1–14.

Jenkins, R. (1989) *European Diary, 1977–81*, London: Collins.

Ludlow, P. (1982) *The Making of the European Monetary System*, London: Butterworth.

McMahon, C. (1979) 'The long-run implications of the European Monetary System', in Trezise (1979).

Mundell, R. A. (1969) 'Toward a better international monetary system', *Journal of Money, Credit and Banking*, **1**: 625–48.

Mundell, R. A. (1972) 'The optimum balance of payments deficit', in Claassen, E. and Salin, P. (ed.) *Stabilization Policies in Interdependent Economies*, Amsterdam: North Holland.

Mussa, M. (1979) 'Empirical regularities in the behaviour of exchange rates and theories of the foreign exchange market', *Carnegie-Rochester Conference Series on Public Policy*, **11**: 9–58.

Solomon, R. (1979) 'Comments', in Trezise (1979).

Spaventa, L. (1979) 'Comments', *Bulletin de la Banque Nationale de Belgique*, **1**: 144–5.

Sumner, M. T. (1980) 'The operation of monetary targets', *Carnegie-Rochester Conference Series on Public Policy*, **13**: 91–130.

The Times (1978) 11 July.

Trezise, P. H. (ed.) (1979) *The European Monetary System: Its Promise and Prospects*, Washington, DC: The Brookings Institution.

Triffin, R. (1979) 'The American response to the European Monetary System', in Trezise (1979).

Van Ypersele de Strihou, J. (1979) 'Comments', *Bulletin de la Banque Nationale de Belgique*, **1**: 134–43

Vaubel, R. (1978) *Strategies for Currency Unification: The Economics of Currency Competition and the Case for a European Parallel Currency*, Tubingen: J. C. B. Mohr.

Vaubel, R. (1979) *Choice in European Monetary Union*, Ninth Memorial Wincott Lecture, London: Institute of Economic Affairs.

Vaubel, R. (1980) 'The return to the new European Monetary System: objectives, incentives, perspectives', *Carnegie-Rochester Conference Series on Public Finance*, **13**: 173–222.

Weber, A. (1991) 'Reputation and credibility in the European Monetary System', *Economic Policy*, **12**: 57–102.

Williamson, J. (1977) *The Failure of World Monetary Reform, 1971–74*, Sunbury-on-Thames: Nelson.

Discussion of Chapter 3

Christopher Allsopp

George Zis, in this useful chapter tracing the political and economic background to the European Monetary System (EMS), argues (a) that the exchange rate regime was an unexpected success, but (b) that the underlying political commitment was such that success should have been anticipated. He goes on to pose the question whether similar mistakes are now being made, for similar reasons, about the prospects for EMU. I would see this argument (in terms of description, although not prescription) as firmly in what used to be called the 'Monetarist' as opposed to the 'Economist' camp. In the context of monetary integration the so-called 'monetarists' believed that it was possible to put the cart before the horse. The horse of technical detail and of political and institutional change would follow once the cart of EMU was in place. Political acts with political commitment would force the pace.

There is much to agree with in the arguments put forward. The political positions of France and Germany were, as described, crucial in the institution of the EMS and have been equally important in the Maastricht Treaty and the formation of EMU among the eleven. In this comment, however, I argue that what happened with the EMS (more strictly, with the ERM) was (a) not as unexpected as suggested in the paper and (b) not so much of a success. Indeed, while it is true that the EMS led on, via the Delors Plan and the Maastricht Treaty, to EMU, it is also arguable that it was the predictable failures of the ERM, spectacularly in 1992–93, that sharpened the commitment to monetary union for those countries that decided to join (as well as demonstrating the potential difficulties for those that stayed out).

THE PHASES OF THE EMS

The significance of the EMS, and the nature of the arguments that surrounded it, changed over time. To an extent, this supports George Zis' arguments. The system was not set in stone, and it did adapt, partly because the political commitment was strong. (Some analyses about its likely effects turned out to be spectacularly wrong. For example, in the UK, nearly all initial comment suggested that if sterling were to join it would lead to overvaluation and a deflationary bias: in the event, the pound, outside the system, rose and rose in 1979 and 1980 far above the level at which it would have started.)

In the first phase, up to about 1987, the ERM, in fact, operated extremely flexibly. Initially, there was not much option given that its birth coincided with the second oil crisis and a marked change in US policy, from Carter and a weak dollar to Reaganomics and a soaring dollar. What is remarkable is that the intention to avoid the problems of the 'Bretton Woods' breakdown, with wider bands and timely realignments, proved to be successful. The system operated more-or-less as a crawling peg. Otherwise, it appeared to be welcomed as providing support to generally restrictive policies. The tensions were extreme only in the case of the 'Mitterand experiment' in France, which was abandoned in favour of the *franc fort* policy and the EMS with marked effects on the political credibility of the latter.

In the period after 1987 up to the breakdown in 1992/93, the ERM became a very different system. There were no more realignments and the accent was increasingly on the exchange rate regime as a disciplining device and on credibility – elements that were reinforced with the signing of the Maastricht Treaty in 1991. Meanwhile, the system was coming under increased pressure. One source of this was the commitment to remove capital controls within the single market programme. Another, obviously, was the major shock of German reunification. The basic point surely is that as the regime changed from a flexible system supported by capital controls to an inflexible, fixed exchange rate system without capital controls, it became, in effect, an accident waiting to happen. And when it did happen, it happened for just the 'technical' reasons that many of the early critics had focused upon.

BREAKDOWN

The chapter skirts over the breakdown in 1992/93 arguing that it was 'inextricably linked' with the fate of the Maastricht Treaty. This is surely too simple a view. The tensions due to increasing inflexibility and especially due to German reunification were there anyway. And the nature of the breakdown illustrates and exemplifies many of the different concerns of the early critics. A superficial sketch might go as follows:

- In Italy, relative inflation meant that international competitiveness was being seriously eroded – a situation that came to look unsustainable to market operators. This was surely the classic problem of fixed but adjustable exchange rates, with delayed adjustment leading to sure-thing speculation and enforced devaluation.

- In the UK the most serious problem was the need to match German interest rate policy, in a situation of recession. (Competitiveness was also an issue, but not, in my view, as important as the inappropriate monetary stance). The political impossibility of raising interest rates to fight exchange rate weakness – due in large part to a Tory party divided on European issues – also led to sure-thing speculation and crisis. Importantly, monetary policy did change markedly after the crisis. What the UK experience illustrates most clearly is the difficulties that can arise from a one-size-fits-all monetary policy in a situation where the limits of fiscal policy had effectively been reached.

- France survived speculative attacks in 1992 but succumbed in 1993. In France the 'fundamentals' did not suggest a need for realignment. The crisis nevertheless occurred illustrating further the fragility of fixed exchange rate systems when capital mobility is high. Although the system broke, France's monetary and exchange rate policy did not in fact change once the crisis was over.

- Generally, the system did not cope well with the large asymmetric shock of German reunification. This was, of course, a one-off event. But other shocks could happen. Moreover, it could be argued that ERM members were lucky not to have faced threatening divergences of national policy priorities through from the early 1980s until 1990.

EVALUATION

So, was the EMS an unexpected success? The answer depends, obviously, on what is meant by unexpected and what is meant by success. This comment has suggested that the system operated flexibly up to the late 1980s so that, given policy adjustments (especially the change in policy in France) and timely realignments, the problems of the 'Bretton Woods' system were largely avoided. Success of a kind, but perhaps not the 'zone of monetary stability' that the architects of the EMS had in mind. When the system became inflexible (in part because of the continuing commitment to monetary integration) and was shocked by German reunification it fell apart in predictable and predicted ways.

The author is surely right to stress the importance of the political commitment of France and Germany. But it is difficult to go along with the idea that the system was too important to fail. It did fail. What is interesting is that the failure led on to monetary union among the eleven. That, perhaps, was unexpected. But, on the author's own arguments, perhaps it should have been predicted.

Are there implications for EMU? The political commitment is there. The author of the chapter would surely agree, however, that it would be dangerous to regard that as in any way a substitute for a well-designed set of institutions and policies capable of withstanding the shocks and conflicts which will undoubtedly occur.

4 Tumbling Giant: Germany's Experience with the Maastricht Fiscal Criteria

Jürgen von Hagen and Rolf Strauch

1 INTRODUCTION

From the first time European Monetary Union (EMU) was officially declared a goal of European integration in 1969, to its realisation thirty years later, Europeans were divided over the question whether the common currency should be the beginning or the end of a process of monetary and fiscal convergence.[1] The former was claimed by the 'monetarists', who argued that the adoption of a common currency would lead to the convergence of price and wage developments and of fiscal performance among the member states. The opposite view was held by the 'economists', who thought that the stability of the common currency could only be guaranteed, if the member states first proved that each could live with fiscal and monetary discipline.

The introduction of a set of formal convergence criteria into the Maastricht Treaty shows that the 'economists' ultimately prevailed. The fiscal criteria in particular were written into the Treaty upon the insistence of the German government. It is an irony of the Maastricht process that the very country that insisted on the need for entry criteria constraining fiscal policy proved unable to meet them except by resorting to emergency measures and budgetary accounting gimmicks at the last minute. Many observers attribute this oddity to the fiscal consequences of German unification, presumably a unique, exogenous shock. In this view, German unification is a classical case of tax smoothing: Germany was right to finance the real investment necessary to rebuild the East German economy with additional public debt. But this view is inconsistent with the nature of the public transfers actually paid to former East Germany since unification, which predominantly served to finance consumption.

In this chapter, we argue instead that the fiscal consequences of German unification were the endogenous outcome of a series of political choices based on short-run strategic considerations that led to the deterioration of public budgeting and budgetary institutions in Germany. The political revolution leading to unification was exogenous, but the measures taken to tackle the resulting economic problems were shaped by West German political concerns and actors. While former Chancellor Kohl and his government were trying to impose tighter budgetary institutions on its European partners, they let Germany's own fiscal institutions slip. As a result, Germany's post-Maastricht (and post-Kohl) fiscal institutions are much weaker than before, and Germany's fiscal policy outlook is a liability rather than a stronghold of stability for the EMU.

Below, we explain how the most critical aspect of the convergence process, the struggle to comply with the Maastricht fiscal criteria, evolved in Germany. Section 2 reviews Germany's performance as judged by the EMI's and the European Commission's Convergence Reports. Germany complied with all but the fiscal requirements. Section 3 presents an account of Germany's post-unification economic developments. Section 4 describes the resource flows to East Germany and the difficulties involved in the tax decisions taken to finance them. In Sections 5 and 6 we analyse the politics behind these fiscal measures. The last section concludes.

2 GERMANY'S RECORD IN THE MAASTRICHT PROCESS

We begin with a review of Germany's assessment in the official reports of the European Commission and the EMI. According to Article 109j of the Maastricht Treaty, these reports had to judge the achievement of a high degree of sustainable convergence by reference to a) the achievement of price stability relative to the three best performing member states, b) the sustainability of the governments' fiscal position, c) exchange-rate stability with respect to other currencies in the EMS and d) the convergence of the long-term interest rate as an indicator for market expectations of a country's inflationary or devaluation risk.

The exchange-rate criterion was no concern for Germany, as the Deutsche Mark was the reference currency of the EMS. Table 4.1 summarises Germany's performance regarding the inflation and interest rate criteria in the last two years before the start of EMU. German inflation was running at about half of the reference value. The long-term interest rate stood at 2.2 percentage points below the permitted rate. Neither one of these criteria posed any problem for Germany's economic policy.

From EMS to EMU

Table 4.1   German inflation and interest rate, 1996–98

	1996	1997	Feb. 1997–Jan. 1998
Inflation (HIPC)			
Germany	1.2	1.5	1.4
Reference value	2.5	2.7	2.7
Interest rate			
Germany	6.2	5.6	5.6
Reference value	9.1	8.0	7.8

Source: EMI (1998).

In contrast, Table 4.2 demonstrates that Germany did not comply with the fiscal sustainability criteria. At the beginning of the 1980s, Germany had had a relatively low level of public debt compared to other European governments. The debt ratio was 31.7 per cent in 1980; by 1983, it had risen to 40 per cent, fuelled by the economic crisis following the second oil shock. The Kohl government which assumed power in 1982 won the general elections in 1983 promising to put the country's public finances in order and to solve Germany's unemployment problem. While the government initially delivered some fiscal consolidation, its efforts in this regard lost force in the second half of the 1980s, although the deficit remained low and reached a small surplus in 1989.[2]

Table 4.2   Germany's fiscal performance, 1989–97

Year	Debt	Surplus	Structural surplus	Expenditures	Revenues
1989	41.8	0.1	0.4	45.0	45.1
1990	43.8	−2.1	−3.4	45.3	43.3
1991	41.5	−3.1	−5.3	48.1	44.8
1992	44.1	−2.6	−4.6	48.8	46.0
1993	48.0	−3.2	−3.4	49.9	46.3
1994	50.2	−2.4	−2.7	49.4	46.8
1995	58.3	−3.3	−3.1	50.1	46.6
1996	60.8	−3.4	−2.8	49.5	45.9
1997	61.5	−2.7	−2.1	48.2	45.4

Source: AMECO. All data per cent of GDP.

Germany's relatively favourable fiscal performance changed with unification. Its structural balance fell from a surplus of 0.4 per cent of GDP in 1989 to a deficit of 5.3 per cent in 1991. This structural worsening was initially hidden by the effects of the unification boom, as the actual deficit rose only to 3.1 per cent in 1991 and fluctuated around 3 per cent in subsequent years. In 1996, Germany's deficit ratio exceeded the Maastricht threshold of 3 per cent by 40 basis points. Accounting gimmicks, such as a special treatment for hospitals in the fiscal accounts, and one-time 'emergency' measures were necessary to reach a deficit ratio of 2.7 per cent in 1997. Judging from the deficit criterion, therefore, it is doubtful whether Germany complied with a 'strict' interpretation of the fiscal criteria, such as the Kohl government had vowed throughout the 1990s to apply in the final decision on EMU.

Meanwhile, the public debt ratio jumped from 41.8 per cent of GDP in 1989 to 61.5 in 1997. With a consistent increase of the debt ratio after 1992, Germany clearly violated the Maastricht criteria, which demanded a sufficient *decline* of the debt ratio.

3 FISCAL CONSEQUENCES OF GERMAN UNIFICATION

The mere dynamics of German unification were stunning. It was only a year from the Leipzig mass demonstrations to the political unification of Germany in October 1990. As a consequence, some critical decisions were taken under immense time pressure and largely led by political and electoral considerations.

A first, important decision was the determination of the conversion rate between the East German Mark and the West German Deutsche Mark. Against the Bundesbank's strong opposition, this rate was fixed at 1:2 for most bank accounts,[3] but for prices, wages, and pensions the conversion rate was set at 1:1 (Bundesbank, 1990). This had immediate fiscal policy implications. As pensions claims in the German social security system are based on the retiree's wage (BMA, 1998) the higher conversion rate resulted in higher demands on social security, both in terms of current flows and in terms of the implicit pension liabilities the system had to take on.

A second, important decision was the immediate and full extension of West Germany's labour market institutions to East Germany, including an unemployment insurance characterised by both a high level and a long duration of unemployment benefits.[4] Until 1993, the replacement rate in the German unemployment insurance was 68 per cent for an unemployed individual with at least one child, and 63 per cent for unemployed without children. These rates were lowered to 67 per cent and 60 per cent, respectively, in the Consolidation Act of 1993. The duration of benefits varies from one year for individuals up to the age of 45 to 32 months for individuals above age 57. When insurance benefits expire, they are replaced by unemployment aid, which has no maximum duration for individuals below age 65, although individuals have to reapply annually. In 1994, replacement rates were lowered from 58 per cent to 56 per cent for individuals with at least one child and from 57 per cent to 53 per cent for unemployed without children (BMA, 1998; Steffen, 1995).

The extension of West German unemployment insurance to East Germany defined the rules of wage bargaining in East Germany in a way that allowed West German employers and labour unions to fend off the competition of low-wage workers from East Germany. Unions feared that competition for the pressure it might exert on the high wage level in West Germany. Employers were equally dismayed with the prospect of low-wage competitors from the new parts of the country. Their collusion was facilitated by the fact that wage negotiations in East Germany were soon taken over by West German unions. Western union leaders presented themselves as acting on behalf of the East German workers, as East German unions had fallen into political disrespect for their association with the communist regime. To eliminate wage competition from East Germany, employers associations and unions in 1991 agreed on a stepwise adjustment of East German wages to Western levels. Several industries – most importantly the steel industry – expected to have the same wage levels in East and West Germany by 1994 (SVR, 1992:107–10).[5] Moreover, unions striving for a very rapid adjustment of wages signed contracts only for less than a year to facilitate re-negotiations and a quick upward move of wages.

Figure 4.1 illustrates the resulting wage movements. From 1990 to 1991 wages in East Germany rose by 18 per cent. This was followed by a wage increase of 32 per cent for 1992 and 19 per cent in 1993. Later on, the wage hikes became more moderate and from 1995 onward real wage growth actually fell below labour productivity gains. Productivity also increased during the process, but far less than wages during the initial phase. Productivity gains peaked at 10 per cent in 1993 and have been around 6 per cent since then.

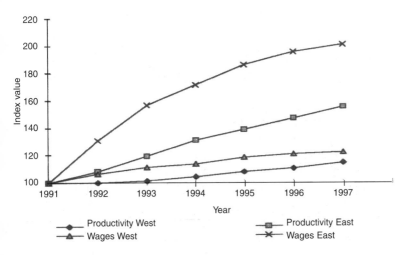

Wages indicate the collective bargaining agreements computed as real hourly earnings; productivity is the GDP produced by a worker per hour.

Figure 4.1   Wages and productivity in East and West
Germany, 1991–97 (Deutsche Bundesbank)

The result of this could only be to price East German labour out of the market.[6] But high wage levels secured high unemployment benefits, which left the unemployed better off staying in the East than moving to West Germany to find employment. Massive unemployment in East Germany was the result (Sinn, 1995; von Hagen, 1998a).[7] Instead of creating jobs in the East, the adjustment process triggered huge social transfers flowing from West to East Germany. As a result, privatisation of East German enterprises became possible only with large wage subsidies.

The federal government responded to the rise in unemployment with an unprecedented level of labour market interventions. In fact, German unification marks the beginning of a 'new era' of labour market policy in the country. Table 4.3 reports the number of participants in different labour market schemes and the unemployment rate for East Germany. Between 183,000 and 388,000 employees, or 2 to 5 per cent of the German labour force, participated in public works programmes from 1991 to 1997. A similar number of employees were enrolled in training programmes. This number fell to 171,000 in 1997 after a peak of 428,000 in 1992. Early retirement and provisional retirement schemes were a third kind of labour market policy. The number of beneficiaries in these programmes increased from 554,000 in 1991 to 853,000 in 1993 and then levelled off to 58,000. At the peak, some 11 per cent of the total labour force benefited from these schemes. An even larger number of individuals were included in programmes supporting part-time work during the initial stage of the transition process. Part-time employees receive a full time-equivalent if their enterprises cut working hours due to a structural change or 'inevitable circumstances' (BMA, 1998). In 1991 1.6 million employees received such transfers, that is 19.6 per cent of the labour force, but the number was continuously and forcefully reduced during the subsequent years to 50 thousand recipients in 1997. The total full-time work equivalent of these measures amounted to almost 20 per cent of the labour force in 1991 and to approximately 11 per cent in more recent years. Taken together, these policies created what became known as a 'secondary labour market' in Germany.

Empirical evidence on the effectiveness of these measures in terms of a reintegration of participants in the labour market is rather disappointing.[8] Only on-the-job-training or training demanded by enterprises seem to have a positive effect on the individual's chances of finding employment. None of the other programmes can be found to have a positive employment impact. In particular, they have failed to re-integrate the long-term unemployed into the labour market (Bertold and Fehn, 1997). Unemployment in East Germany rose from 11.1 per cent in 1991 to more than 18 per cent in 1998, with some regions suffering unemployment rates above 25 per cent. Thus, the interventionist policies were unable to overcome the structural weaknesses of Germany's highly administered labour market. The limited effectiveness of this approach is particularly noteworthy because alternative economic strategies were proposed already at an early stage of unification, but ignored by the Kohl government. Most alternative proposals suggested letting the market determine wages and paying transfers to employees that could not support themselves or their families at the market wage rate, instead of tying transfers to unemployment. This would have helped to overcome the inherited labour market distortions and keep unemployment low in the first place (see Akerlof *et al.*, 1991; Sinn and Sinn, 1991).

Table 4.3   The labour market in East Germany, 1991–97

	1991	1992	1993	1994	1995	1996	1997
Employees in part-time work	1616	370	181	97	71	71	50
Employees in job-creation schemes	183	388	260	281	312	278	235
Employees in training schemes	169	428	351	248	250	238	171
Employees in early retirement – or transitional old-aged schemes	554	811	853	650	374	186	58
Employed persons	7321	6387	6219	6330	6396	6259	6053
Unemployed persons	913	1170	1149	1142	1047	1169	1363
Unemployment rate	11.1	14.4	15.1	15.2	14	15.7	18.1
Participation rate (per cent)	51.7	48.0	47.1	48	48.1	48.1	48.1

Figures are in thousands or in per cent

Source: Deutsche Bundesbank (1998), Autorengemeinschaft (1998).

4 FISCAL IMPLICATIONS

4.1 Transfer Flows

Table 4.4 reports the total net transfers flows paid to East Germany by the various parts of the German government. Total gross transfers rose from DM 139 billions in 1991 to DM 189 billions in 1997. The federal government's share in these transfer flows increased over time. The West German Länder, early on, looked for a financing arrangement which would confine their fiscal burden to predictable amounts. This arrangement was found in the German Unity Fund (Schwinn, 1997: 51–4). The Western Länder paid only small transfers to the East beyond their contributions to this fund, and until the inclusion of the new Länder in the equalisation scheme of the 'Länderfinanzausgleich'. Direct transfers from Western Länder and local governments to their East German counterparts did not exceed 14 billion Deutsche Mark, or 8 per cent of the total transfers in 1994.

From EMS to EMU

Table 4.4   Public gross transfers to East Germany, 1991–98 (bn Deutsche Mark)

	1991	1992	1993	1994	1995	1996	1997	1998*
Federal Budget	75	88	114	114	135	138	131	139
'German Unity' Fund	31	24	15	5	–	–	–	–
EU	4	5	5	6	7	7	7	7
Pension Fund	–	5	9	12	17	19	18	18
Labour Office (BfA)	25	38	38	28	23	26	26	28
Länder and local governments in West-Germany	5	5	10	14	10	11	11	11
Total	*139*	*151*	*167*	*169*	*185*	*187*	*183*	*189*
of which (per cent)								
Social security benefits	40.3	45.0	46.1	43.7	42.7	44.9	44.2	44.4
Subsidies to firms	5.8	6.6	6.6	10.0	9.7	8.0	7.7	8.5
Investment	15.8	15.2	15.6	15.4	18.3	17.6	17.5	17.5
Cash transfers (not classifiable)	38.1	33.1	31.7	30.8	29.2	29.4	30.6	29.6

* indicates preliminary figures as planned in the budget.
Source: Deutsche Bundesbank (1997), BMF (1998).

Table 4.4 also reports the functional distribution of these transfers. The largest share is transfers to private households. Social security payments rose from 56 billion to 84 billion between 1991 and 1996, between 40 and 46 per cent of total gross transfers. A large part of these expenditures were payments from the federal government, which were channeled through the social security system to overcome its financing shortages (see Table 4.5). Moreover, the federal government directly paid for social security benefits under early retirement schemes and unemployment support.

Federal support to the social insurance system would have been even bigger without the transfers made from within the system. These transfers were heavily needed to finance the falling ratio of receipts to expenditures in East Germany. While the revenues of the unemployment insurance collected in East Germany covered 50 per cent of its East German expenditures in 1990, this ratio dropped to 7.2 per cent in 1993 and only increased slightly afterwards, reaching about 10 per cent in 1997 (Table 4.6). A general increase in the unemployment insurance contribution rates led to a surplus of the system in West Germany that was used to cover expenses in East Germany. While the federal government covered deficits in the German

Table 4.5 Financial transfers of the Federal Government (bn DM), 1991–97

	1991	1992	1993	1994	1995	1996	1997
Transfers to East German private households	27.2	32.9	52.6	44.6	44.5	46.3	–
• unemployment aid	0.3	1.5	3.5	4.9	5.7	6.8	–
• early retirement	5.7	5.1	5.0	7.2	8.2	5.6	2.1*
• unemployment ins.	5.9	8.9	24.4	10.2	6.9	13.8	9.6
• pension system	7.7	8.7	10.7	13.5	15.1	16.2	17.4**
• others	7.6	8.7	9.0	8.8	8.6	3.9	–
firms	19.7	22.9	20.2	25.3	25.0	21.6	–
states and communities	9.5	6.6	7.6	7.3	32.6	32.3	–

* This is a preliminary figure as planned in the budget. ** The figure includes a preliminary part as planned in the budget.
Source: Boss (1998), BMF (1998).

pension system throughout the 1990s, the rate of contributions to expenses remains much higher in West than in East Germany. As shown in Table 4.6, this rate fell from around 81 per cent in 1991 to 56 per cent in 1997, as a result of rising unemployment, rising early retirement benefits and rising wage levels. Thus, although social security and unemployment insurance have no explicit geographical dimension, the uneven regional distribution of unemployment and the fact that East Germans did not contribute fully to the pension fund imply that these schemes became channels of massive regional income redistribution (Czada, 1995).

Table 4.6 Ratio of contributions to expenditures for unemployment insurance and pension fund (%)

	Unemployment insurance		Pension fund	
	West	East	West	East
1990	92.6	50.4	86.0	–
1991	148.7	15.2	85.0	80.9
1992	154.4	7.2	83.4	69.4
1993	129.4	7.1	78.9	65.4
1994	133.6	9.0	81.0	62.2
1995	131.1	11.1	80.7	57.8
1996	120.5	10.2	81.8	55.6
1997	127.5	9.5	84.0	56.0

Source: Deutsche Bundesbank.

Public investment in East Germany financed by West German or federal administrations amounts to much less than the transfer payments to individuals, as indicated in Table 4.4. Public investment rose from 22 billion to 33 billion during the period considered, and never exceeded a fifth of the total transfers. This is a clear refutation of the tax-smoothing interpretation of German fiscal policy after unification. Current subsidies to East German enterprises are the third most important transfer category amounting to 8 billion in 1991 and 16 billion in 1997.[9]

Not included in these figures are the expenditures and liabilities incurred by the Treuhand, the East German privatisation agency. The Treuhand financed its expenditures through privatisation proceeds and borrowing in the capital market. The agency was allowed to raise capital market funds in order to take over liabilities of the former socialist firms as well as to guarantee private loans these firms made. Table 4.7 gives some details. From 1990 to 1994, the Treuhand channelled between 6 and 47 billion Deutsche Mark annually into East German industries and labour markets. In the last two years of its existence this is equivalent to 46 per cent of the federal transfers to the East German Länder. Interest payments on the debt inherited from former socialist firms only account for a small part of the overall expenditure level. Thus, in 1993 the interest paid to the debt processing fund came close to one-fifth of the Treuhand's expenditures. In general, privatisation proceeds never sufficed to cover expenditures and the Treuhand experienced rising deficits due to its spending on other activities.

Table 4.7   The Treuhand expenditures, revenues and debt (bn DM), 1990–94

	Second half of 1990	1991	1992	1993	1994
Expenditures	5.9	27.6	41.2	46.6	46.6
Revenues	1.6	7.7	11.6	8.5	9.5
Balance	−4.3	−19.9	−29.6	−38.1	−37.1
Liabilities from socialist enterprises	9.8	5.5	37.8	23.4	1.9
Change of debt	14.1	25.3	67.4	61.5	36.3
Interest paid to the debt processing fund	–	1.1	7.7	4.2	2.7*
Interest on own debt	4.4	9.9	8.3	9.9	10.3

* Not included in the preceding two lines.

Source: Boss (1998: 3).

4.2 Financing the Fiscal Expansion

In the very early debate over German Union, it was assumed that the financing needs of East Germany would be transitory and that the East German economy would pick up after a while. In this view, unification would ultimately be self-financing and the initial increase in public spending could be financed largely by government borrowing. The preceding stabilisation of Germany's public debt in the 1980s supported that view, as did the initial unification boom that increased government revenues. Only when it became clear that the transfer flows were going to be permanent, did the government have to resort to raising tax rates to start financing the increased public spending. Even then, the federal government never developed a consistent financing strategy for German unification. One can find different reasons for this default. First, the government probably wanted to avoid an open recognition that it had destroyed the East German labour market. Second, the rising tax burden triggered a public debate about Germany's attractiveness as a business location from 1993 onward. Since the government never mobilised the political strength to cut spending, it had to engage in revenue raising activism under conflicting goals. The result was a financing strategy that can best be characterised as a process of muddling through (Sturm, 1998a).

The changes to the 'solidarity surcharge' on personal income tax are a telling example for the conflicting orientations of tax policy. Introduced in 1991, when the additional financing needs could no longer be denied, it was presented as a temporary measure and abolished in 1992. But the continued financing needs forced the Government to re-impose it in 1995, at a rate of 7.5 per cent. This time it was introduced indefinitely; but political struggles within the government coalition centred around it in subsequent years. The Liberal Democrats pushed for the abolition of the surcharge arguing that it increased an already excessive tax burden. But the Christian Democrats were not willing to reduce public spending accordingly. In the end, a lower tax rate of 5.5 per cent was adopted in 1998 (Bundesbank, 1997; SVR, 1995, 1997).

Table 4.8 presents a summary of the tax measures introduced by the federal government between 1991 and 1997. A short glance at this table reveals the multitude of tax initiatives affecting almost any major tax category, some with reductions of the tax rates, other with increases, still others with tax exemptions. Most changes occurred in income and corporate income tax laws.

Table 4.8 Tax changes from major tax initiatives for selected tax categories, 1991–97

Tax Initiative	Income tax	Corporate tax	Solidarity tax	Trade tax	Wealth tax	Value added tax	Inheritance tax	Motor vehicle tax	Capital income tax	Others
General Tax Law 1991	x	x	x	x	x	x		x		x
General Tax Law 1992	x			x	x	x	x		x	
Zinsabschlagsgesetz (1992)	x	x			x				x	
Consumer and Common Market Law (1992)	x	x		x						x
Consolidation Pact (1993)	x	x	x	x	x	x	x	x	x	x
Standortsicherungs-gesetz (1993)	x	x		x			x		x	x
Consolidation and Growth Pact (1993)										x
Tax Evasion and Tax Simplification Law (1993)	x	x		x	x	x	x	x	x	x
Social Care Insurance (1994)	x									
Value added Tax Changes and other Laws (1994)	x		x	x		x				
General Tax Law (1996)	x	x	x	x	x	x	x			
Housing Construction Programme (1996)	x		x							
General Tax Law (1997)	x	x	x	x		x	x			
Tax Support for New Länder (1997)	x	x				x				

Source: SVR (1995), BMF (1997, 1998).

Given the usual lag structure of changes in income and corporate income tax laws, these initiatives affected revenues over the subsequent years. The Bundesbank (1997) warned that the amount of tax exemptions induced an erosion of the tax base. The mounting complexity of the tax system and the rising tax burden are also regarded as the main reasons for the increasing tax evasion. This can be observed from Table 4.9. The table shows that the share of corporate income tax in total tax revenues fell significantly between 1991 and 1995. Furthermore, the assessed part of income tax, which contains tax rebates from business and personal allowances, was reduced to a negligible part of total revenues. Both developments can be attributed largely to the tax deductions for investments in East Germany (see Deutsche Bundesbank, 1997; Scharrer *et al.*, 1998).

Table 4.9   Share of income and corporate income tax

Year	Tax revenues	Income tax	Income tax ('veranlagte Einkommensteuer')	Corporate tax
	Share of GDP	Share of Taxes to Total Tax Revenues		
1991	21.6	48.5	6.7	5.2
1992	22.1	48.6	6.1	4.6
1993	22.1	49.0	4.8	4.0
1994	22.1	46.7	3.5	2.7
1995	22.2	45.0	1.8	2.4
1996	21.2	42.5	1.6	3.9
1997	20.4	42.4	0.8	4.5

Source: Deutsche Bundesbank.

These revenue shortfalls not only presented a problem in themselves, but also caused a reduced predictability of revenue flows and, hence, fiscal planning capacity. As the Council of Economic Advisors (SVR, 1997) put it, revenues were uncoupled from economic growth, which made it increasingly difficult to forecast revenues. The figures reported in Table 4.10 indicate the problems which the tax forecasting committee had in recent years to predict the actual revenues.[10] Repeatedly, it overestimated future revenues by double-digit billion amounts. Even the Spring and Fall estimates of the current year were often higher than the actual outcome, although the forecast error is smaller. This complicated fiscal planning and produced unexpected financing gaps leading to emergency measures, as well as extraordinary attempts to raise revenue. Thus, Finance Minister Waigel made use of his prerogative to block expenditures in March 1995, and again in June 1997 (SVR, 1996: 138, 1997: 121). One of the most obvious signals of the government's troubles in meeting the Maastricht criteria was its attempt to force the Bundesbank to revalue its gold reserves against accounting conventions in May 1997, and cash in the resulting accounting profits.

Table 4.10   Tax forecasts – deviations from actual values, 1991–97

Year	Difference between forecast and actual outcome			Actual outcome
	November previous year	May current year	November current year	
1991	12.3	10.9	2.2	661.9
1992	13.5	3.2	2.6	731.7
1993	−12.1	0.7	3.4	749.1
1994	3.9	1.2	2.5	786.2
1995	−35.1	−31.5	−5.4	817.3
1996	−31.7	−10.0	−5.0	800.0
1997	−24.8	−6.8	2.0	797.2

Source: SVR (1997: 116, 121).

5 POLITICAL FACTORS

The decomposition of the political system in the former GDR started at the beginning of the electoral campaign for the West German federal elections in 1990. Therefore, short term electoral reasoning became a strong element in a situation of general uncertainty about the economic fundamentals and consequences of unification. Together with the fear of massive migration from East Germany, election considerations were probably the main determinant for the speed and the terms of agreements on the Economic, Monetary and Social Union between the West and the East German governments. Economic reasoning and cautious policy advice were suppressed.

Earlier in 1989, electoral expectations for the governing coalition had looked rather bleak. The Christian and Liberal Democrats were trailing behind the Social Democrats in public opinion polls from the fall of 1989 to the spring of 1990. (Schwinn, 1997: 55) Working towards rapid unification strongly improved the position of the government parties; probably that was what Chancellor Kohl felt when he proposed his 10-point programme for a confederation of the two parts of Germany as early as November 1989. While the government had been in a defensive position before, merely reacting to the agenda set by the Social Democrats, the prospect of unification immediately changed its strategic position. Moreover, rapid unification under favourable terms promised a new electorate for the governing parties, at least at a later stage of the unification process. Both the favourable conversion rate for the monetary union and the terms of the social union that included the extension of Western labour market institutions must be seen against the background of these considerations. It is noteworthy, for example, that proposals of a more moderate conversion rate and a slower transfer of social institutions met stronger resistance from the federal government than from East German policy makers involved in the negotiations of the treaties in 1990.[11]

As indicated above, it was initially assumed that the economic transition was going to be a self-financing process. The Christian Democrats could employ this argument and a strategy of pure optimism concerning the burden of reunification, claiming the 'track record' of delivering the West German economic miracle after World War II and, more recently, of improving the country's economic stance during the 1980s. The Social Democrats, in contrast, could not effectively attack the position, because their admonitions for a more cautious unification strategy were often equated in the public debate with an attitude of spoiling the unique opportunity for unification.

As a result of these political factors, the financial arrangements provided by the first Treaty on Economic, Monetary and Social Union in 1990 were insufficient to sustain the unification process. Later in the course of 1990, when it became obvious that the unification costs were likely to be higher than initially estimated, the government could not change the political agenda any more without a tremendous loss of credibility. Thus, the unsustainable financial arrangements driven by electoral opportunism were carried forward into the Reunification Treaty.

The point is illustrated by the following episode. In August 1990, the last Finance Minister of the GDR, Walter Romberg, a Social Democrat, presented a forecast of the fiscal implications of unification for the East

German Länder during the coming years. Given the generous regulations of the social union, he predicted a sky-rocketing increase in public debt and asked for more transfers to East Germany. Yet strong pressures from the West German government eventually led the East German head of government, Lothar de Maizière, a Christian Democrat, to refrain from including this forecast in his official bargaining position in the negotiations of the Unification Treaty. Although most political actors, including the Western Ministry of Finance, knew that East German Länder and local governments did not have nearly enough resources to comply with the legal demands of the social union (Schwinn, 1997: 81–3), the political campaign prevented the adoption of an adequate financing arrangement, because that would have made the costs of unification explicit.

6 INSTITUTIONAL WEAKNESSES: THE DEMISE OF BUDGETING IN GERMANY

Decisions to spend other people's money are at the heart of fiscal policy. Above the level of local governments, public policy programmes typically involve an incongruence between those who pay and those who benefit. Political economy research shows that this leads to a spending and deficit bias, as policy makers try to attract as much funds paid by other people as possible for the benefit of their constituencies. Good budgetary institutions are critical to keep the political interests that produce fiscal profligacy in check and to keep these biases small.[12]

Germany's budgetary institutions at the federal level were traditionally among the strongest in European comparisons (von Hagen, 1992). Important characteristics of the traditional German budget process were the comprehensiveness of the budget, that is, the rule to make decisions with financial implications within the framework of the budget process, the relatively strong position of the finance minister relative to the other members of cabinet, based on a constitutional right to veto spending decisions, and the binding force of the budget law, that is the fact that supplementary budgets and in-year changes were rare. Given the importance of budgetary institutions to maintaining sustainable public finances (Perotti *et al.*, 1998), a significant aspect of German unification is that the government undermined and circumvented the traditional institutions. The resulting institutional deterioration plays a significant part in explaining the financial troubles of the German government after unification.

Table 4.11   Public debt in the 1990s (as percentage share of GDP)

	Federal govern- ment	Local govern- ments (West)	Local govern- ments (East)	ERP- fund	German unity fund	Kreditab- wicklungs- fonds	Erblasten- tilgungs- fonds	The Treuhand
1989	22.1	21.6	–	0.3	–	–	–	–
1990	22.3	20.3	–	0.4	0.8	1.1	–	0.6
1991	20.6	18.1	0.6	0.6	1.8	1.0	–	1.4
1992	19.8	17.8	1.4	0.8	2.4	3.0	–	3.5
1993	21.7	18.4	2.4	0.9	2.8	3.2	–	5.3
1994	21.4	18.3	3.3	0.8	2.7	3.1	–	6.1
1995	22.0	18.4	4.0	1.0	2.5	–	9.6	–
1996	23.8	18.3	4.3	1.0	2.4	–	9.4	–
1997	25.0	17.7	4.4	0.9	2.2	–	8.9	–

Source: Deutsche Bundesbank.

A first indication of this institutional deterioration is the use of resource flows not subject to the stringency of the formal budget process. The increased use of special funds by the federal government to finance German unification is the first, most obvious phenomenon in this regard. Table 4.11 gives a breakdown of the development of Germany's public debt after 1989.[13] While the federal government's debt only rose by 3 per cent of GDP in the wake of unification, the combined debt of the German Unity Fund, the ERP fund and the 'Erblastentilgungsfonds' rose quickly to 12 per cent of GDP, or almost half of the federal government's official debt. The Treuhand alone incurred an impressive debt of over 6 per cent of GDP, an amount of liabilities resulting in an increase of public debt from 0.6 per cent to 6.1 per cent of GDP in just five years. Additional funds, such as the 'Sondervermögen' (special asset fund) of the railways were used to hide away large amounts of public debt.

Significantly, the use of such funds implied that the decisions over a large part of the transfers paid to East Germany were not subject to the scrutiny of legislative control. The control of the otherwise powerful budget committee in Parliament was largely circumvented by the fact that the special funds did not appear in the budget. As a result, the committee's control powers became effective only when the changes in fiscal stocks and flows finally began to have an impact on the federal budget. A second phenomenon is the increased use of tax expenditures indicated above. While the budgetary effect of tax expenditures is the same as that of explicit subsidy payments, they are harder to control in the budget process, because they do not appear as an expense in the budget law.

The Treuhand is a particularly significant case as regards the loss of financial controls in the German government. *De jure*, it was an independent federal agency under the supervision of the Ministry of Finance and subject to the scrutiny of a special parliamentary committee. *De facto* the Ministry of Finance exercised partial control, at best, over its activities. The 'THA-Leitungsausschuß', an advisory committee to the Ministry of Finance working in the Treuhand, emerged from a group of comptrollers who were sent to Berlin to check the Treuhand's activities before it became an integral part of the government apparatus in October 1990. Later, this group monitored the privatisation projects of the Treuhand and made pertinent recommendations. But this did not yield effective control over the general financing situation, which could also not be enforced by the Ministry of Finance itself. Requests of the Ministry concerning the usage of funds the Treuhand borrowed in the capital markets or received from other sources were not necessarily answered. For example, the Treuhand's president Birgit Breuel flatly refused to produce information on the credit commitments which the Treuhand had made to firms taking over ex-socialist enterprises, commitments that reached an amount of Deutsche Mark 20 billion (Czada, 1994a: 40).

Nor was the Treuhand Committee in parliament able to exercise financial control, although it was vested with the formal authority to do so. According to the law, the committee had to agree on the amount of debt the Treuhand was allowed to raise. However, it had no control over the ways the money was spent. Although the committee put much effort into its control function, it did not effectively work as a 'safeguard of the purse'. A conflict between the Treuhand and the committee in 1993 illustrates the point. In June 1993, the Treuhand demanded an expansion of its credit limit by eight billion DM to finance some measures settled in the negotiations for the Consolidation and Solidarity Pact between the Federal Government and the Länder. When the committee approved seven billion DM, the Treuhand threatened to limit its commitments to public work agencies. The committee was eventually forced to concede to the Treuhand to avoid risking the consolidation package (Czada, 1994a: 35).

A second indication of the institutional deterioration is the increasing loss of influence of the Ministry of Finance over the financial decisions involved in German unification. During the initial unification process the

Ministry of Finance lost fiscal control due to its own drafting of the first treaty on social, economic and monetary union. In the treaty the West German government made financial commitments to its Eastern counterpart without having the legal authority and instruments to control the usage of the corresponding funds. The Ministry's unlucky role during this stage of the unification process may have further undermined its political position[14] which was generally weak due to Kohl's inclination to concentrate power in the Chancellor's office (Bundeskanzleramt). In fact, a Task Force on reconstruction in the Chancellor's office instead of the Ministry of Finance participated in most important decisions concerning the reconstruction of the East German Länder.

Moreover, a variety of informal decision-making forums sprang up under Chancellor Kohl's government. One example was the 'round tables' involving representatives of the parties in parliament, social groups, and the Chancellor's office to discuss issues such as labour market policies (Czada, 1994b). Ultimately, the agreements reached at these 'round tables' had financial implications, which, it seems, were often not fully considered by the participants, but which were later presented as unchangeable. The most important of these co-ordination circles was the 'Ludewig Round Table', where the prime ministers of the new Länder or their delegates, a representative of the Treuhand, and State Secretary Ludewig, acting as the representative of the Chancellor's office, discussed transition issues and policies, such as public work programmes and investment subsidies. This informal circle also took definite decisions and drafted fiscally relevant laws. Among other decisions, it set the eligibility criteria for public guarantees of private debts incurred by firms in Eastern Germany (Czada, 1994a: 41). In addition, the contacts emerging from these meetings were often used to furnish financing strategies for rescues of single enterprises in East Germany (Czada, 1994b: 257).

A third indication of the institutional deterioration is the increased 'ad-hoccery' of the fiscal measures, within or outside the pre-established setting of the budget process. Particularly prevalent in the early years of the 1990s was the Chancellor's tendency to promise financial aid to special interests and groups complaining of being particularly hurt by the transformation process. At the time, the German press was musing about the standard 'Chancellor billion' that anyone complaining seemed to be able to obtain. A particularly ironic aspect of this financial ad-hoccery was revealed to the public when the Chancellor complained that the German banking industry was not paying the government an amount of Deutsche Mark 10 billion the bankers had allegedly promised to spring for the good of German unification.

Finally, while German governments between 1952 and 1980 had resorted to supplementary budgets only four times, the Kohl government presented seven supplementary budgets between 1990 and 1997 (Sturm, 1998). Budget freezes and the last-minute revision of the budget proposal in December 1994 are similar signs of weakening budget management (ibid.). These incidents show that the Kohl government's fiscal policy increasingly became one of reactive budgeting rather than a consistent budgetary strategy.

Evidently, then, the Kohl government did not use the opportunity of the Maastricht process to strengthen Germany's budgetary institutions, as a number of other EMU member states did.[15] When the time of reckoning finally came in 1997, the government had resort to one-off measures and budgetary gimmicks to meet the very fiscal criteria it had verbally touted for so long to persuade the German public of the benefits of EMU. While the European Commission recognised that Germany's deficit ratio was by 20 basis points due to one-time measures, a German institute estimates that the budgetary gimmicks accounted for 40 basis points. Adding these to the official ratio of 2.7 per cent, an honest fiscal account would have caused a violation of the deficit criterion (DIW, 1998).

7 CONCLUSION

Germany's fiscal policy in the 1990s is characterised by a perplexing degree of schizophrenia. On the European front, the Kohl government spent every effort to insist on tight fiscal policies and on hardening the fiscal constraints embedded in the Maastricht Treaty. Domestically, in contrast, the same government showed a growing disregard for sound fiscal policies and for the rules set by the existing budgetary institutions. Disastrous financial decisions taken out of electoral opportunism were never reversed or replaced by a more long-term orientated financial strategy. The 1990s, therefore, leave Germany with a large fiscal problem that still awaits a sustainable solution. The fact that such a solution will ultimately involve reforms including in Germany's labour market institutions does not, of course, make it more politically palatable nor increase the chances that it will be provided by the left-wing government elected in 1998. The weakening of Germany's budgetary institutions in the 1990s is a significant negative legacy of the Kohl era, and one that risks resulting in a continued lack of German fiscal discipline in years to come.

One might argue that the rules of EMU will force Germany to attack its fiscal problems, anyway. But it seems doubtful that the constraints of the Stability Pact will be enforced by the EMU, if the very country that imposed them shows itself unwilling or unable to respect them. If this turns out to be correct, the weakening of Germany's fiscal institutions in the 1990s may have adverse consequences on fiscal discipline beyond the country itself.

NOTES

1. See Fratianni and von Hagen (1992) for a review of the pre-Maastricht debate over EMU.
2. For a more detailed discussion, see Perotti *et al.* (1998)
3. A preferential rate of 1:1 was applied to small savers, the vast majority of the East German population.
4. In contrast, the US unemployment insurance, for example, combines a high replacement rate and a short duration of benefits, while the UK system has a low replacement rate and long duration (Nickell, 1997).
5. After years of steady economic growth labour unions also made strong demands for wage increases in the West.
6. Anecdotal evidence suggests that unions deliberately took this into account. For example, the former chairman of the metal workers' union, F. Steinkühler argued: 'We knew that there would be firms which could not pay the negotiated wage increases due to their low productivity... And we knew someone had to pay... Everyone wanted reunification – the government, society, all political parties. Therefore everyone has to pay. This means that when firms with low productivity cannot afford these wage increases, then the Treuhand has to pay, that is, the government' (quoted in Burda and Funke, 1993: 551).
7. Theoretical models emphasise the role of unemployment benefits for the level of structural unemployment (see among others Driffill and Miller 1998). Empirical findings strongly confirm that high replacement rates in combination with their 'long-term' duration cause high levels of structural unemployment, above all if no effective active labour market policies are in place bringing people back to work (see Nickell, 1997; Siebert, 1997).
8. A literature overview and additional evidence is provided in Hübler (1997) and Berthold and Fehn (1997). See also Buttler and Emmerich (1995) and Heinelt *et al.* (1994).
9. According to Table 4.4, between 50 billion and 56 billion DM per year cannot be ascribed to any of these transfer categories, they include wage compensation for public employees and other transfers.
10. In the German budget process, tax revenues are forecast by a committee composed of the Ministry of Finance, the Ministry of Economic Affairs, the

6

0m EMS to EMU*

Ministries of Finance of the Länder, local government associations, the
Bundesbank, the Council of Economic Advisors and leading national research
institutes.
11. A particularly illuminating account of the negotiations is the biographic
essay of Tietmeyer (1994) who lead the negotiations for the West German
government.
12. For a review of this literature, see von Hagen (1998b), and Alesina and Perotti
(1997).
13. See Boss and Rosenschon (1996) and Kilian (1993) for a description of the
different funds and their functions.
14. See the biographic essay of Wolfgang Schäuble, head of the Chancellor's
office. He presents an episode where he employed this argument to counter
Waigel's assertion that the Unification Treaty bears 'unpredictable financial
risks' (Schäuble, 1993: 121–2).
15. See, for example, Hallerberg and von Hagen (1998).

REFERENCES

Akerlof, G. A., Rose, A., Yellen, J. L. and Hessenius, H. (1991) 'East Germany in
from the cold: the economic aftermath of currency union', *Brookings Papers
on Economic Activity*, pp. 1–101.
Alesina, A. and Perotti, R. (1997) 'Budget deficits and budget institutions', paper
presented at the NBER/ZEI Conference on Budgetary Institutions and Fiscal
Policy, Bonn, June 1997.
Autorengemeinschaft (1998) 'Der Arbeitsmarkt in der Bundesrepublik Deutschland
in den Jahren 1997–98', in *Mitteilungen aus der Arbeitsmarkt- und Berufs-
forschung*, **31**: 5–58.
Berthold, N. and Fehn, R. (1997) 'Aktive Arbeitsmarktpolitik – wirksames Instru-
ment der Beschäftiungspolitik oder politische Beruhigungspille', *ORDO*, **48**:
412–35.
Boss, A. (1998) *How Germany Shouldered the Fiscal Burden of the Unification*,
Kiel: Kiel Institute of World Economics, Kiel working paper No. 851.
Boss, A. and Rosenschon, A. (1996) 'Öffentliche Transferleistungen zur
Finanzierung der deutschen Einheit: Eine Bestandsaufnahme', Kiel: Institut für
Weltwirtschaft, Kiel Discussion Papers 269.
Bundesministerium für Arbeit und Soziales (BMA) (1998) *Übersicht über das
Sozialrecht*, 5th edn, Bonn: BMA.
Bundesministerium der Finanzen (BMF) (various issues) *Finanzbericht*, Bonn:
BMF.
Burda, M. and Funke, M. (1993) 'German trade unions after unification: third
degree wage discriminating monopolists?', in *Weltwirtschaftliches Archiv*,
129(3): 537–60.

Buttler, F. and Emmerich, K. (1995) 'Kosten und Nutzen aktiver Arbeitsmarkt-spolitik im ostdeutschen Transformationsprozeß', in Gutmann, G. (ed.) *Die Wettbewerbsfähigkeit der ostdeutschen Wirtschaft - Ausgangslage Handlungser-fordernisse, Perspektiven*, Berlin: Duncker and Humbolt, pp. 61–94.

Czada, R. (1994a) 'Die Treuhandanstalt im politischen System der Bundesre-publik', in *Aus Politik und Zeitgeschichte*, B43–44/94, pp. 31–42.

Czada, R. (1994b) 'Schleichweg in die 'Dritte Republik': Politik der Vereinigung und politischer Wandel in Deutschland', in *Politische Vierteljahresschrift*, **35**: 245–70.

Czada, R. (1995) 'Der Kampf um die Finanzierung der deutschen Einheit', Cologne: MPIFG, MPIFG Discussion Paper 95/1.

Deutsches Institut für Wirtschaftsforschung (DIW) (1998) 'Entwicklung des Staats-defizits im Jahre 1997 – Ein (notwendiger) Blick zurück', in *Wochenbericht* (25/98).

Deutsche Bundesbank (March 1990, October 1996, August 1997, April 1998) *Monthly Report*, Frankfurt am Main: Deutsche Bundesbank.

Driffill, J. and Miller, M. (1998) 'No credit for transition: the Maastricht Treaty and German unemployment', CEPR Discussion Paper No. 1929, London: CEPR.

European Monetary Institute (1998) *Convergence Report: Report Required by Article 109j of the Treaty Establishing the European Community*, Frankfurt: EMI.

Fratianni, M. and von Hagen, J. (1992) *The European Monetary System and Euro-pean Monetary Union*, Boulder: Westview Press.

Hallerberg, M. and von Hagen, J. (1998) 'Electoral institutions and the budget process' in Fukasaku, K. and Hausmann, R. (eds.) *Democracy and Decentral-ization in Latin America*, Paris: OECD.

Heinelt, H., Bosch, G. and Reissert, B. (eds) (1994) *Arbeitsmarktpolitik nach der Vereinigung*, Berlin: Sigma.

Hübler, O. (1997) 'Evaluation beschäftigungspolitischer Maßnahmen in Ost-deutschland', in *Jahrbücher für Nationalökonomie und Statistik*, **216**: 22–44.

Kilian, M. (1993) *Nebenhaushalte des Bundes*, Berlin: Duncker and Humbolt.

Nickell, S. (1997) 'Unemployment and labor market rigidities: Europe versus North America', in *Journal of Economic Perspectives*, **11**: 55–74.

Perotti, R., Strauch, R. and von Hagen, J. (1998) *Sustainability of Public Finances*, London: CEPR.

Sachverständigenrat (SVR) zur Begutachtung der Gesamwirtschafltichen Entwick-lung (various issues), *Jahresgutachten*, Stuttgart: Metzler-Poeschel.

Scharrer, H.-E., Wohlers, E., Weinert, G., Hinze, J., Krägenau, H., Wetter, W. and Winkler-Büttner, D. (1998) *Nachhaltigkeit: Beurteilung der Konvergenz ausgewählter Mitgliedstaaten im Vorfeld der Europäischen Wirtschafts- und Währungsunion*, Hamburg: HWWA, Report No. 179.

Schäuble, W. (1993) *Der Vertrag. Wie ich über die deutsche Einheit verhandelte*, Munich: Knaur.

Schwinn, O. (1997) *Die Finanzierung der deutschen Einheit*, Opladen: Leske and Budrich.

Siebert, H. (1997) 'Labor market rigidities: at the root of the unemployment in Europe', in: *Journal of Economic Perspectives*, **11**(3): 37–54.

Sinn, G. and Sinn, H.-W. (1991) *Kaltstart*, Tübingen: J. C. B. Mohr (Paul Siebeck)

Sinn, H.-W. (1995) 'Schlingerkurs: Lohnpolitik und Investitionsförderung in den neuen Bundesländern', in: Gutmann, G. (ed.) *Die Wettbewerbsfähigkeit der ostdeutschen Wirtschaft – Ausgangslage Handlungserfordernisse, Perspektiven*, Berlin: Buncker and Humbolt, pp. 23–60.

Steffen, J. (1995) 'Die wesentlichen Änderunen in den Bereichen Arbeitslostenversicherung, Rentenversicherung, Krankenversicherung und Sozialhilfe (HLU) in den vergangenen Jahren', mimeo.

Sturm, R. (1998) 'Finanzpolitik am Ende oder vor der Wahl? Akteure, Instrumente und Blockaden in der Finanypolitik', in: Andersen, U. (ed.) *Der Deutsche Steuerstaat in der Finanzkrise*, Schwalbach: Wochenschau Verlag.

Tietmeyer, H. (1994) 'Erinnerungen an die Vertragsverhandlungen', in Waigel, T. and Schell, M. (eds) *Tage, die Deutschland und die Welt veränderten: Vom Mauerfall zum Kaukasus: Die deutsche Währungsunion*, Munich: Ferenczy byat Bruckmann, pp. 57–117.

von Hagen, J. (1992) *Budgeting institutions and fiscal performance*, Brussels: European Commission DG-II, Economic Paper 92.

von Hagen, J. (1998a) 'East Germany: the economics of kinship' in Desai, P. (ed.) *Going Global: Transition From Plan to Market in the World Economy*, Cambridge: MIT Press.

von Hagen, J. (1998b) *Budgeting Institutions for Aggregate Fiscal Discipline*, Bonn: ZEI, Policy Paper B9–01.

5 France and the Maastricht Criteria: Fiscal Retrenchment and Labour Market Adjustment

Stephen Bazen and Eric Girardin

INTRODUCTION

A widely held view in France is that the sacrifices made in order to qualify for entry into EMU have been huge. The process had already started in the 1980s with the U-turn in macroeconomic policy in March 1983. A decisive choice was then made in favour of a restrictive macroeconomic stance on both the fiscal and monetary fronts, in order to maintain the franc within the ERM. According to this view, French monetary policy was entirely geared to the franc–mark parity, in order to import credibility from the Bundesbank. This entailed rising and persistent unemployment, a long period with no increase in real wages, and so on. The Maastricht convergence process was the crowning of this painful process, with a historic slashing of the budget deficit, and a killing of inflation.

Our objective is to assess the extent to which such a process really occurred in the 1980s and 90s. We will not deal with monetary policy since this was the subject of another paper (Bordes *et al.*, 1997) where we showed that after 1993 French monetary policy did indeed target the exchange rate *vis-à-vis* the mark, but other concerns, such as competitiveness *vis-à-vis* the dollar zone, certainly played a non-negligible role. Rather we want to focus here on two aspects which played a major role in determining the compliance with the Maastricht criteria, and which will continue to occupy the centre-stage even after the start of EMU, that is, both fiscal consolidation and labour market changes.

In the first section, we intend to examine the precise nature of the fiscal retrenchment implemented in the middle of the 1990s, to determine the impact of fiscal developments on household behaviour and to assess the likelihood that fiscal consolidation will prove durable.

95

Changes in the labour market are closely linked to fiscal developments, both because the high level of unemployment is one of the causes of the budget deficits, and because certain fiscal measures directly impact on the level of employment.

In the second section, we describe how various labour market variables have evolved during the 1980s and 90s, and go on to test whether wage setting behaviour has been modified in the process of convergence.

1 FISCAL POLICY AND ITS MACROECONOMIC EFFECTS

The overall assessment of the French situation by the EU Commission in its 1998 Convergence report is quite upbeat when it notes that since 1995 both the capping of public expenditure and the rise in the burden of taxation 'have laid the bases for a gradual and durable improvement in public finances during the following years' (EC, 1998, p. 108).

It is worth examining carefully the stages which characterised this fiscal adjustment and determining whether the success of such a programme should only be measured by its ability to cut the current deficit.

1.1 Was there a Large-scale Fiscal Retrenchment?

When the Maastricht treaty was agreed upon at the end of 1991, the French fiscal situation seemed relatively healthy. Gross public debt was only 40 per cent of GDP, the budget deficit was close to its cyclically adjusted level, in as much as output was not far from its potential level (see Table 5.1), and there was even a (primary) surplus when interest payments on public debt were removed. However, the recession was starting to bite, with GDP growth of only 0.8 per cent in 1991. This would be followed by 1.2 per cent in 1992 and −1.3 per cent in 1993. The high level of real interest rates (Table 5.1) in the wake of German unification played a major role here. The sharp fall in investment and the nearly complete stop in consumption growth are particularly noteworthy.

Did the process leading to French compliance with the Maastricht budget deficit criterion represent an episode of large-scale fiscal adjustment?

In the available literature (Alesina and Ardagna, 1998; Cour *et al.*, 1996) fiscal adjustment, which should reflect discretionary action by budgetary authorities, is measured by the change in the cyclically adjusted (or structural) primary deficit of the general government.

Table 5.1   Macroeconomic performance (%)

	1990	1991	1992	1993	1994	1995	1996	1997
Effective exchange rate	5.8	−2.1	3.3	2.3	0.7	3.6	0.2	−3.5
GDP real growth rate	2.5	0.8	1.2	−1.3	2.8	2.1	1.6	2.3
Output gap*	3.2	2.0	1.2	−2.0	−1.1	−1.0	−1.5	−1.2
Unemployment rate	8.9	9.5	10.4	11.7	12.3	11.6	12.3	12.4
GFCF growth	2.8	0.0	−2.8	−6.7	1.3	2.8	−0.5	0.4
Private consumption growth	2.7	1.4	1.3	0.2	1.4	1.7	2.0	0.9
Ex post long-term real interest rate [a]	6.5	5.8	6.2	4.6	5.6	5.7	4.4	4.6
Inflation rate								
CPI	3.4	3.2	2.4	2.1	1.7	1.8	2.0	1.2
RPI	1.4	0.8	−0.3	−0.5	0.8	1.7	−1.1	−0.4

* percentage points; [a] deflated by CPI.

Source: OECD, *Economic Outlook.*

Movements in the cyclically adjusted primary budget deficit as measured by OECD show a period of fiscal expansion over the period 1991–94
followed by fiscal retrenchment over 1995–97 (Table 5.2). The IMF
measure indicates an even sharper fiscal retrenchment.

Table 5.2   Measures of fiscal stance (% GDP)

	1990	1991	1992	1993	1994	1995	1996	1997
Actual deficit	1.6	2.1	3.9	5.8	5.8	4.9	4.1	3.0
Primary deficit	−0.8	−0.5	1.1	2.6	2.4	1.3	0.6	−0.3
Cyclically adjusted deficit								
(OECD)	2.3	2.1	3.6	3.8	4.4	3.7	2.7	1.7
(IMF)	2.8	2.3	3.4	3.2	3.7	3.1	1.9	0.9
Interest on public debt	2.4	2.4	2.7	2.9	3.1	3.3	3.4	3.3
Cyclically adjusted primary deficit (OECD)	−0.1	−0.3	0.9	0.9	1.3	0.4	−0.7	−1.6
(IMF)	0.4	−0.1	0.7	0.3	0.6	−0.2	−1.5	−2.4

Source: OECD, *Economic Outlook*, December 1998, except row 4: IMF *World Economic
Outlook*, October 1998.

From EMS to EMU

From 1.6 per cent of GDP in 1990, the actual budget deficit reached 5.8 per cent in 1994. This increase was due almost equally to discretionary and cyclical factors since the rise in the structural deficit was close to 2 per cent of GDP while the cyclical part rose by 2.3 per cent (of GDP). The French experience stands out since over the 1990–94 period the structural deficit fell in many European countries (by 3.6 per cent of GDP in Italy, 3.5 per cent in Belgium and 3.0 per cent in the Netherlands) allowing the rise in their actual deficit to be limited (1.9 per cent, 0.6 per cent and 1.3 per cent respectively). The peculiarity of the French case in the first half of the 1990s can be explained by the fact that the expansion in structural deficits had already begun in the late 1980s at the time of the start of economic expansion. The fiscal stance did not change when the economy slowed down in the early 1990s. The sharp improvement over 1995–97, which led to a reduction of almost 2.8 per cent (of GDP) in the actual deficit, was mostly due to discretionary factors since the cyclically adjusted deficit fell by 2.7 (OECD) or 2.8 (IMF) per cent of GDP.

The debt/GDP ratio increased by more than a third during the fiscal expansion period (1994 compared to 1990), and it increased by a further fifth during the retrenchment period. The overall rise of 22.5 percentage points was due both to the primary deficits over the period 1992–96 and to dynamics specific to the debt/GDP ratio in as much as the rate of growth was continuously smaller than the level of the interest rate (Table 5.3).

Table 5.3 Dynamics of public debt: determinants of the changes in the debt/GDP ratio (% GDP)

	1993	1994	1995	1996	1997
Total change *of which*:	5.5	3.2	4.2	2.9	2.4
Primary surplus	2.4	2.2	1.1	0.3	−0.6
Interest / GDP growth	3.0	1.7	2.1	2.4	1.8
Stock–flow adjustment	0.2	−0.7	1.0	0.2	1.2
Level of gross debt/GDP	45.3	48.5	52.7	55.7	58.0

Source: European Economy, no. 65, 1998.

A period of large-scale fiscal adjustment is defined by Alesina and Perotti (1997) as (a) 'a year in which the cyclically adjusted primary deficit

falls by more than 1.5 per cent of GDP', or (b) 'a period of two consecu-
tive years in which the cyclically adjusted primary deficit falls by at least
1.25 per cent in both years' (op. cit. p. 220).

Table 5.4   Change in cyclically
adjusted primary deficit

	1995	1996	1997
OECD	−0.9	−1.1	−0.6
IMF	−0.8	−1.3	−0.9

Source: Table 5.2.

Table 5.5   Efficiency ratio of fiscal adjustment*

	1995	1996	1997
OECD	1.0	0.7	1.8
IMF	1.1	0.6	1.0

* Ratio of the (*ex post*) change in the actual budget deficit to
the (*ex ante*) change in the cyclically adjusted primary deficit.

Source: Table 5.2 and Table 5.4.

Using either the IMF or the OECD measure of the fiscal impulse
(Table 5.4) the French case never meets either definition (a) or definition
(b) over the 1995–97 period. In other words there was not a large-scale
fiscal retrenchment.

The efficiency of the fiscal adjustment (Table 5.5) can be assessed by
computing the ratio of the (*ex post*) change in the actual budget deficit to
the (*ex ante*) change in the cyclically adjusted primary deficit. Using the
OECD measure for a large sample of countries, Cour *et al.* (1996) found
an average efficiency ratio of 0.6, but reaching 1.5 in some countries, and
sometimes negative. In the French case, this ratio increased according to
the OECD measure, and reached an extremely high level in 1997.

1.2 Is Fiscal Adjustment Likely to be Successful?

In order to shed more light on fiscal adjustment, one should examine the composition of the fiscal retrenchment and its effects on the economy.

1.2.1 The composition of fiscal retrenchment

Fiscal retrenchment should have started already in 1994. The budget prepared for that year was supposed to be a restrictive one. This would have implied a freeze in real public expenditure. Even with receipts increasing slightly this would have led to a fall in the government budget deficit. Actually, economic growth being higher than planned, revenues increased sharply. This bonanza was unfortunately not used to cut the deficit but to finance new social expenditure, leaving the deficit at its planned level. This was indeed a missed opportunity. Besides, early in 1994, the government took charge of the stock of social security debt. These two factors led to yet another rise in the public debt to GDP ratio to 48.4 per cent.

Fiscal retrenchment started in 1995. The outgoing government had planned to reduce the budget deficit by freezing public expenditure in real terms. This would have implied mainly a cut in public investment and in transfers to local governments, but no change in taxes (OECD, 1997). The revised budget presented by the incoming government represented a major shift in priorities. A rise in selected public expenditure would be financed by sharp tax increases and a cut in some 'non-priority' spending. The increase in the tax burden amounted to some 1 per cent of GDP at a yearly rate. This involved a rise in the standard rate of VAT (from 18.6 to 20.6 per cent), and an exceptional 10 per cent increase in both the wealth tax and the profits tax. In spite of these two series of measures, net fiscal receipts in value terms increased by the same rate as in 1994, that is 3.7 per cent. In other words, when the exceptional measures are left out, net fiscal receipts increased only by 1.7 per cent, that is, only half the rate of growth of market value added. The rise in public expenditure was targeted on the long-term unemployed and the young, as well as on social housing and small firms. The slowdown in the rate of growth of public expenditure is noteworthy, from 4.6 per cent in 1994 to 2.1 per cent in 1995, even although interest service on public debt still increased at a high rate (10.8 per cent). Such a slowdown was generated mainly by a fall in capital expenditure. On top of this, the deficit in the social security budget did not fall, both because of the slowdown in economic activity and the increase in health expenditure.

The fiscal stance adopted in 1996 was aimed at significantly reducing the budget deficit. It is striking to find here a package which is very similar to the one prepared for 1995 by the outgoing government, that is, a reduction in public investment and the stabilisation in real terms of state transfers to local authorities. Moreover the wage scale of civil servants was frozen. The changes to tax rates were marginal. Eventually fiscal receipts were lower than planned because of a disappointingly low rate of GDP growth.

The novelty contained in the budget for 1997 involved the freezing of nominal public expenditure. This would imply an across-the-board reduction for most ministries and a marginal cut in public employment (5,600). The objective was to use such a freeze to reform (and reduce) direct taxation. The French income tax system is indeed characterised by a narrow base and a highly progressive scale. The reform aimed at broadening the base and reducing tax rates.

In 1997, mid-year, the budget deficit was forecast to reach 3.6 per cent by the year-end. A package was implemented including the freezing of public expenditure representing FF 10 billion, and an increase in revenues based on a 15 per cent rise in business taxes and a reform in the taxation of capital gains for businesses. As a result the share of taxes and social security contributions in GDP increased by 0.4 percentage points. The resulting fall in the government deficit to 3 per cent of GDP stems also both from a slowdown in the rate of increase of public expenditure (to 2 per cent) and the much publicised payment by France Telecom of a lump sum (0.46 per cent of GDP) in exchange for the commitment by the state to pay pensions of those Telecom employees who are civil servants.[1]

Table 5.6 Composition of the public sector borrowing requirement

	1991	1992	1993	1994	1995	1996	1997
Total (billion of F)	142.3	277.4	401.5	423.6	372.2	323.4	243.0
of which:* (%)							
State:	83.2	81.8	80.6	82.4	82.2	90.2	110.0
Local governments:	9.6	8.6	3.5	3.4	3.1	2.0	−6.7
Social security:	13.0	17.3	22.6	15.9	18.2	14.6	20.0

* The sum is higher than 100 since other central government agencies were all along in surplus. In 1997, such a surplus amounted to 20% of the overall deficit.

Source: European System of National Accounts, *INSEE rapport sur les comptes de la nation*, various years.

The social security deficit and its fluctuations played a substantial role in the dynamics of the general government deficit. The rise in the former accounted for more than a third of the increase in the deficit between 1991 and 1993. By contrast, the improvement in the situation of local governments' budgets is noteworthy (see Table 5.6).

France is differentiated at the international level by its relatively high level of per capita health expenditure given its standard of living. Overall, since 1960, health expenditure in France has been rising more rapidly than GDP; as a proportion of GDP it more than doubled from 4.3 per cent in 1960 to 9.8 per cent in 1993. This increase has been particularly sharp during the early 1990s when GDP per head levelled off while per capita health expenditure carried on rising quickly. Such a rise is due predominantly to a quantity effect and not to the increase in the cost of providing health services. The ageing of the population does not seem to play a major role in the French case, while the increase in the supply of services linked to technical progress may be an important explanatory factor (INSEE, 1995).

A plan to reform social security was presented at the end of 1995. This relied on a new tax, aimed at repaying the accumulated social security debt (250 billion francs over the subsequent 13 years), broadly based on all types of incomes. Moreover social security contributions would be levied on pensioners and some of the unemployed. In addition family allowances were frozen. The main institutional novelty included an annual control by Parliament, with the latter voting the social security budget, as of the end of 1996. In the interim the annual rise in prescriptions by practitioners was capped at 2.1 per cent. The reform also involved the creation of regional agencies to control the financing of hospitals in charge of negotiating medium-run contracts with both private and public hospitals. These measures were supposed to reduce drastically the deficit in the social security budget, by 36 billion francs in 1996 and 59 billion in 1997. However, the slow implementation of this reform package plus the low rate of economic growth implied that in 1996 the actual deficit was hardly reduced.

In 1997, the task of cutting the social security deficit was tackled by partly transferring the source of financing from household contributions to direct taxes. Other measures involved both a rise in revenues and a cut in expenditure. Overall the ceilings set for the rise in health expenditure were not broken.

1.22 Composition and durability of fiscal retrenchment

Recent theoretical work (see the survey by Henin, 1997) has highlighted the possibility that the macroeconomic effects of large-scale fiscal retrenchment programmes could be the opposite to small-scale fiscal adjustment packages. Giavazzi and Pagano (1990, 1995) thus uncovered examples of cases (Sweden) with non-linearities in the consumption function: the impact of a fall in government transfers can change sign when the reversal in the fiscal stance is substantial and permanent enough. A systematic comparative study (Cour *et al.*, 1996; see below) found some supportive evidence of such behaviour for a number of countries.

The theoretical literature shows that the composition of the large-scale fiscal adjustment matters for its success. Thus a fall in public expenditure can signal that a threshold has been reached in the growth of public expenditure, such that a cut in spending will generate expectations of a fall in taxes (Bertola and Drazen, 1993). By contrast, fiscal adjustment relying on a rise in tax rates may signal that this expenditure threshold has not been reached, and lead to a fall in consumption, since agents anticipate higher future taxes (Manasse, 1996). A similar argument can be presented for a threshold level of public debt (Sutherland, 1997).

Recent empirical literature has emphasised that the composition of the fiscal retrenchment determines both the durability of the budget deficit reduction and the nature of the macroeconomic effects of the fiscal package. There is evidence that a durable reduction in a deficit accompanied by expansionary effects on the economy can be achieved when the fiscal retrenchment is implemented mainly through cuts in public expenditure, particularly bearing on (a) transfers and social security, and (b) wages and employment. Such a programme thus tackles the two items of public expenditure which have been regularly increasing over the recent period. A successful 'type 1' package (as dubbed by Alesina and Perotti, 1997) would hardly involve any rise in the tax burden and at best might even imply a fall in taxes on households. By contrast, a soon to be reversed fiscal retrenchment programme, which is likely to have restrictive effects on the economy, would very often involve a rise in the overall tax burden, especially with respect to social security contributions and household taxes. The expenditure side of such a 'type 2' package (Alesina and Perotti, 1997) would exclusively involve a cut in public investment, with other components of public expenditure remaining immune from the cuts.

When assessed in the light of available prior evidence, the fiscal retrenchment programme implemented in France since the mid 1990s

Table 5.7 Fiscal adjustment: size and composition (% of GDP)

| | BEFORE: 1990–94 | | | | | DURING: 1995–97 | | | CHANGE |
	1990	1991	1992	1993	1994	1995	1996	1997	1997/1994
Total primary expenditure	47.6	48.0	49.4	51.7	51.0	50.6	50.9	50.4	-0.6
Transfers	25.6	26.3	27.3	28.7	28.2	28.2	28.5	28.4	0.2
Government wages	13.2	13.4	13.8	14.4	14.3	14.4	14.5	14.4	0.1
Non-wage/government current consumption	4.8	4.9	5.2	5.5	5.2	5.0	5.1	5.0	-0.2
Public investment	3.6	3.6	3.5	3.2	3.2	3.2	3.1	3.1	-0.1
Total revenues	49.0	49.0	48.9	49.6	49.2	49.8	50.9	50.9	1.7
Indirect taxes	15.1	14.7	14.5	14.6	14.9	15.1	15.9	15.8	0.9
Social security contributions	21.0	21.0	21.3	21.6	21.1	21.3	21.6	21.0	-0.1
Direct taxes	8.9	9.3	9.0	9.2	9.4	9.5	10.0	10.6	1.2
of which: Income tax on households:	4.2	5.0	5.0	5.2	5.2	5.26	5.42	5.8	0.5
Profit tax on business:	2.1	1.8	1.4	1.4	1.5	1.57	1.67	2.0	0.4
Other	4.0	4.0	4.1	4.2	3.7	3.7	3.7	3.7	0.0

Source: INSEE (rapport sur les comptes de la nation, 1998–99) and EC (*European Economy*, 1998, no. 65).

belongs more to a type 2 fiscal adjustment programme (Tables 5.7 and 5.8). Indeed, the programme relied to a very large extent on tax increases (representing 1.8 percentage points of GDP, out of a 2.6 per cent cut in the primary deficit) which are typical of a type 2 fiscal adjustment package. The elements pertaining to a type 1 programme are a very small cut in transfers and a substantial cut in non wage government current consumption.

However, both the rise in public sector wages and the fall in social security contributions (as a share of GDP) are negative elements under the two types of fiscal programmes.

Table 5.8   Characteristics of the French fiscal retrenchment programme (% GDP)

	Type one	Type two
positive	0.1% cut in transfers 0.4% cut in non-wage government consumption	0.3% cut in public investment 0.5% rise in profit tax on business 0.9% rise in indirect taxes
negative	0.1% rise in public sector wages	0.3% fall in social security contributions

Source: Table 5.7.

In order to assess the likely success of the fiscal adjustment programme, we should track the context and effects of fiscal consolidation on macroeconomic variables, both real and financial. Since fiscal consolidation cannot yet be judged *ex post* in the French case, it is useful to compare the movements of these variables before and during consolidation with what it was in successful and unsuccessful cases of fiscal retrenchment in previous experiences for other countries, as documented by McDermott and Wescott (1996). The procedure used by the latter consists in correcting for the effects of the world business cycle, by measuring the variables as differences from weighted averages of industrial countries.

We consider here the path of macroeconomic variables for the year preceding fiscal action and for the two-year period during which fiscal action took place. We then see to what extent the French experience is closer to previous successful or unsuccessful episodes of fiscal consolidation. It seems best to consider 1994 as the year preceding fiscal action in France (column b, Table 5.9). For the two-year period of fiscal retrenchment, we take the average of either 1995 and 1996 or 1996 and 1997.

Table 5.9 Macroeconomic background and effects of French fiscal action

	One year before*				Two years during consolidation*			
	France		Successful	Unsuccessful	France		Successful	Unsuccessful
	(a)	(b)	(c)	(d)	(e)	(f)	(g)	(h)
Real GDP growth (%)	-2.3	-0.1	-0.18	0.11	-1.2	-1.6	0.10	-0.71
Employment growth (%)	-1.3	-0.8	-0.18	0.06	-1.4	-2.3	0.10	-0.71
Unemployment rate (change in %)	1.3	1.4	2.12	0.55	–	0.1	1.90	0.84
Real short term interest rate (%)	5.4	4.4	2.44	0.09	4.4	1.6	2.06	0.52
Real long term interest rate (%)	4.9	5.4	1.34	0.15	5.1	4.4	1.06	-0.27
Real private consumption (change in % GDP)	1.5	-1.4	-0.40	0.40	-0.1	-0.2	0.22	-0.14
Real private investment (change in % GDP)	-5.4	-1.5	-0.02	-0.54	-1.2	-1.0	0.80	-0.76

(a) 1993 ; (b) 1994 ; (e) Average 1995–96 ; (f) Average 1996–97

* Deviation from the average of OECD countries, except for consumption and investment.

Source: columns (c), (d), (g) and (h): McDermott and Wescott (1996).

With respect to the starting point, the French case seems closer to successful experiences for nearly all variables, that is negative GDP and employment relative growth, a large change in the unemployment rate, high real short-term or long-term interest rates as well as the fall in private consumption. The only dissenting element is the large fall in private investment, which would make the French case closer to unsuccessful previous experiences.

When considering the period of fiscal consolidation itself – columns (e) and (f) – the movements of all activity variables seem to make the French experience similar to an unsuccessful case. Indeed we notice negative relative GDP and employment relative growth, a fall in the GDP share of consumption and investment and a very small rise in unemployment. The only element which brings the French case close to a successful episode is the (positive) level of real interest rate differentials.

Overall, the *ex ante* assessment of the likelihood of success of the French fiscal retrenchment programme is that the initial situation seemed very favourable but the economic performance during the consolidation does not look promising. The assessment by the EU Commission that we quoted initially thus seems rather optimistic when viewed in the light of previous experiences of fiscal consolidation.

1.3 Fiscal Variables and Consumption Behaviour

Giavazzi and Pagano (1990) working on Ireland and Denmark, had found some evidence in favour of 'non-Keynesian' (that is, negative) effects on private sector savings of drastic cuts in government consumption. In later work on a panel of countries, with multiplicative dummies for fiscal policy variables during periods of fiscal adjustment, Giavazzi and Pagano (1995) showed that cuts in transfers and tax increases can have non-Keynesian or neo-Ricardian (Barro, 1974) effects on household consumption. Focusing on a specific country (Sweden), Giavazzi and Pagano (1995) also showed that a standard consumption function overpredicted private consumption (by 5 to 6 per cent in 1992 and 1993). They attributed (without a formal test of this hypothesis) this negative error to large-scale fiscal expansion in Sweden in the early 1990s. Private consumption would have fallen because current tax cuts would have led to expectations of higher taxes tomorrow.

It is worth considering here to what extent such non-Keynesian behaviour by French households could rather have been generated by a 'Maastricht effect'. With public deficits reaching nearly twice the ceiling set by the fiscal criteria, the probability of restrictive fiscal policies rose sharply because of the need to meet these criteria very quickly. The rise in taxes can thus be seen as imminent and not likely to be shifted to future genera- tions,[2] and households would respond by saving today in order to be able to pay such taxes in the medium run.

The existing work on consumption behaviour in the French case stresses the peculiarities of the early 1990s. Indeed a robust result of esti- mated consumption functions up to 1990 showed that real disposable income and inflation were the main determinants of French household consumption (Cadiou, 1995; Bonnet and Dubois, 1995). These determi- nants predicted a fall in the savings rate over the 1990–93 period, but instead (Table 5.10) it rose from 12.2 to 14.1 per cent. Two competing explanations were provided to account for this rise: the first relies on precautionary savings linked to the rise in unemployment, the second puts forward the effects of financial liberalisation[3] attributing a major role to short-term bank credit to households. Available evidence (Sicsic and Villetelle, 1995), focusing on the period up to 1994, seems to favour the latter element, which would be able to account for the 'missing consump- tion' of the early 1990s.

In its official report on the year 1995, the French Statistical Institute (INSEE, 1996), trying to explain such missing household consumption, mentioned the neo-Ricardian view, whereby faced with a sharply rising budget deficit, households would have increased their savings rate as a response to forecast future tax increases required by the rise in current deficits. The Institute suggested that while:

> available empirical work in the French case does not validate over the past [i.e. before 1990] such behaviour by households, one cannot exclude the conclusion that the response by households to a worsening of public sector deficits as sharp as we have seen from 1991 onwards would be stronger than in the past. However this remains to be proved. (INSEE, 1996, p. 77)

Table 5.10   Household savings rate (% gross disposable income)

1990	1991	1992	1993	1994	1995	1996	1997
12.2	13.1	13.6	14.1	13.6	14.5	12.8	13.0

Source: OECD, *Economic Outlook.*

The strategy we adopt consists in building on the result of such previous work in order to see to what extent the specification of the French household consumption function which proved satisfactory up to the early 1990s is stable over the subsequent period and if not, to what extent fiscal variables can account for such instability.[4]

The general specification of the consumption function that we use, à la Davidson *et al.* (1978), is as follows:

$$\Delta c_t = \alpha_0 + \alpha_1 \Delta c_{t-1} + \alpha_2 \Delta y d_t + \alpha_3 (c_{t-1} - y d_{t-1}) + \alpha_4 \Delta 4 p_{t-1}$$
$$+ \alpha_5 \Delta(CRE - yd) + \alpha_6 \Delta(BS - yd) + \alpha_7 (SBS - yd)_{-1} + \alpha_8 \Delta(TRA - yd)_{-1} \qquad (1)$$

where (with all variables in logarithms):

c: real household consumption
yd: real household disposable income
p: household consumption deflator
CRE: short-term bank loans to households
BS: public sector budget surplus
SBS: fiscal impulse
TRA: public transfers
Δ: quarterly difference operator
$\Delta 4$:   annualised quarterly difference.

Estimating cross-country consumption equations similar to (1), Cour *et al.* (1996) used dummy variables for the budget surplus or its change, and found that large-scale fiscal retrenchments are accompanied by a slightly higher growth of consumption. They also noted that the change in the total budget surplus appears significant (with a positive coefficient) only during large-scale episodes, while there is no level effect, which implies that the influence of fiscal policy on consumption is significant only in the short run.

Estimating an equation such as (1) without fiscal policy variables, over the 1971–97 period with quarterly data, we confirm the results obtained in previous work (mentioned above), to the effect that short-term bank credit to households is a significant determinant of French consumption (Table 5.11, equation *(a)*) while the rise in unemployment does not seem to play a significant role.

Using recursive instrumental variables, we identify a degree of instability (of equation (a) in Table 5.11) at the beginning of 1993, with a fall in household consumption that such a model is unable to account for (Figure 5.1).

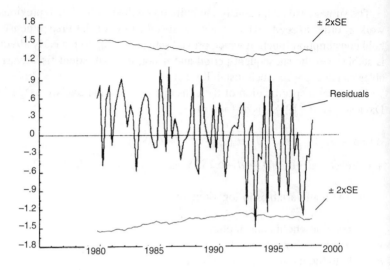

Figure 5.1   Recursive (one step ahead) residuals
for household consumption equation

Several methods are available for the cyclical adjustment of budget deficits. The OECD measure of the structural deficit defines the latter as the deficit associated with the growth in previous year's public expenditure in line with potential GDP and with the growth in previous year's revenue in line with actual GDP. The IMF measure takes as the benchmark not the previous year but the year when output was considered to have reached its potential level. Both measures suffer from the somewhat arbitrary procedure used to obtain potential output. A third, less arbitrary, measure was suggested by Blanchard (1993) and avoids such a procedure by computing what the budget deficit of the current year would be with no change in the unemployment rate compared to the previous year. One thus has to correct the budget deficit for the effects on taxes and transfers of changes in the unemployment rate.

In order to get a Blanchard type measure of the fiscal impulse with quarterly data, we implement a simplified version of the method suggested by Alesina and Perotti (1995, 1997) by regressing the general government budget surplus (as a share of GDP) on a constant and the current unemployment rate.[5] The fitted equation is then used to compute the level of the budget surplus (BBS) at the previous year's level of unemployment. The measure of fiscal impulse (SBS) is the difference between BBS and the actual budget surplus during the previous year. We implement this procedure over the 1970:1–1997:3 period.

Table 5.11 Household consumption function, 1971:4–1997:3

Dependent variable: Δc	*(a)*	*(b)*	*(c)*
Cst	−0.017	−0.015	−0.014
	(−3.88)	(−3.54)	(−3.31)
Δyd	0.41	0.45	0.38
	(1.95)	(2.14)	(1.87)
Δc_{-1}	−0.33	−0.29	−0.27
	(−3.85)	(−3.37)	(−3.25)
$\left[\Delta\dfrac{CRE}{yd}\right]_{-1}$	0.48	(0.43)	0.40
	(3.85)	(3.41)	(3.27)
$\Delta\Pi_{-1}$	−0.076	−0.08	−0.08
	(−3.15)	(−3.33)	(−3.23)
$(c-yd)_{-1}$	−0.15	−0.14	−0.135
	(−4.83)	(−4.63)	(−4.55)
9194 SBS_{-1}			−0.19
			(−1.62)
9597 SBS_{-1}			0.24
			(1.11)
9194 ΔBS		0.56	0.6
		(2.76)	(2.96)
9597 $\Delta TRANS_{-1}$		−0.61	−0.78
		−1.81)	(−2.25)
Specification $\chi^2(7)$	4.33	4.15	4.46
	[0.74]	[0.76]	[0.72]
ARCH 4	F(4,89) 0.63	F(4,87) 0.64	F(4,84) 0.62
	[0.64]	[0.63]	[0.64]
Normality $\chi^2(2)$	6.57	4.36	4.52
	[0.03]	[0.11]	[0.10]
Heteroscedasticity X_i^2	F(10,86) 0.80	F(16,76) 1.20	F(18,73) 1.31
	[0.62]	[0.29]	[0.20]
$X_i * X_j$	F(20,76) 1.31	F(43,49) 0.81	F(35,38) 0.71
	[0.19]	[0.75]	[0.86]

Instrumental variable estimation. Additional instruments: Δyd with eight lags
9194 SBS   = Multiplicative dummy for Blanchard fiscal impulse (1 over 1991–94)
9597 SBS   = Same but for 1995–97 (1 over 1995–97)
9194 Δ BS   = Multiplicative dummy for change in actual surplus (1 over 1991–94)
9597 Δ TRANS   = Multiplicative dummy (1 over 1995–97) for change in transfer payments.

Source of the seasonally adjusted data used: OECD, except for CRE: Bank of France.

A much better fit is obtained for the consumption function when the equation is augmented for fiscal policy variables than when these variables are absent (Figure 5.2 focusing on the 1990s obtained with both equation (a) and equation (c) in Table 5.11). These variables are entered with multiplicative dummies. Thus the one-period fiscal impulse à la Blanchard (as a share of GDP), obtained with the procedure detailed above, enters with a (weakly) significant negative coefficient over the 1991 through 1994 period. This implies that a loose fiscal policy, as occurred over this period in France, leads in the long run to a fall in household consumption. In other words this provides evidence for the Ricardian or expectational effect of a worsening of public finances, that the French Statistical Institute was hinting at. Over the 1995–97 period the same variable is not at all significant. The second non-Keynesian influence of fiscal policy over the 1991–94 period comes through the current change in the actual government budget surplus with a positive sign: that is, household consumption rises by 0.6 per cent when the government budget surplus as a share of disposable income, rises by 1 percentage point. Finally, over the 1995–97 period, a 1 per cent fall in transfer payments (as a share of personal disposable income) leads to a 0.8 per cent rise in household consumption over the next quarter. The latter can be interpreted as a typical anti-Keynesian effect. We also tried many other fiscal variables, such as the ratio of government consumption over public investment, but these never proved significant.

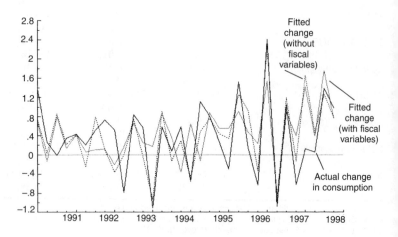

Figure 5.2   Fit of the estimated consumption function
over the 1990s with and without fiscal variables

Overall, the evidence for the expectational effect over the 1992–94 period matches the result of our comparative analysis of the French situation before the start of the fiscal retrenchment programme. Indeed, we see here that it is conceivable that fiscal policy had become so loose that consumers were increasing their savings as a response to such a deterioration. Earlier we saw that the initial fall in GDP or employment growth (relative to industrial countries) was such as to make fiscal retrenchment likely to succeed.

By contrast, we also saw that all the indicators of the macroeconomic performance during the fiscal retrenchment period (that is 1995 to 1997) pointed to a likely lack of durable success of the fiscal adjustment. Such a prospect was reinforced by the fact that the reduction in the budget deficit was implemented more through tax increases than through cuts in public consumption, since international evidence shows that such a strategy has previously proved unsuccessful in durably cutting fiscal deficits. This argument is further reinforced by the finding that the fiscal retrenchment programme was not a large-scale one. In the present econometric exercise, we find that over the fiscal consolidation period, the cyclically adjusted budget surplus has no influence on household consumption. This evidence would also point to the lack of success of the fiscal adjustment. However, the negative assessment of the fiscal adjustment is mitigated by the anti-Keynesian effect of the fall in government transfers on private consumption, which is quite substantial.

The lesson from these various pieces of evidence is that in France fiscal retrenchment does not seem able to stimulate output via anti-Keynesian effects.[6] This has strong implications for the future. Since the Stability (and Growth) Pact caps budget deficits, France in EMU will have to rely on other types of mechanisms to soften the impact of asymmetric shocks. At this point, progress in labour market flexibility can play a major role.

The doubts raised on the medium-run durability of the fiscal adjustment are compounded by worries on the long-run perspectives with respect to the pension system. Projections in this area are conditional on a number of assumptions, in particular involving the relative levels of interest rates and real growth rates, but broadly speaking they imply (see for example Leibfritz *et al.*, 1995) that within the next three decades, net public debt (as a share of GDP) could be multiplied by a factor of 2 or 2.5. This illustrates the fact that the acceptance of France Telecom future pension liabilities by the state in return for cash in order to comply with the Maastricht budget criteria may represent a typical case of 'short termism'.

2 DEVELOPMENTS IN THE FRENCH LABOUR MARKET

High and persistent unemployment rates in France are often attributed to the lack of flexibility of the labour market. The basic facts would at first sight support this view:

a. more than 90 per cent of workers are covered by collective agreements and the national minimum wage directly affects the pay of around 12 per cent of employees;
b. firing regulations and labour laws are very formal and penalise adjustment;
c. business taxes and employers' social security contributions are high;
d. unemployment benefits are relatively generous.

It is tempting to draw the following conclusions from these observations: wages will be inflexible downwards and adjust slowly to labour market and other shocks; turnover will be low and job flows small; the rate of job creation will be limited; unemployment spells will tend to be long.

However, while one may be able to find evidence in support of some of these expected consequences, it is also the case that the French labour market can appear quite flexible in a number of ways. The key issue of course is not whether businessmen, politicians or international organisations bemoan the kind of formal rigidities listed above, but whether these factors prevent the labour market from adapting to changed economic circumstances brought about by the move towards monetary union in Europe. In this section, we examine how employment, unemployment, wages and prices have evolved and point to a number of fundamental changes that have taken place in the process of wage setting in the French economy.

2.1 Employment and Unemployment

Figure 5.3 shows the familiar rise in French unemployment which roughly quadrupled in the twelve-year period from 1974 to 1986 from less than 3 per cent to around 11 per cent. Thereafter there was a short period in which it fell and after 1990 it rose to 12 per cent and has since hovered around that rate. The composition of French unemployment is quite different from that in the United Kingdom, for example. Females represent the majority of the unemployed, although male and female unemployment vary in a similar manner over the period. The number of unemployed aged under 25 is similar to the number of males unemployed up to 1984 but declines thereafter due to special employment measures and employment creation in general, and stabilises at around 600,000 (20 per cent of the total unemployed) after 1991.

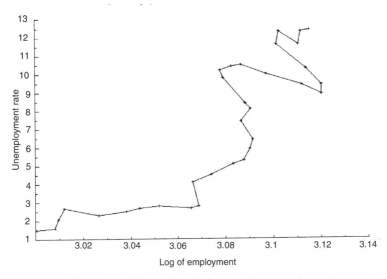

Figure 5.3 The relationship between the unemployment rate and the logarithm of employment in France, 1965–97

In employment terms, the French economy has never been a large net creator of jobs. Figure 5.3 also shows how the logarithm of salaried employment has evolved over the period 1965–97 and even when the French economy was growing at rates of 3 per cent of more in the early part of the period, salaried employment grew by an average of 1.65 per cent per annum. In subsequent periods, the rate has been slower: 1975–85 0.48 per cent and 1986–97 0.66 per cent. Somewhat paradoxically, in terms of job flows, job creation rates are much higher in France than in the United Kingdom and are slightly higher than in the United States (Table 5.12).

Table 5.12   Gross job creation and job destruction, 1984–91*

	France		United Kingdom		United States	
	1984–89	*1989–91*	*1987–89*	*1989–91*	*1984–88*	*1989–91*
Gross job creation	13.9	13.7	9.0	8.0	13.2	12.6
Gross job destruction	−12.8	−13.9	−5.1	−6.4	−10.0	−11.1
Net job creation	1.2	−0.2	3.9	1.6	3.2	1.4

* Flows expressed as a percentage of the employment stock.

Source: OECD Jobs Study, 1994.

Another important aspect of employment growth in France is the role of the public sector. In the period since 1980 public sector employment has grown at a faster rate than salaried employment in the private sector. At the same time the share of self-employment has declined. A further feature of job creation in recent years is the preponderance of assisted employment through various special measures – particularly for the young and long-term unemployed – and the increasing use of temporary employment contracts.

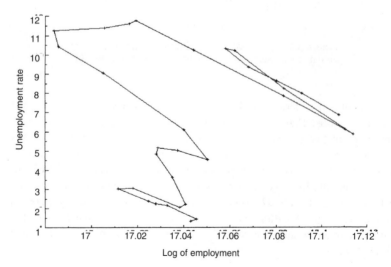

Figure 5.4   The relationship between the unemployment rate and the logarithm of employment in the United Kingdom, 1965–97

In net terms, the relation between changes in employment and unemployment is not clear-cut. In Figure 5.3, the unemployment rate is plotted against the logarithm of salaried employment. Again, the period up to 1974 stands out as one of steady employment growth and a constant rate of unemployment. There then followed a period (1975–82) in which the unemployment rate trebled to 8 per cent while at the same time employment increased by 3 per cent. Unemployment then rose further to 10 per cent before the creation of more than one million jobs in net terms in the late 1980s brought it down to 9 per cent. Thereafter unemployment rose to 12 per cent on the back of further job loss in the early 1990s. Compared to the United Kingdom, employment and unemployment changes have been less dramatic (see Figure 5.4) but France has been left with a high and persistent rate of unemployment.

2.2 Wages and Prices

Nominal wage inflation has followed price inflation down from the double digit rates of the period running from 1975 to the early 1980s (see Figure 5.5 – the definitions of the variables are provided below). By the end of the 1980s, price inflation had stabilised at around 2 to 3 per cent and has since fallen further. Wage inflation increased at a slightly higher rate but has also stabilised. The process of disinflation has been accompanied by a dramatic fall in the share of wages in value-added, which implies that real wages have grown less slowly than labour productivity (see Figure 5.6). This contrasts with the period following the first oil price shock when real wage increases outstripped productivity growth. The question of how and why the share of wages fell so dramatically after 1985 (by about ten percentage points) is addressed in papers by Blanchard (1997) and Caballero and Hammour (1998). A number of possibilities are considered, including changes in relative factor supplies, biased technological change and changes in the distribution of economic rents. According to the two studies cited it would appear to be the latter phenomenon – whereby firms have managed to appropriate an increasing share of economic rents – that is responsible.

Overall, on an annual basis real wages have never fallen, although in a number of years, they have hardly increased. However, the aggregate picture hides a number of factors pointing to a degree of downward flexibility. First, in the period 1991 to 1996, between a quarter and a third of year-round employees experienced a reduction in their nominal earnings

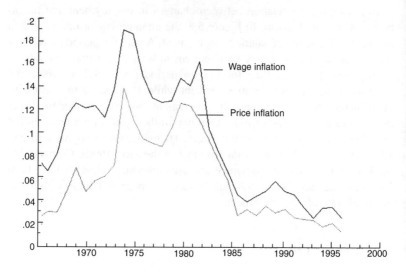

Figure 5.5   Wage and price inflation

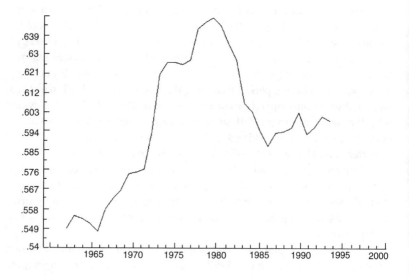

Figure 5.6   The share of wages in value-added

(INSEE, 1997). While this is often associated with changed working conditions (ending shift work, no longer working weekends) there is also an unexplained element. Second, since the late 1980s collectively bargained wage rates at the lower end have fallen below the value of the legal minimum wage in the majority of principal collective agreements. Employers' groups refused to renegotiate the lowest wage rates following increases in the minimum wage, since the whole collectively bargained wage structure would shift upwards due to the manner in which most wage scales are determined (a system of coefficients applied to a base wage). Instead, centralised collective agreements lagged behind and were supplemented by local, company-level agreements in certain cases. These observations suggest that wage fixing mechanisms do not always correspond to the stylised view derived from the formal framework mentioned above.

The picture that emerges from the developments laid out above is that the French labour market is one where unemployment is proving hard to reduce, but where inflationary pressures have been checked. There is evidence of the upper hand in collective bargaining having been acquired by employers, and the share of income paid as wages has been reduced substantially. The extent to which these developments are due to convergence to the criteria set out in the Maastricht treaty or whether they were the consequences of fundamental changes that were already underway before 1991 is examined in the next sub-section.

2.3 Econometric Analysis

In view of the observations made on the basis of the evolution of a number of aggregate variables presented graphically above, in this sub-section a small system of equations is estimated in order to derive a simple aggregate wage relation. This is then tested to see whether there is any evidence of structural breaks in the wage setting mechanism during the 1980s and early 1990s. Previous attempts at estimating the aggregate wage relation in France have produced varying results (see Henin, 1997). In relation to the effects of the European Monetary System, Artus and Salomon (1996) for example find strong effects of productivity, German inflation rates and German relative (to French) wages but no role for the unemployment rate. Anderton and Barrell (1993) find a strong effect from unemployment, expected and past price inflation and long-run productivity growth, but no role for the tax wedge. Barrell *et al.* (1994) find that in addition to the latter findings, the replacement rate and union density are significant. Artis and Ormerod (1996) find that past real wages, expected inflation, unemployment and a trend are the main determinants of nominal wage growth in France but that the relationship changes from the second quarter of 1983 onwards (up to 1991, the end of their estimation period).

In this sub-section the aim is to test using a simple wage relation whether there are structural breaks in the processes determining wages in aggregate. The following variables were obtained from the OECD Business Sector Database 1998/2 for the period 1965:1 to 1997:4 for the whole economy: total compensation of employees (W^*); number of employees (E); average number of hours worked per employee (H); the private consumption deflator (P); real GDP in market prices (Q); and the rate of unemployment (u).

Using these basic variables, the following were created following the practice adopted in the modelling of aggregate wage equations:

$$w = log(W^* / (ExH)) \quad q = log(Q / (ExH)) \quad p = log(P)$$

so that w represents the log of the hourly nominal wage and q the log of hourly labour productivity.

It is clear from the graphs presented earlier that the long-term relationship between real wages and productivity is not a stable one, that is the share of wages is not a constant, and this suggests that the kind of error correction relationship based on a constant share of wages is not going to be appropriate.

An initial vector autoregression was estimated for the period 1966:2 to 1983:4 using five lags ($k = 5$) on each of the variables that constitute the vector $X_t = (w_t \, p_t \, g_t \, u_t)'$ in the following system written in the error correction form:

$$\Delta X_t = \pi X_{t-k} + \sum \alpha_i \Delta X_{t-i} + \Phi D_t + \varepsilon_t$$

where ε is a vector of independently and identically distributed errors. It was apparent that a number of outlier observations gave rise to estimated residuals that were large for a small number of periods and so five dummy variables were included (in the vector D along with a constant) for certain quarters in the years 1968, 1973, 1974, 1978 and 1982. Their inclusion improved the statistical properties of the estimated system, and the results of diagnostic tests are presented in Table 5.13.

Table 5.13   Diagnostic tests on initial system, 1966:2–1983:4

	Δw	Δp	Δg	Δu	System
AR(5,40)	0.916	0.131	1.174	1.544	0.881(80,89)
ARCH(4,37)	1.085	0.393	0.131	1.714	NA
Normality(2)	1.263	2.262	1.523	3.991	12.16 (8)

AR(.,.) is an F test for autocorrelation; ARCH(.,.) is an F test for autoregressive conditional heteroscedasticity and Normality is a χ^2 test for normality. The corresponding degrees of freedom are in parentheses. NA indicates that the test statistic could not be calculated due to insufficient degrees of freedom. Estimation and testing carried out using PCFIML Version 8 (Doornik and Hendry, 1994).

From this basis we proceeded to test the existence of cointegrating (that is, long run) relationships between the variables using the Johansen procedure, and the test results are presented in Table 5.14. On the basis of these tests, we conclude that there are probably two cointegrating vectors among the variables in X.

Table 5.14   Cointegration statistics, 1996:2–1983:4

	P=0	P=1	P=2	P=3
Test for cointegration				
Maximum eigenvalue test	32.71**	21.62*	14.18*	0.049
Trace statistic test	68.56**	35.85**	14.23	0.049
Eigenvalues	0.369	0.262	0.181	0.0007

In each column the cointegration test statistics apply to the null hypothesis that there are P or fewer cointegrating vectors. One (two) asterisk(s) indicate that the null hypothesis is rejected at a 5%(1%) significance level.

The two cointegrating vectors are :

$$C1 = p - 0.545\ w - 0.310\ g + 0.068\ u$$
$$C2 = w - 1.006\ p - 3.924\ g + 0.165\ u$$

The first of these would appear to be a long-run price equation while the second resembles a long real wage equation of the form:

$$w - p = 3.924\ g - 0.165u.$$

Unemployment thus exerts a strong negative influence in the long run on nominal wages – a one point increase in the unemployment rate reduces real wages by 16.5 per cent other things being equal. Clearly the other variables are not unchanging, as during the period covered productivity rose at annual average rate of 3.2 per cent.

The main aim of the current exercise is to see whether the wage setting process in France has been modified during the period before and after the signing of the Maastricht treaty. To this end we use the results obtained for the period up to the final quarter of 1983 to forecast the different variables in the unrestricted VAR over the subsequent period. This cut-off point is chosen to coincide with the policy shift towards the control and reduction of price inflation. A number of changes took place around this time as a result of this shift, one of the most notable being the change in real interest rates from being negative or zero, to being positive and substantial. Predictions of the individual variables w, p and u in first differences are presented in Figure 5.7. Visual inspection of these plots reveals that nominal wage inflation is quite well predicted by the estimated system up until the end of the 1980s after which the model over-predicts what happens. For price inflation, the model over-predicts almost immediately after the estimation period ceases, indicating that the change of policy stance represented a regime change. The most successful forecasts seem to be given for the unemployment rate. Thus the tentative conclusions are as follows: the process of disinflation from the mid 1980s represents a change of regime which is at odds with the processes determining price inflation prior to 1984. However, the wage setting process continued to function in a reasonably similar manner as prior to 1984 at least until 1990. Whether the taming of wage inflation is a consequence (albeit indirect) of fiscal retrenchments and slow economic growth associated with exchange rate discipline and high real interest rates remains to be established.

In order to concentrate on the 1990s, the system was re-estimated using data for the period 1966:2 to 1989:4, and predictions estimated for the remaining period up to 1997:4 (see Figure 5.8). The diagnostic tests suggest that the system is not unduly misspecified. However, as with the previous model, the estimated wage relation fails to track the evolution of nominal wages during the 1990s, reinforcing the notion that there is a structural break in the wage setting process.

As a final step, a further system was estimated for the period 1984:1 to 1997:4, and diagnostic statistics are presented in Table 5.15. Given that the VAR for this sub-period appears to be well specified, we proceeded to test for the existence of a long-run relationship between the variables – see Table 5.16.

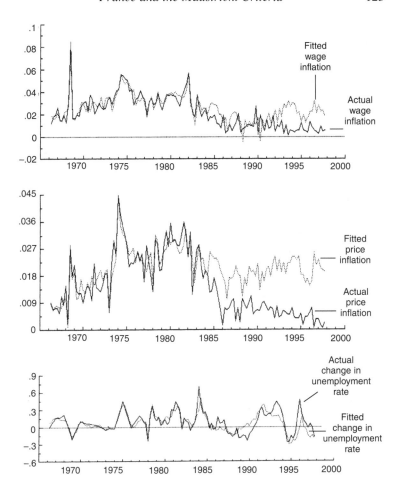

Figure 5.7 Actual, fitted and predicted values of wage inflation, price inflation and change in unemployment for model, 1966:2–1983:4

Table 5.15 Diagnostic tests on the system, 1984:1–1997:4

	Δw	Δp	Δg	Δu	System
AR(4,31)	0.383	0.392	0.276	0.630	0.963(64,64)
ARCH(4,27)	0.380	0.386	0.220	0.451	na
Normality(2)	0.867	0.016	1.844	0.016	4.078 (8)

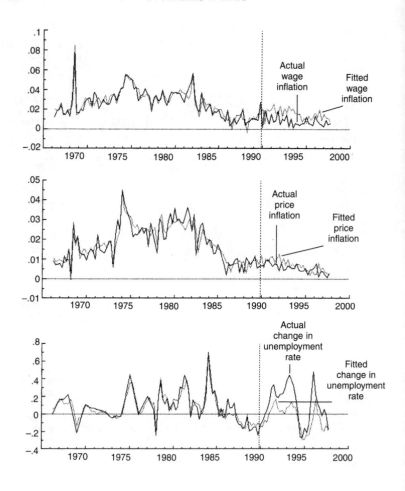

Figure 5.8   Actual, fitted and predicted values of wage inflation, price inflation and the change in unemployment for model, 1966:2–1989:4

Table 5.16   Cointegration statistics, 1996:2–1989:4

Test for cointegration	P=0	P=1	P=2	P=3
Maximum eigenvalue test	31.41*	14.29	2.028	0.059
Trace statistic test	53.79*	22.38	8.087	0.059
Eigenvalues	0.429	0.225	0.134	0.001

From the cointegration tests, it would appear that there is only one long-run relationship between the variables in the longer period, and this has the form of a long-run real wage equation:

$$w–p = 0.746\ g – 0.006\ u$$

(The cointegrating vector is in fact: $C1=w – 0.986p-0.746g+0.006u$). The coefficients are substantially different from those obtained for the period up to 1983 and suggest that changes in the unemployment rate and productivity have a far more limited effect on nominal and real wages. We therefore tentatively conclude that wage setting behaviour has changed during the period 1983–97 following the shift in economic policy towards bringing inflation under control and maintaining the value of the franc in the exchange rate mechanism in the latter part of the 1980s, even although the predictions of the model estimated up to 1983 seem to be accurate.

The message that emerges from this limited econometric analysis is that there have been changes in the operation of the French labour market during the 1980s in particular, but also in the period during which the convergence to the nominal criteria set out in the Maastricht treaty was achieved.

CONCLUSION

Overall, the picture presented of the situation of the French economy at the start of EMU is mixed. On the one side inflation is well under control (0.3 per cent in 1998, a historic floor), the trade balance is in large surplus, and France is, by the size of its economy alone, the second pillar of the new European area. However, the negative elements seem destabilising. They concern potential difficulties with the government deficit and the persistently high level of unemployment. The very high (from an international perspective) level of employment in the public sector and the associated wage costs have proved impossible to reduce. In spite of renewed efforts, health expenditure still represents a threat to the sustainability of the social security budget. Finally, pension liabilities of the public sector raise doubts on the ability for budget deficit ceilings under the Stability Pact to be met in the long run. This means that on the budget front, the difficult decisions in France seem to lie ahead of us rather than behind us.

With respect to unemployment, the seeming impossibility of bringing it down through substantial net job creation, has meant that policy has been directed towards special employment measures for the young and long-term unemployed and the reduction of working time. Both of these measures contribute to the budget deficit in that the state picks up all or part of the bill. This interdependence between the two main weaknesses in the French economy has led many in France to expect EMU to provide a macroeconomic stimulus and thus an external solution to these domestic economic problems.

NOTES

1. When France Telecom was privatised, all employees maintained the status of civil servants. Those recruited since privatisation are normal private sector employees.
2. The 'future' in the intertemporal government budget constraint becomes almost 'next year'.
3. For an econometric study of the impact of financial liberalisation on French household consumption behaviour, see Girardin *et al.* (1997), as well as Bordes *et al.* (1995).
4. After the first version of this paper was written, we came across the paper by Cotis *et al.* (1997) who estimate a French household non durable consumption equation and test for the new relevance of the effect of some fiscal policy variables in the early 1990s. However, our work differs in a number of ways. First, their estimation period stops in mid-1995, so that they are unable to test for the possible effects of fiscal retrenchment over 1995–97. Second, they acknowledge problems in breaking the budget surplus into structural and cyclical components with the effect that they do not address empirically the question of their differential impact on consumption. Third, they seem content with using OLS while our preliminary tests showed that the results obtained by using such a method are not robust when checked with instrumental variable techniques. Fourth, they use a different strategy from the one we put forward, since they ignore the results of the work by Sicsic and Villetelle (1995) showing the crucial role played by consumer credit in explaining French consumption behaviour in the early 1990s, that is. since they do not check for the role of this variable their tests of the effects of fiscal variables are not very reliable.
5. Alesina and Perotti use annual data but we need to work on higher frequencies in order to include the cyclically adjusted surplus in our consumption function. This explains why we do not disaggregate the components of the budget surplus before filtering them.
6. Eichengreen and Wyplosz (1998) reach the same conclusion.

REFERENCES

Alesina, A. and Perotti, R. (1995) 'Fiscal adjustment: fiscal expansions and adjustment in OECD Countries', *Economic Policy*, **21**: 205–48.

Alesina, A. and Perotti, R. (1997) 'Fiscal adjustment in OECD countries: composition and macroeconomic effects', *IMF Staff Papers*, **44**(2): 210–48.

Alesina, A. and Ardagna, S. (1998) 'Tales of fiscal adjustment', *Economic Policy*, **27**: 487–545.

Anderton, R. and Barrell, R. (1993) 'The ERM and structural change in European labour markets: a study of ten countries', NIESR discussion paper, No. 40.

Artis, M. and Ormerod, P. (1996) 'Another look at the "EMS Effect" in European labour markets', in De Grauwe, P., Micossi, P. S. and Tullio, G. (eds) *Inflation and Wage Behaviour in Europe*, Oxford: Oxford University Press.

Artus, P. and Salomon, R. (1996) 'The EMS, credibility and disinflation: the French case', in De Grauwe, P., Micossi, P. S. and Tullio, G. (eds) *Inflation and Wage Behaviour in Europe*, Oxford: Oxford University Press.

Barrell, R., Pain, N. and Young, G. (1994) 'Structural differences in European labour markets', in R. Barrell (ed.) *The UK Labour Market: Comparative Aspects and Institutional Developments*, Cambridge: Cambridge University Press.

Barro, R. (1974) 'Are government bonds net wealth?' *Journal of Political Economy*, 82: 1095–117.

Bertola, G. and Drazen, A. (1993) 'Trigger points and budget cuts: explaining the effects of fiscal austerity', *American Economic Review*, **83**: 11–26.

Blanchard, O. (1993) 'Suggestion for a new set of fiscal indicators', OECD Working Paper.

Blanchard, O. (1997) 'The medium run', *Brookings Papers on Economic Activity*, **2**: 89–158.

Bonnet, X. and Dubois, E. (1995) 'Peut-on comprendre la hausse imprévue du taux d'épargne des ménages depuis 1990?', *Économie et Prévision*, **121**: 39–58.

Bordes, C., Girardin, E. and Marimoutou, V. (1995) 'Les effets de variatins de taux d'intérêt dans le nouvel environnement financier français', *Revue Économique*, **46**(3): 635–44.

Bordes, C., Girardin, E. and Marimoutou, V. (1997) 'Fonction de réaction de la nouvelle Banque de France et intégration Européenne', working paper, University Montesquieu-Bordeaux IV.

Caballero, R. and Hammour, M. (1998) 'Jobless growth: appropriability, factor substitution and unemployment', *Carnegie-Rochester Conference Series on Public Policy*, **48**: 51–94.

Cadiou, L. (1995) 'Le mystère de la consommation perdue', *Revue de l'OFCE*, **53**: 147–64.

Cotis, J. P., Crepon, B., L'Horthy, Y. and Meary, R. (1997) 'Are automatic stabilizers still effective? The French case in the Nineties', in Hairault, J. O., Henin,

P. Y. and Portier, F. (eds) *Public Policies, Business Cycles and Macroeconomic Stability: Should we Rebuild Built in Stabilizers?*, Boston: Kluwer Academic Publishers, pp. 255–80.

Cour, P., Dubois, E., Mahfouz, S. and Pisani-Ferry, J. (1996) 'The cost of fiscal retrenchment revisited: how strong is the evidence', Centre d'Études Prospectives Internationales (CEPII) working paper No. 96–16.

Davidson, J., Hendry, D. Srba, F. and Yeo, S. (1978) 'Econometric modelling of the aggregate time-series relationship between consumers expenditure and income in the UK', *Econometric Journal*, **88**: 338–48.

EC (1998) Convergence Report, Brussels, European Commission.

Eichengreen, B. and Wyplosz, Ch. (1998) 'The Stability Pact: more than a minor nuisance', *Economic Policy*, **26**: 65–114.

Giavazzi, F., and Pagano, M. (1990) 'Can severe fiscal contractions be expansionary?', NBER Macroeconomics Annual.

Giavazzi, F., and Pagano, M. (1995) 'Non Keynesian effects of fiscal policy changes: international evidence and the Swedish experience', NBER working paper, No. 5332.

Giorno, C., Richardson, P., Roseveare, D. and Van den Noord, P. (1995) 'Estimating potential output, output gap and structural budget balances', OECD Economics Department working paper, No. 152.

Girardin, E., Sarno, L. and Taylor, M. P. (1997) 'French private consumption: 1970–94: the effects of real interest rates, liquidity constraints and financial deregulation', Working paper, University Montesquieu-Bordeaux IV.

Henin, P. Y. (1997) 'Soutenabilité des déficits et ajustements budgétaires', *Revue Économique*, **48**(3): 371–96.

INSEE (1995) *L'économie française, édition 1995: Rapport sur les comptes de la nation de 1994*, Le Livre de Poche.

INSEE (1996) *L'économie française, édition 1996 : Rapport sur les comptes de la nation de 1995*, Le Livre de Poche.

INSEE (1997) *L'économie française, édition 1997 : Rapport sur les comptes de la nation de 1996*, Le Livre de Poche.

Leibfritz, W., Roseveare, D., Fore, D. and Wurzel, E. (1995) 'Aging populations, pension systems and government budgets: how do they affect saving?', OECD Economics Department, working paper, No. 156.

Manasse, P. (1996) 'Are taxes too low?', *Journal of Economic Dynamics and Control*, **20**: 1263–88.

McDermott, C. J. and Wescott, R. P. (1996) 'An empirical analysis of fiscal adjustment', *IMF Staff Papers*, **43**(4): 725–53.

OECD (1997) 'France', *OECD Economic Studies*, February.

Sicsic, P. and Villetelle, J.-P. (1995) 'Du nouveau sur le taux d'épargne des ménages?', *Économie et Prévision*, **121**: 59–64.

Sutherland, A. (1997) 'Fiscal crises and aggregate demand: can high public debt reverse the effects of fiscal policy', *Journal of Public Economics*, **65**: 147–62.

6 The Prodigal Son or a Confidence Trickster? How Italy got into EMU

Vincenzo Chiorazzo and Luigi Spaventa*

INTRODUCTION

The improbable should not be mistaken for the impossible.[1] By mid-1996 the probabilities assigned to Italy's admission to the third stage of EMU were nil, or slim at best. The country did not fulfill any of the entry conditions. The general government deficit exceeded by some four points the Maastricht standard. The fact that in June 1996 a new government led by Mr Prodi set for 1997 a deficit target far above the required 3 per cent was interpreted as the official recognition that admission was out of reach.

The government's attitude and strategy suddenly changed in the late summer of 1996, when a supplementary financial plan introducing additional deficit cutting measures to achieve a 3 per cent deficit target in 1997 was submitted to and swiftly approved by Parliament. With inflation converging towards the reference value, re-admission to the EMS was obtained in November. The budget package was greeted with scepticism or derision, especially abroad: the objection was that, while insufficient to achieve the target, it consisted mostly of one-off or window-dressing measures. The outcry was louder when the government had to propose further interventions in March 1997.

In the end, however, the 1997 deficit was lower than 3 per cent; it appeared moreover that, with some minimal efforts, this result would be sustainable over time. Fulfilling all the criteria but that on debt, Italy gained admission in May 1998. In view of the stark contrast between forecasts and outcome, Italy's admission to EMU is, in a way, an intriguing story, on which this chapter attempts to shed some light.

*   The authors wish to thank Dr Carlo A. Ciampi, Minister of the Treasury, who kindly provided some information relevant for section 1 of this chapter.

Section 1 provides a chronicle of the events that led to the unexpected dash for entry and a description of the hostile environment that surrounded the Italian government's efforts.

In section 2 we try to answer the obvious question: how was this possible? In a messy way, a substantial structural adjustment had already been achieved in the first half of the 1990s. But by 1996 the real problem lay with a high interest burden that dwarfed the corrections of the primary surplus. The imminence of EMU opened the prospect of two alternative outcomes, both to some extent self-fulfilling: joining at the outset would accelerate interest rate convergence and provide a sizeable bonus on interest expenditure; any delay would cause that bonus to be lost. The Italian government understood this and behaved accordingly. It was in a way a confidence trick – but one that could succeed only because of earlier adjustment.

Italy's fiscal adjustment in the 1990s falls within the category of 'strong fiscal corrections' according to the standard definition in the literature. Lasting, however, for years, it lacked credibility until recently, and was accompanied by a steep rise of taxation. An unsatisfactory growth performance was its inevitable cost: but, as we argue in section 3, in a European context, that cost was relatively modest considering the size of the adjustment.

1 ECONOMICS, POLITICS AND DIPLOMACY

The first column of Table 6.1 summarises Italy's position at the beginning of 1996. The crisis of March 1995, when it was feared that Italy would default on its debt, was over.[2] The lira exchange rate, which had depreciated by 20 per cent in four weeks, recovered, and the spread of the BTP (the Italian long-term bond) on the German Bund, which had soared to 670 basis points, returned to the levels of the end of 1994. The prospects of Italy's admission to EMU, however, remained bleak.

Between 1995 and 1996 the drive towards a start of EMU in January 1999 regained momentum and the issue of compliance with the Maastricht conditions for admission suddenly became relevant. Italy was nowhere near to fulfilling any of the five criteria. The general government deficit, although on a downward trend since 1991, was still at 7.7 per cent. The debt/GDP ratio had stabilised, but was more than double the reference value. Inflation, although surprisingly subdued considering the spate of exchange rate depreciations and the rise in indirect taxes, was still far above the required level and so was the long-term interest rate on government

Table 6.1   Italy's convergence process

	1995	1996	1997
Inflation rate			
– yearly average	5.4	4.0	1.9
difference from convergence criterion	2.7	1.5	−0.9
– year end	5.6	2.9	1.8
Interest rates			
– yearly average of long-term rates	12.2	9.4	6.7
difference from convergence criterion	2.5	0.3	−1.0
– spread BTP-Bund at year end	4.83	1.81	0.33
– average cost of public debt	9.5	8.9	7.9
Lira/DM depreciation (+)/appreciation (−)			
– yearly average	14.4	−9.8	−4.3
– year end	9.2	−11.4	−1.5
General government deficit (ratio to GDP)			
outcomes	7.7	6.7	2.7
plans			
– 1995		7.5	4.4
– 1996 June		6.7	5.4
– 1996 October		6.6	3.0
General government debt (ratio to GDP)	124.2	124.0	121.6
Probability of Italy's admission (year end) *			
– in 1999	0.127	0.524	0.96
– by 2001	0.223	0.171	0.04

* See note 2 at the end of the chapter.

Sources: Banca d'Italia, Relazione Annuale (1998); Ministero del Tesoro, Documento di Programmazione Economico-Finanziaria (various years).

bonds. A few months after the 1994 general elections the Berlusconi government had been replaced by an interim government supported by the left; new elections appeared imminent. Political uncertainty and the extent of the lira depreciation made the prospect of re-entering the exchange rate mechanism of the EMS remote. Not surprisingly, the probabilities assigned to Italy's admission – even late admission – were slim when judged by the markets,[3] nil in the eyes of our European partners,[4] as well as of economists and opinion makers. Dornbusch's unqualified judgment that 'Italy is surely off the list for immediate consideration' as 'it is inconceivable that [it] can clean up in time',[5] sums up a prevailing view, justified by the fact that the government's official deficit target was 4.4 per cent for 1997.

The outcome of the April 1996 elections was a centre-left government headed by Mr Prodi, with Mr Ciampi at the helm of the Treasury. The new government's three-year financial plan, presented in June, left the previous government's deficit target for 1997 unchanged, deferring the fulfillment of the 3 per cent condition to 1998: as this implicitly ruled out the chance of admission in 1999, some were disturbed;[6] but on the whole that decision was generally well received and even supported by the governor of the Bank of Italy.[7] At the time the following passage in the planning document received little notice, or was considered mere lip service:

> The strategy of budget policy does not allow for an acceleration in the timing of adjustment... This choice does not imply that the government has given up the possibility of submitting Italy's candidature for entry... [The] commitment [is] to check in the autumn if it is possible to speed the timing of compliance with the... criteria, depending on the cyclical situation and the conditions of the financial markets.[8]

Mr Ciampi meant what he wrote, as he explained to the managing director of the IMF at the G7 meeting in Lyon in June and to Mr Waigel shortly after. His aim was to gain admission in 1999, but he would rather wait for the autumn to announce the supplementary adjustment that was required, hoping for a more favourable macroeconomic environment and especially relying on continued convergence of interest rates. Mr Waigel was also informed of this strategy that Italy intended to seek re-admission to the ERM in the autumn: in Ciampi's words, Waigel reacted not so much with hostility as with incredulity.

In a letter to Chirac and Kohl (6 September) Prodi expressed his will to enter EMU at the outset, noting that a guarantee of Italy's participation, by allowing a steep decline in interest rates, would make the required adjustment 'not so dramatic'.[9] A sensible economic point, but politically a weak one, especially with the Germans who insisted that credibility should be gained at home, rather than granted from outside.

The urgency of a fresh initiative on the fiscal front became evident after a bilateral meeting with the Spanish government in Valencia, on 23–24 September. The Italian feelers as to the possibility of a joint initiative to soften the entry conditions met with a *fin de non recevoir*: Spain, it was replied, would make it without any need to bend the rules.[10] The Italians left Valencia knowing that they could expect no support in a quest for a lenient application of the criteria and risked being left out alone. This convinced Prime Minister Prodi that it was time to move and to move quickly: five days after Valencia, supplementary measures for 25 trillion lira were announced to attain the 3 per cent deficit target in 1997.[11]

On the strength of this announcement, Ciampi immediately notified the Germans that Italy would apply for re-admission into the ERM in the near future. Waigel asked that Italy's case be examined only after approval of the new budget, at least on a first reading, and hence after Finland's admission that was decided on 12 October.

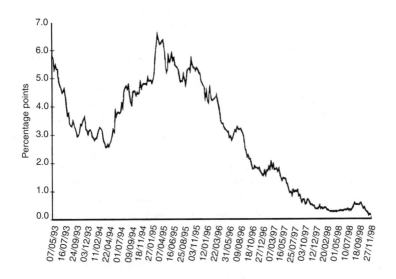

Figure 6.1   The BTP/Bund spread (OECD, European Commission and European Monetary Institute)

The decline in the BTP/Bund spread by almost 130 basis points between mid-September and mid-November (Figure 6.1) showed that the markets took a favourable view of Italy's last minute dash. Not so a number of commentators at home and abroad, who were quick to point out that the supplementary measures embodied little, if any, structural corrections.[12] The *Financial Times*, in particular, published a number of scathing articles on Italy's fitness to participate in the ERM, let alone in EMU.[13] 'No to the fudge romana' was the editorial *cri de coeur* on 20 November, accompanied by a Lex column entitled 'Roman numerals': allowing the French to use the transfers from France Telecom to the Treasury to cut their deficit 'inevitably... has encouraged those even worse placed to follow suit', but 'Italy's latest efforts go beyond what can be accepted' as the proposed 'tax package does not deserve scrutiny in other European capitals' and in any case is not 'enough for Italy to qualify for the first round'.

Italy's re-admission to the ERM in late November was a complicated affair, that lasted two days. Ciampi's objective was a central parity of Lit 1000 per DM. Earlier, the Union's central bankers, convened by the president of the European Monetary Institute, had agreed to a Lit 970 parity. Mr Tietmeyer, in the absence of Mr Waigel, insisted on 950 and would not budge above 970. In the end Mr Ciampi's obstinacy prevailed and the outcome was considered his success:[14] on 25 November the ECOFIN accepted the lira back into the fold at a central parity of Lit 990 per DM.

With participation to the ERM fulfilling one of the conditions required for admission[15] and inflation falling (Figure 6.2), Mr Prodi became determined to join in 1999 and pledged to resign in case of failure. This cheered the markets (the BTP/Bund spread fell to 150 basis points at the beginning of 1997) but failed to improve the politicians' and media's mood towards Italy:[16] if anything, it caused growing disquiet in many quarters. True, the prospect of leaving Italy out, alone, with the inevitable domestic political consequences that would follow, was a source of honest embarrassment, not only in Paris, but also in Bonn. German politicians were however under the pressure of their electorate's hostility to a single currency that included the lira. Not unimportantly, moreover, the British had a covert interest in a narrow EMU, with at least another large country out of the single currency. Finally, with the 1996 deficit higher than expected, fears that the September supplementary measures may not be sufficient to attain the 3 per cent target in 1997 appeared justified.

All this helps to understand the developments in the public debate between the end of 1996 and the summer of 1997. The Germans hardened their attitude: in repeated official pronouncements it was promised that 'zero after the comma' would be required, with no leniency allowed in the interpretation of the criteria; a prominent banker said that 'if Italy is admitted it could be a time bomb within the union', while Professor Horst Siebert forecast that the DM could plunge to 2 to the dollar if EMU were extended south of the Alps. It was then suggested that Italy would swallow the pill of delayed admission more easily if it were given company, and Spain was selected as the natural candidate.[17] More interestingly, rumours intensified that diplomacy was at work to provide Italy with an acceptable compromise that would delay its entry.

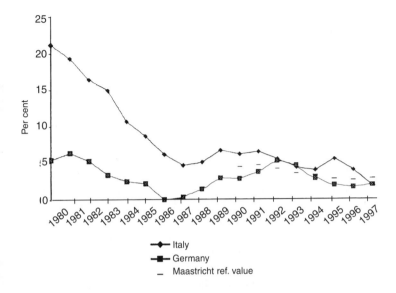

Figure 6.2   Consumer price inflation: Italy and Germany

Some of these rumours were sheer fancies, others were more plausible. The *Financial Times* (5 and 7 February) reported a detailed blueprint of a compromise solution attributed to unnamed central bankers and Treasury officials. 'To assuage German fears while offering Italy the necessary certainty that it could join EMU... on January 1, 2002...', the trick was, according to 'a senior monetary source', 'to allow the Germans to say that Italy is out of the first wave of EMU members, while making the Italians feel comfortable enough to say they are more or less in'. The relieved comment was that 'the artful compromise now being drawn... will gently put an end' to 'dangerous false hopes in Italy – and false fears in Germany': 'Italy's Prodi government has played an elaborate confidence trick, but confidence is finally waning. The bond markets fell for it... [but] reality was bound to impinge'.

What is remarkable in all this is that proposals like those reported by the press were never presented, formally or even informally, to the Italian government.[18] Clearly, the wishful thinking of some had been transformed into news, with the likely purpose of playing a confidence trick in reverse. Actually, spreads widened again and it became apparent that additional deficit cutting measures were needed to meet the 3 per cent target. As these measures were enacted, there followed an outcry. Being a patchwork of anticipations of later revenues and postponements of expenditures – it was pointed out – they would produce no lasting improvement and would never be accepted by our partners. Francesco Giavazzi asked Minister Ciampi to withdraw the mini-budget and face squarely the prospect of late admission.[19] Franco Modigliani joined in and, in an open letter to Ciampi,[20] asked: 'is it not better otherwise to resign?' As Ciampi himself recognises, that was the moment when he feared that the credibility bonus on interest rates would be lost and Italy would not make it. The press reported more rumours (attributed to unquoted official sources) regarding initiatives to separate 'hard currency sheep... from soft currency goats' and Italian suggestions that the launching of EMU be delayed by twelve months.[21]

Once more the press and the anonymous sources quoted therein were disappointed. The favourable monthly returns of the State sector accounts made the 3 per cent objectives within reach. A convincing convergence programme was submitted to the EU Commission. Inflation fell to 1.7 per cent in the summer, well within the Maastricht standard. Interest rates thus resumed their decline: the spread on the Bund fell from more than 190 basis points at the end of March to 30–40 at the end of the year.

In the end the 1997 general government deficit was 2.7 per cent, below target, with a decline of 2.5 points of the debt/GDP ratio. All the Maastricht conditions but that on debt were met. Italy's admission was a foregone conclusion for the markets and, in spite of some rearguard battles,[22] a grudgingly accepted outcome for some of our partners. In March, at the ECOFIN Council in York, Ciampi understood that he was safely at home. Talking to the President of the Bundesbank over drinks he sensed that the latter was relaxed, as never before: the implicit blessing was made apparent when Tietmeyer asked Ciampi who would be the Italian candidate for the executive board of the ECB.

So, one may say, all is well that ends well. But *how* did it end well? How was a 4 points cut in the deficit achieved in one year without much apparent pain? Only by sleight and trickery, as some have maintained all along? Surely, this cannot be the whole story, for, if it were, the price would be exacted in the following years – and, so far, it has not. We shall attempt to clarify this issue in the following section.

2 TRICKS OR SUBSTANCE? THE ANATOMY OF FISCAL ADJUSTMENT

2.1 Fiscal Adjustment in the Period 1990–96

The Italian fiscal adjustment began in the early 1990s, as shown by Table 6.2 which reports yearly data of the general government accounts for the period 1990–97.[23] The primary balance went into surplus for the first time in 1991 (or 1992, if cyclically adjusted data are used). That surplus grew each year, with the exception of 1994. Between 1990 and 1996 the actual improvement was slightly less than 6 per cent of GDP; 7.5–8 per cent if cyclically adjusted data are considered.

These are no mean results. The adjustment of the primary balance was almost uninterrupted and above 1.5 per cent in four years out of six.[24] These undeniable quantitative results usually meet with two powerful criticisms. First gradualism prevailed: hence it was never felt that the problem of the fiscal imbalance was anywhere near solution. Year after year, huge corrections were announced, only for it to be realised a few months later that the targets would not be attained and that a mid-year mini-budget was required. Moreover, budget plans would often consist of a complicated patchwork of measures the structural component of which was difficult to detect. Even the size of the announced correction was often misleading, as it compared the target with an arbitrarily computed trend, rather than with the previous year's outcome.[25] Second, tax increases played a far greater role than expenditure cuts in the improvement in the primary balance: while it is far from certain that the short-term adverse Keynesian effects of tax rises are higher than those of expenditure cuts,[26] it is accepted that a rising tax burden impairs economic efficiency in the long run.

Certainly, Italy's way of facing its fiscal problem in the period 1990–96 does not compare favourably with episodes of sizeable, expenditure-based and front-loaded corrections in other countries. To draw from this a summarily negative judgment would, however, be unwarranted.

The fiscal imbalance of a high debt country must be corrected with a high *and* lasting primary surplus. This is what Italy has done in the 1990s. As shown by Table 6.3, in 1996 the Italian primary surplus exceeded that of most European countries. Since the mid 1990s, moreover, a surplus of the order of 4.5 per cent is projected to persist over time, irrespective of further major corrections. A seemingly messy succession of measures, some of which were replacing earlier ones of a temporary nature, thus appears to have produced structural effects.

Table 6.2 Italy: general government accounts (ratio to GDP)

		1990	1991	1992	1993	1994	1995	1996	1997	1990/1997
1	*Primary balance*	-1.7	0.1	1.9	2.6	1.8	3.6	4.1	6.8	*8.5*
	– cyclically adjusted (a)	-2.8	-0.8	1.5	3.6	2.4	3.6	4.5	7.2	*10.0*
1.1	*Revenues*	42.7	43.8	46.5	48.3	45.7	45.9	46.4	48.8	*6.1*
	– cyclical component	0.8	0.6	0.3	-0.7	-0.4	0.0	-0.3	-0.3	
	memo item: tax burden (b)	39.6	40.6	43.0	44.4	41.7	41.9	42.4	44.3	*4.7*
1.2	*Primary expenditures*	44.3	43.7	44.6	45.7	43.9	42.3	42.3	42.0	*-2.3*
	– Transfers to households	18.3	18.3	19.3	19.5	19.5	19.0	19.3	19.6	*1.3*
	– Government consumption	17.6	17.6	17.7	17.6	17.1	16.1	16.3	16.3	*-1.3*
	– Capital	5.6	4.7	4.7	5.0	4.1	4.7	4.0	3.5	*-2.1*
2	*Interest*	9.5	10.2	11.5	12.1	11.0	11.3	10.8	9.5	*0.0*
3	*Total expenditures*	53.8	53.9	56.1	57.8	54.9	53.6	53.1	51.5	*-2.3*
	– cyclical component	-0.3	-0.3	-0.1	0.3	0.2	0.0	0.1	0.1	
4:1–2	*Overall balance*	-11.1	-10.1	-9.6	-9.5	-9.2	-7.7	-6.7	-2.7	*8.4*
	– cyclically adjusted (EC)	-12.2	-10.9	-9.9	-8.6	-8.6	-7.7	-6.3	-2.2	*10.0*
	– cyclically adjusted (OECD)	-11.9	-10.6	-9.6	-8.4	-8.3	-7.3	-5.8	-1.7	*10.2*
	– cyclically adjusted (IMF)	-12.0	-11.0	-9.6	-8.5	-7.8	-6.8	-5.4	-1.3	*10.7*
	Memorandum items:									
	Accounting measures	na	na	-0.09	0.38	0.19	-0.83	0.35	0.64	
	– on primary balance	na	na	-0.05	0.42	0.19	-0.85	0.33	0.52	
	– on interest payments	na	na	0.04	0.04	0.00	-0.02	-0.02	-0.12	
5	*Debt*	98.0	101.5	108.7	119.1	124.9	124.2	124.0	121.6	*23.6*

(a) actual primary balance + cyclical component estimated by European Commission (Autumn 1998), (b) including social security contributions.

Sources: Ministero del Tesoro, Relazione generale sulla situazione economica del Paese (1997); OECD, Economic Outlook (various years); Imf, World Economic Outlook (various years).

Table 6.3 Primary balances and primary expenditures – ratios to GDP

	Primary balances		Primary expenditures	
	1991	1996	1991	1996
Belgium	3.8	5.3	44.1	44.4
France	0.9	−0.3	48.1	51.2
Germany	−0.4	0.3	45.4	45.4
Italy	0.1	4.1	43.3	41.9
Netherlands	3.3	3.3	49.5	45.4
Spain	−0.5	0.5	40.9	39.8
United Kingdom	0.4	−1.1	37.8	38.3

Source: European Commission.

Table 6.4 Composition of the changes of the primary balance – General Government – ratios to GDP

	1990–94	1994–96	1996–97
Government consumption	**−0.5**	**−0.8**	**0.0**
– of which: compensation to employees	−0.7	−0.4	0.1
Transfers to households	**1.2**	**−0.2**	**0.3**
– of which: pensions	1.6	0.0	0.5
Other current expenditures	**0.4**	**−0.5**	**−0.2**
Capital expenditures	**−1.5**	**−0.1**	**−0.5**
Total primary expenditures	**−0.4**	**−1.6**	**−0.3**
Revenues	**3.0**	**0.7**	**2.4**
– of which: direct taxes	0.5	0.3	0.7
indirect taxes	1.1	0.2	0.3
Change in primary balance	**3.5**	**2.3**	**2.7**
Memorandum item: tax burden *	2.1	0.7	1.9

* including social security contributions.

Source: Ministero del Tesoro, Relazione generale sulla situazione economica del Paese (1997).

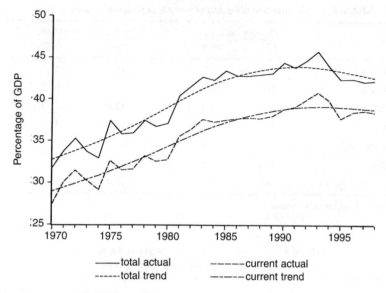

Figure 6.3   Trends in Italy's primary expenditure

While it is a fact that almost two thirds of the increase in the primary balance was due to higher revenues (the tax burden inclusive of social security contributions increased by 2.8 points between 1990 and 1996), it would not be correct to conclude that nothing was done on the expenditure side – although it is certainly true that more could have been and should be done. As shown by Table 6.4, expenditure cuts were almost irrelevant in the subperiod 1990–94, but played a much larger role in 1994–96 (70 per cent of the change in the primary balance). Second, and more importantly, since the 1960s successive layers of permissive legislation had set total and current primary expenditure on a steeply rising trend, as shown by Figure 6.3, where actual data are corrected with a Hodrick-Prescott filter. The measures taken in the first half of the 1990s appear to have stopped, or even curbed this trend. Thus employment in the public sector, which had increased by 13.6 per cent in the 1980s, fell by 0.7 per cent between 1990 and 1994, and by 1.5 per cent between 1994 and 1996. Two reforms of the overgenerous Italian pension system were enacted in 1992 and in 1995. The first essentially lowered the intercept;

the second flattened the trend.[27] Thus pension expenditure, as a ratio to
GDP, rose in the first subperiod, but remained unchanged in the second.
The rising trend of transfers to households for health care was also
corrected and there was a modest decline of its share to GDP over the
period (–0.6). Finally, it must be noted that the ratio of primary expenditure to GDP is lower in Italy than in other major European countries
(Table 6.3), while that of current transfers to households (including
pensions), although higher than in Germany, is at the average level of
continental Europe (around 20 per cent). The need for further measures to
curb pension expenditure is of course undisputed,[28] considering the
projected trend even after the corrections and the high level of social
security contributions. Our point is that measures were indeed taken on
the expenditure side: if the rising trend of public expenditure had
persisted, the increase in revenues could not, by itself, have produced the
lasting correction which we now observe.

2.2 Two Alternative Outcomes

In the early 1990s the correction of the primary balance was offset to a large
extent by a growing interest burden, so that the improvement of the overall
balance was modest. As shown by Tables 6.2 and 6.5, the average cost of
debt peaked at 11 per cent and the share of interest payments on GDP rose
to 11–12 per cent: the result of soaring interest rates and the high and short-
lived outstanding debt.[29] In that period Italy found itself in a situation
familiar to scholars and dreaded by policymakers: the prospect of a vicious
circle of self-feeding debt growth, with the primary surplus having to rise
ever faster merely to keep the overall deficit ratio unchanged. Even though
an unchanged deficit ratio is in principle compatible with the eventual
stabilisation of the debt ratio, instability is likely to arise much earlier as the
market perceives that the required increases in the primary surplus become
politically unfeasible. Each year's debt-stabilising primary surplus together
with the average cost of debt are computed in Table 6.5: even correcting for
the cycle, the former approached 10 per cent in 1993.

The situation improved considerably in the following years. With the
increase of the primary surplus, the decline in interest rates and the
economy's recovery, debt stabilisation was achieved between 1994 and
1995. More importantly, the primary surplus obtained with the succession
of measures taken since 1991 was there to stay, as shown by trend projections produced by the government and by private research institutions. But

Table 6.5 Italy: debt stabilisation

	1990	1991	1992	1993	1994	1995	1996	1997
Average cost of debt	10.2	10.6	11.2	10.8	9.2	9.5	8.9	7.9
Nominal growth rate	10.0	8.9	5.2	3.2	5.7	8.2	5.7	4.2
Primary balance (ratio to GDP)								
– debt stabilizing *	0.5	3.4	8.7	12.4	7.4	2.9	3.9	4.6
– difference with actual	2.1	3.3	6.8	9.8	5.6	-0.7	-0.2	-2.3
Change in debt/GDP ratio	2.2	3.5	7.2	10.4	5.8	-0.7	-0.2	-2.4
Memo item: average residual life of public debt (years)	2.5	2.9	2.9	3.3	4.7	4.5	4.5	4.6

The main components of the stock-flow adjustment are the privatisation proceeds, the changes in the value pf debt denominated in foreign currency, the difference between the nominal and the issue value of bonds and the changes in the Government's net holding of financial assets.

* computed applying the following formula: $a^*(t) = (i(t) - g(t)^*(1-0.5i(t))^* D(t-1)/Y(t) + s(t)$ where $a^*(t)$: debt-stabilising primary balance; $i(t)$: average cost of public debt defined as (Interests)(0.5*(D(t)+D(t-1))); $g(t)$: nominal gdp growth rate Y(t): nominal gdp at current market prices; D(t): General Government Gross Debt (Maastricht definition); s(t): stock-flow adjustment, namely D(t)–D(t–1)– general government deficit.

Sources: Ministero del Tesoro and authors' computations.

these results were far from decisive. The decline in interest rates and hence in the cost of debt was largely due to the convergence game played by the markets. The moods of markets are, however, volatile and the risk that they may abruptly change was high. The tequila effects of the Mexican crisis at the end of 1994 provide a glaring example. As the flight to quality took the shape of a massive movement of funds into Deutsche Mark denominated assets and as the Deutsche Mark strengthened *vis-à-vis* the dollar, the bonds of Europe's periphery (Italy, Spain, Sweden) were severely hit in the first quarter of 1995, with a dramatic rise in their spreads over the Bund and Italian bonds were hit more than others (see Figure 6.1). It was a passing episode, but it was a warning of the potential fragility of the convergence process. The prospect of EMU introduced a new variable, that could spell either greater risk or an unprecedented opportunity.

As long as EMU appeared remote – in the years between the ratification of the Treaty of Maastricht and the first half of 1995 – interest rate convergence, although fragile, was dictated by the markets' appraisal of the improvement of economic fundamentals. As the move towards the single currency resumed its momentum and it became clear that no safe home would be provided to the currencies of those countries not admitted with the first batch, the nature of the game changed: interest rate spreads came to depend on the probabilities assigned by the markets to the prospect of joining the single currency at the outset. Of course, as has been frequently observed, a deficit target of precisely 3 per cent has little objective economic meaning; and, at any rate, it should not matter much whether it is achieved in one or in two years, provided the progress is real and sustainable. But, once it was decided that the criterion should be precisely met in 1997, and not later, mere reference to fundamentals became insufficient and any 'objective economic meaning' was lost. For given fundamentals, or to be more precise for a given trend of improvement of the primary balance, two distinct equilibrium outcomes became possible: one in which a decline in interest expenditure induced by a fall of interest rates would give a substantial contribution to the reduction of the overall deficit; another in which the same efforts of primary correction would be frustrated by the persistence of higher levels of interest expenditure and exposure to external shocks. Because (and only because) a substantial correction was already accomplished, the 3 per cent criterion thus acquired in a way a self-fulfilling nature: a quick move to comply with it on time would provide a sizeable bonus that would otherwise be lost.

The Italian government understood, albeit belatedly, that this was the bet and behaved accordingly.

2.3 The 1997 Bet and its Pay-off

The government was very careful not to rely publicly on the effects of the hoped-for decline in interest rates, in order not to expose itself to the accusation of trickery. The assumptions regarding interest rates and the projections of interest expenditure for 1997 and especially for 1998 erred very much on the side of caution, both in the 1996 revised financial plan for 1997 and in the following documents.[30] The whole attention was concentrated on delivering the additional correction that would make it possible to meet the criterion, only implicitly relying on the interest rate bonus that would result from forcing the 'good' outcome.

The initial purpose of the September 1996 revision was to achieve the 3 per cent target by means of an improvement in the primary balance of some 3 points of GDP – 2 more than in the June document – and a reduction of interest expenditure of 0.7 points. The enacted correction was a shrewd blend of the following items: a moderate dose of additional structural measures; the imposition of cash limits, with the twin purpose of imposing some discipline on the spending behaviour of lower levels of government and of postponing expenditure in the year of Maastricht; accounting revisions in line with criteria set earlier or agreed to by Eurostat; last, but perhaps most important, a temporary income surtax (familiarly called Eurotax), levied in 1997 with the commitment to pay back 60 per cent of it in the future.[31]

Those who fiercely criticised the Eurotax for its one-off nature and even more for the promise to pay part of it back after Italy's entry in the single currency[32] missed its political importance. First, it was the ultimate signal of the government's commitment to gain admission, for, after imposing a levy explicitly aimed at achieving this objective, the government would be compelled to resign in case of failure. Second, the need for this extra effort 'for Europe' was recognised and accepted politically and by the public: a symptom (another symptom) that the aim of not being left 'outside Europe' was widely shared in the country.

In the end, the primary surplus actually achieved in 1997 was on target, with an increase of 2.7 per cent of GDP over the 1996 level. As shown by Table 6.6, little more than one point was due to one-off measures (more than half due to the Eurotax); 0.6 points to accounting revisions (only 0.3 in terms of changes, as the revisions were extended backward to earlier years) affecting both the primary balance and interest expenditure; and 0.9 points to the postponement of expenditures (0.3 points for changes).[33] The target for the overall deficit was over-fulfilled: 2.7 per cent instead of 3, due to a decline of interest payments larger than projected. The bet was already paying off, but more was to come later.

Table 6.6 Italy: contributions to the 1997 fiscal adjustment (percentage of GDP)

1996 deficit	6.7	
1997 deficit	2.7	
Change	**4.0**	
Contributions		
Interest	**1.3**	
Primary	**2.7**	
– Personal income taxes	0.4	
– Corporate income taxes	0.6	
– Social security contributions	0.4	
– Other current receipts	0.5	
– Capital receipts	0.4	
– Eurotax	*0.6*	
– other	*−0.2*	
– Current primary expenditure	−0.1	
– Gross fixed investments	−0.1	
– Other capital expenditure	0.6	
permanent measures	*1.6*	
one-off measures	*1.1*	

Memorandum items:	Effects on	
	1996–97 change	1997 level
Accounting revisions	0.3	0.64
Postponement of payments	0.3	0.89

Source: Istat and authors' evaluations.

It has been observed with some reason that the endeavour to pursue fiscal adjustment relaxed in 1998 – in other EU countries no less than in Italy. In Italy the primary balance target was undershot by 0.5–0.6 points (and the primary surplus fell by 1.7 points), largely due to a decline in the tax burden. In spite of this, however, and in spite of much lower growth than forecast (1.3 per cent real instead of 2.5), the overall balance was more or less on target and unchanged with respect to 1997. What happened, of course, was that interest expenditure fell more than projected and this reduction was sufficient to offset the shortfall in the primary surplus. It is also remarkable that the Asian crisis, very much unlike the Mexican crisis, did not affect the convergence process: Italian spreads on Germany, in line with the rest of Europe, including France, only rose by a handful of basis points at the time of the LTCM collapse.

In the end, between 1996 and 1998 a 4 points decrease in the overall deficit was achieved with a mere one point increase in the primary surplus. Thus the bet has paid off handsomely, and not only in the short run. OECD (1998) computed the 'tax gap', that is the tax change, required to keep the deficit at an average 1 per cent over the cycle in some European countries:[34] the gap is positive for most other countries (and particularly high for Germany), but is slightly *negative* for Italy, implying that, in the case of Italy, fulfillment of budget conditions near to those required by the stability pact would be practically painless.

The Italian 'Stability Programme' submitted to the Council and the Commission in December 1998, on the other hand, targets a general government deficit of respectively 2, 1.5 and 1 per cent in the three years 1999–2001, to be achieved with some modest corrections to keep the primary surplus at 5.5 per cent and with interest payments declining from 7.5 to 7 to 6.5 per cent of GDP. Once more the interest projections err on the side of caution even on a conservative estimate. This is probably done deliberately and may serve one of three purposes: it may shelter the government from the consequences of an unplanned shortfall of the primary surplus; or it may allow the government some room to lower the tax burden with a planned reduction of the target primary surplus; or it may insure compliance with a rigid interpretation of the Stability Pact (balanced budget by 2002). The former possibility would be a waste, as, given the tax burden, it would signal a permissive attitude towards expenditure: the benefits, if any, would be short lived. The second possibility would yield longer-term benefits. It is a moot point whether this second possibility should be sacrificed to the third.

3 ADJUSTMENT AND GROWTH

As pointed out in section 2, the Italian adjustment displays some unattractive features. It was protracted in time (six years), so that the public got used to expecting more doses of the same medicine, and stronger doses were announced than were actually administered. Joining EMU moreover was believed to require even more tears and sweat – and success was uncertain until the very end. Finally, tax increases played a great role in the improvement in the primary surplus. In a varying degree, these are ingredients for the production of traditionally Keynesian recessionary effects.

Table 6.7 Fiscal adjustment and growth performance, 1992–97 (cumulated changes)

	1992–95		1996–97		1992–97	
	EU	Italy–EU	EU	Italy–EU	EU	Italy–EU
(Ratios to GDP)						
Primary correction	–0.2	3.7	2.2	1.0	2.0	4.7
Current revenues	0.8	0.8	0.3	2.6	1.1	3.4
Current primary expenditure	1.6	–3.0	–1.1	2.0	0.5	–1.0
(%)						
GDP growth	6.0	–1.5	4.5	–2.3	10.8	–4.0
Private consumption growth	5.1	–5.1	4.0	–0.6	9.3	–5.9
Employment	–3.0	–2.4	0.5	–0.2	–2.5	–2.6

Source: European Commission and authors' computations.

As is to be expected, the Italian growth performance in the period was disappointing in terms of both output and employment, as evidenced by Table 6.7. The yearly average growth rate in Italy over the six years 1992–97[35] was 0.6 per cent lower than that of the European Union. The output gap increased in Italy more than in the EU. The employment performance was only slightly less disappointing. As net exports did very well, giving a hefty positive contribution to growth, domestic demand was responsible for this outcome. While non-residential investment did not do too badly, households' consumption in Italy lagged very much behind that in the rest of the EU: the remarkable exception was 1997, when consumption grew faster while investment fell far more than in the EU.

Households' current real disposable income collapsed in 1993, a recession year when moreover the tax burden peaked and real wages fell; although it improved in the following years, it never recovered to earlier levels. The fall in household saving only partially offset the effects of reduced disposable income. Even the unexpected recovery of private consumption in 1997, in spite of the Eurotax, can be explained in different ways. First, owing to the sharp drop in inflation, real disposable income corrected for the effect of inflation on the sizeable financial wealth of Italian families actually rose. (Conversely, the real value of debt increased, and this may have something to do with the fall of fixed investment that occurred at the same time.) Second, a temporary fiscal incentive to buy new cars scrapping the old ones accounts for half-a-point increase in consumption in 1997. As the latter was phased out and as the effect of lower inflation on households' financial wealth ceased to operate in 1998, consumption growth slowed down again.

Granted that the Italian fiscal adjustment exacted a heavy price in terms of output and employment, was this price so peculiarly high considering the size of the adjustment and in comparison to what happened in other EU countries? In Figure 6.4 we plot the differences between the annual average change in primary balances in each of the 14 EU countries (excluding Luxembourg) and the EU weighted average change against each country's average annual GDP growth differential with the EU weighted average. We consider the six-year period, beginning with the 1992/1991 changes and ending with 1996/95. We have excluded 1997, the Maastricht year when primary surpluses increased steeply in some countries and in the whole area and when window-dressing and accounting measures played an important role everywhere.

Ideally, virtuous non-Keynesian cases should find their place in the first quadrant (more than average primary correction and more than average growth) and perverse ones in the third (less than average correction with less than average growth). The second and the fourth quadrant belong, within limits, to the Keynesian norm. We find only one positive non-Keynesian case, Finland, but two rather perverse ones, Sweden and France. Ten countries are in the Keynesian norm. Ireland is clearly an outlier: its extremely fast relative growth has clearly nothing to do with the modest relative deterioration of its primary budget after the remarkable fiscal adjustment accomplished in earlier years. The performance of Greece is clearly superior to that of Italy (an average relative primary correction of 1.2 points for the former and of 0.7 for the latter with approximately the same negative growth differential). But, if we compare the size of the relative fiscal correction and that of the growth differential, it may be surmised that both Italy and Greece did better than Belgium, Spain and Germany and possibly Portugal and Austria. If we extend the period to 1997, Italy, Greece and Finland fare better, while Germany shifts to the perverse third quadrant; France's unhappy position remains unchanged.

The *ex post* relationship between relative fiscal adjustment and relative GDP growth performance shown in Figure 6.4 is open to an important objection. As net exports contribute to GDP growth, exchange rate competitiveness plays a relevant role: hence the comparison does not control for the positive effects of exchange rate depreciations in countries that, like

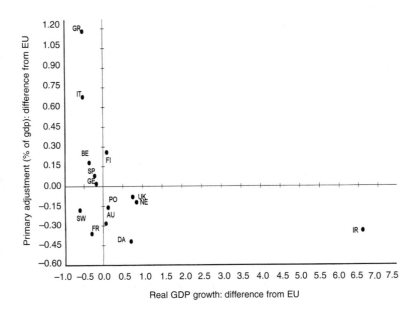

Figure 6.4   Relative fiscal correction and relative growth performance, 1992–96

Italy, managed to keep inflation under control. The existence and the extent of Keynesian effects are best evaluated for domestic demand in general and for consumption in particular. Hence in Figure 6.5 we perform the same exercise as in Figure 6.4, considering for each country consumption growth (instead of GDP growth) differentials with the EU average. Unsurprisingly, the position of Italy, Spain and especially Finland (no longer un-Keynesian) worsens, while that of Germany (but not that of France) improves. Surprisingly, Greece becomes a virtuous non-Keynesian case. All in all, however, the cost of the Italian correction still appears relatively low: if one dared to draw a regression line, Italy would be well above it.

In conclusion, at least at first sight Europe appears to display some Keynesian features which Italy has shared to a moderate extent. At first sight, of course, because a simple visual comparison of relative fiscal effort and relative growth performance cannot and does not lead very far.

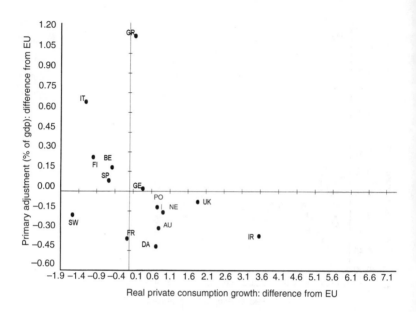

Figure 6.5   Relative fiscal correction and relative growth performance, 1992–96

CONCLUSION

Italy gained admission to EMU with an unexpected and unexpectedly successful last minute effort, defying widespread adverse expectations, technical disbelief and political hostility. We asked in the title whether Italy was a truly repentant prodigal son or a confidence trickster. Our answer is that, yes, it did play some confidence trick; but that trick could succeed and be accepted because, and only because, most of the deserving work of fiscal adjustment had already been done in earlier years. The additional trick played in 1997 was to set in motion the virtuous mechanism of a fast and steady decline in interest expenditure. The exercise was not perhaps performed entirely according to the rule book, but in 1997 that book was neglected by all. In the end it served its purpose and was grudgingly applauded. Sticking to the rules at the cost of delaying entry, as some asked, would have produced the undesirable result of making the deficit reduction more difficult and more costly. There were, in jargon, two equilibria: the conditions for a good equilibrium did exist and were wisely exploited.

The protracted process of adjustment undoubtedly had a cost in terms of employment and growth. In spite of its undesirable features, however, it is far from obvious that that cost was unduly high: if anything, comparison with other countries provides some casual evidence to the contrary.

The fiscal adjustment that has been accomplished can be sustained without much effort in the next few years. In the longer term, however, it will be jeopardised by rising pension expenditure unless timely measures are taken. Before then, the pressing need to lower the distortionary burden of taxation and social security contributions will require further efforts of correction on the expenditure side.

NOTES

1. This is an imprecise quote from P. G. Wodehouse, *Leave it to Psmith.*
2. These rumours often found support in the views expressed by eminent economists. Thus Rudi Dornbusch in one of his newsletters stated bluntly that the question was not *whether* Italy would default, but *when.*
3. There are several ways of computing such probabilities from market interest rates, of which the best known has been the JP Morgan EMU calculator. Different methods yield different results, but they all share considerable elements of arbitrariness. The one reported in the table, from Favero *et al.* (1998), is in our view the most satisfactory, because, unlike the others, it allows for the possibility of a late entry.
4. On 21 September 1995 it was reported that the Bundestag's press office after a meeting of the Finance parliamentary committee attributed to Mr Waigel the following: 'Italy, though a founder of the European Community, will not be able to make it.'
5. See Dornbusch (1996a and b).
6. An outspoken critic was Commissioner Mario Monti: see *Corriere della Sera*, 28 June 1996.
7. In his parliamentary hearing Mr Fazio said that 'a stronger correction would affect negatively the economy's growth'. (Commissioni riunite 5a del Senato della Repubblica e V della Camera dei Deputati, Audizione del Governatore della Banca d'Italia, 9 luglio 1996).
8. See Camera dei Deputati (1996)
9. See Prodi's interviews to *Il Sole 24 Ore*, 30 December 1998 and to *Il Messaggero*, 31 December 1998.
10. Mr Aznar's position was expressed with undiplomatic *machismo* to the *Financial Times* on 30 September 1996: 'His earnestness about the Maastricht goals... he says, is the message he gave... to Mr Romano Prodi... when they met in Valencia. Mr Aznar made it clear that he would have no truck with any joint southern European approach to try to bend the criteria or the timetable. "He wanted Spain and Italy to walk together holding hands toward Maastricht", he

says, of Mr Prodi. "I'm not interested in holding hands. I told him we'd be there right from the start".'

11. The importance of the Valencia bilateral meeting is confirmed by an interview by Prodi to the *Financial Times*, 2 October 1996. 'In little more than two weeks, Mr Romano Prodi... has radically altered his ideas on participation in European monetary union... [He] used to feel it would not be a "tragedy" if Italy were a bit late in meeting the Maastricht criteria... but the government clearly became alarmed at the prospect of being left behind...' Though rejecting Aznar's account reported in note 9, he said: 'The change occurred... when I saw that other countries were making a serious effort to address their budget deficit... I realised Italy too could not miss the appointment' and he acknowledged that 'a significant contributory factor was his meeting in Valencia last month...'

12. See for instance the letter of Professors Alesina and Perotti to the *Financial Times*, 24 September 1996 and the columns of Professors Penati and Giavazzi in the *Corriere della Sera* (30 September, 4 October and 23 November 1996), where it was taken for granted that the deficit would in the end exceed the target substantially and the government was accused of deluding the country.

13. 'ERM entry for Italy', 16 October 1996: 'Ever optimistic, Italy hopes for a fudge. But many Germans are desperately seeking ways to exclude countries that have failed to demonstrate the requisite fidelity to a stability oriented policy. Italy is at the top of the list of undesirables... Instead of throwing everything into a helter-skelter rush to cut deficits and enter the ERM, Italy might do better to concentrate on sustained fiscal tightening.' On 11 November Barry Riley ('Economic costs of Italy's financial success') resurrected the ghost of debt restructuring, voicing 'the nasty thought that Italy's quickest and most direct route to EMU would be first to write down its debt by half', and invented the new ghost of a secession of the rich North from the rest of the country.

14. A vivid account of the Ecofin meeting, with a great deal of reliable inside information, was provided by the *Financial Times* of 26 November 1996.

15. Under a somewhat generous interpretation (for Finland as well as for Italy), as the two-years' membership required by article 109j.1 of the Treaty was not satisfied with reference to 1 January 1999.

16. A good example is the disaster scenario painted by Anatole Kaletsky, 'L'Italie et l'euro: le ver dans le fruit', *Le Monde*, 10 December 1996.

17. In the words of Dresdner Bank's Mr Lipp, 'Spain can make it, Italy probably not. But it does not work politically to have Spain take part in EMU without Italy. The political art and task for Germany and France now is to convince Spain to forgo joining EMU at the start.' This quote and the quotes in the text are from the *International Herald Tribune* and the *Financial Times*, 3 February 1997.

18. The Italians were always careful not to give the impression that they might be interested in a fall-back solution. Hence they accepted without discussion the unsatisfactory exchange rate arrangements of the ERM2 (between the 'ins' and the so-called 'pre-ins'), agreed at the ECOFIN Council in Verona on 12 April 1996 (see on this Spaventa, 1996).

19. See Francesco Giavazzi, *Corriere della Sera* 18 and 27 March 1997. There were many other slightly milder criticisms: for example Luigi Spaventa, *La Repubblica*, 27 March 1997.
20. *Corriere della Sera*, 30 March 1997.
21. *Financial Times*, 7 April 1997 and *Il Sole-24 Ore*, 16 April 1997. The Italian suggestion of a delay was attributed to Mr Dini, the foreign minister, at the Noordwijk council. See also Dornbusch (1997).
22. The last battle was fought by the Dutch, whose finance minister Zalm asked for the presentation and preliminary parliamentary approval of the economic and financial programme for the years 1999–2001.
23. From 1992 onwards the data are revised to include the effects of the accounting corrections (detailed in a memo item) allowed by Eurostat in 1997.
24. It terms of the primary balance it would then fall within the category of an 'aggressive policy action' (see McDermott and Wescott, 1996). This does not apply however to the overall budget balance.
25. As the IMF article IV consultation mission noted in 1995, this measurement of adjustment 'gives a misleading impression of the fiscal effort, since much of the so-called adjustment it includes is required merely to compensate for the expiry of one-off measures and avoid backsliding'.
26. On the effects of the composition of fiscal adjustment see Alesina and Perotti (1995, 1997), Alesina and Ardagna (1998), Giavazzi *et al.* (1998) and, with reference to EU countries, Caselli and Rinaldi (1998).
27. The reforms lowered the projected peak of pension expenditure by some 7.5 point of GDP. The trend is now flat until 2003 and it rises gently in the next decades.
28. See Franco and Munzi (1997).
29. At the beginning of the 1990s the sum of floating rate debt and of debt with residual life up to one year was some two-thirds of total and the average residual life of debt was less than three years, as reported in Table 6.5.
30. The assumed interest rate on the 12-month Treasury bill exceeded the actual rate by 200 basis points in 1997 and by almost 300 in 1998. A similar caution was displayed in the projections of long-term rates. The May 1997 document reported the 10-year BTP/Bund differential computed from market forward rates at a time when Italy's admission was considered uncertain. The May 1997 projections and outcomes for the spread are the following:

Date	Forward rate projection	Effective
22.08.97	1.26	0.96
10.11.97	1.18	0.65
18.02.98	1.10	0.38
09.05.98	1.03	0.23

31. The commitment is being honoured: by mid-1999 the 60 per cent of the Eurotax will be paid back.

32. See section 1. If one considers fudges, the accounting revisions agreed upon by Eurostat for Italy and the Eurotax are hardly the worst. For vivid descriptions of the French and Belgian fudges, see *Financial Times*, 19 September 1997 ('The magic of Maastrichtian mathematics', 'A slice of French fudge') and *The Wall Street Journal Europe*, 3 January ('Belgium Cooks Its EMU Books') and 15 January 1997 ('Belgian Bookkeeping'). The German off-budget treatment of some important items of general government expenditure is known and accepted.
33. Though the year's corresponding appropriations were left unchanged, at least part of the delays in spending have had an indirect structural effect: the short-term discipline introduced by that means has allowed a reduction in future appropriations.
34. The basis of the methodology is Blanchard *et al.* (1990), extended to the EU by Franco and Munzi (1997).
35. For the sake of comparisons with the EU 1991 should be taken as the base year, because it is the first year in which statistics for united Germany are available.

REFERENCES

Alesina, A. and Perotti, R. (1995) 'Fiscal expansions and adjustment in OECD countries', *Economic Policy*, 21.
Alesina, A. and Perotti, R. (1997) 'Fiscal adjustment in OECD countries: composition and macroeconomic effects', *IMF Staff Paper*.
Alesina, A. and Ardagna, S. (1998) 'Tales of fiscal adjustment', *Economic Policy*, 27: 487–545.
Blanchard, O., Chouraqui, J., Hagermann, R. P. and Sartor, N. (1990) 'The sustainability of fiscal policy: new answers to an old question', OECD *Economic Studies*, 15.
Camera dei Deputati (1996) *Documento di programmazione economico-finanziaria relativo alla manovra di finanza pubblica per gli anni 1997–99*.
Caselli, P. and Rinaldi, R. (1998) 'La politica fiscale nei paesi dell'Unione Europea negli anni novanta', *Temi di Discussione*, Banca d'Italia, 7.
Dornbusch, R. (1996a) 'Euro fantasies', *Foreign Affairs*, September/October.
Dornbusch, R. (1996b) *World Economic Letter*, 3 September.
Dornbusch, R. (1997) *Dornbusch Letter*, 2 May.
Favero, C. A., Giavazzi, F., Iacone, F. and Tabellini, G. (1998) 'Extracting information from asset prices: the methodology of EMU calculators', manuscript, November.
Franco, D. and Munzi, T. (1997) 'Ageing and fiscal policies in the European Union', *European Economy*, 4.
Giavazzi, F., Jappelli, T. and Pagano, M. (1998) 'Searching for non-Keynesian effects of fiscal policy', IGIER *Working Papers Series*, 136.

McDermott, C. J. and Wescott, R. F. (1996) 'An empirical analysis of fiscal adjustment, *IMF Staff Paper*, 4.

OECD (1998) *Economic Outlook*, December.

Spaventa, L. (1996) 'Coexisting with Euro: prospects and risks after Verona', in Kenen, Peter B. (ed.) *Making EMU Happen, Problems and Proposals: a Symposium, Essays in International Finance*, August.

Discussion of Chapters 4, 5 and 6

John Driffill

These three chapters provide fascinating accounts of how France, Germany and Italy met the Maastricht criteria and got into EMU. They expose a number of sharp contrasts and similarities between the experiences of the three countries. A surprising contrast stands out and strikes the reader immediately, in some ways confirming but in other ways overturning stereotypical views of the countries in question. The account of Italy, in the South, is one of superficial disarray covering deeper currents of systematic change. By contrast Germany, in the North, is presented as a country in which, behind the stern facade, discipline and order were less than might have been expected. France, between the two, is shown as a country in which the road to EMU was strewn with unexpected obstacles, but in which there is closer correspondence between the surface show and the deeper forces at work.

For all three countries, there are a number of common elements and important issues which come through. One is the problem of the workings of the labour market, its flexibility, and the level of the natural rate of unemployment or the NAIRU. All three have problems related to persistently high unemployment. Another is the looming issue of publicly funded pensions and its consequences for taxation and public borrowing. Again, all three will face problems in the future of financing heavy public unfunded pension obligations. In all three countries there were elements of creative accounting, or window dressing, typically short-term measures which will add to future problems, undertaken in order to make the public debt figures look more acceptable. But each country is shown to have its own peculiarities. In the Italian case it is clearly the very high level of the national debt. For France it is the overvaluation of the exchange rate resulting from the *franc fort* policy (I would argue, although this is not the view proposed by the authors). And in the German case it is the political and fiscal consequences of reunification.

The Italian case is fascinating. Chiorazzo and Spaventa paint a thrilling picture of sailing close to the wind, daring gestures, cool nerves, scrapes, and near misses, with a happy ending. (At least so far. Of course we have not yet seen the ending, only that the first round has ended happily with

Italian membership of EMU.) The essential ingredient is that for Italy there were clearly multiple equilibria of this game, and this was clearly perceived by key figures in Italian governments. The financial markets' confident expectations of entry into EMU would reinforce expectations of low future inflation and low interest rates, cutting the cost of debt service, substantially reducing the deficit, and enabling Italy to qualify on the Maastricht criteria. Fear of non-entry would raise fears of future inflation, raise interest rates, and thereby raise the cost of servicing the national debt, leading to a higher deficit, making qualification for entry into EMU more difficult. Thus beliefs were self-confirming. Sustaining confidence in Italy's entry was paramount. This was just achieved in the end, although Italy had a very close shave. At various times in the approach to EMU sceptics and critics confidently declared that Italy could not qualify and should not be allowed to join. These eminent voices, including those of the *Financial Times* and Professor Rudi Dornbusch, were eventually proved wrong. Chapter 6 cocks an elegant and well-informed snook at them, and the reader is bound to share the authors' evident pleasure in doing so.

While inflation rates were low, and on that criterion Italy comfortably qualified, its record of exchange rate stability was on the margin, as were interest rates (which depended on expectations of joining), the national debt to GDP ratio was very high but falling, and the deficit was very marginal. The chapter argues that the Eurotax, which has been widely dismissed as a piece of window dressing, was in fact an important signal of the government's commitment to take the measures necessary to secure entry, and the public's willingness to accept this tax was a demonstration of the widespread approval of the pro-EMU policy. Chapter 6 argues force-fully that while on the surface the many changes in taxation and government spending appear to be piecemeal, small, and unfocused, they have had the effect of a cumulative and lasting improvement in the state's fiscal position. The case is largely convincing, although the summary representa-tion of it in Figure 6.3, which portrays the trend in government expenditure as a share of GDP as having turned the corner since 1990 or thereabouts, having grown consistently from 1970 until then, leaves some concern that on these data it may be too soon to be really confident. The forecast peak in state pension obligations has been reduced from 23.27 per cent of GDP in 2040 to 15.79 per cent of GDP in 2032, a substantial reduction, which nonetheless leaves very heavy future obligations.

The German case stands out in marked contrast to the Italian one. The diagnosis offered by von Hagen and Strauch is that the policy process in Germany was undermined by various consequences of reunification in a number of unintended and incidental ways. While Germany was keen to impose fiscal discipline on other potential members of EMU, and took a hard line on the rigorous application of the Maastricht criteria for EMU entry, within Germany controls on government expenditure and taxation were being eroded. The national debt rose from 41.8 per cent of GDP in 1989 to 61.5 per cent in 1997. The deficit was over 3 per cent in 1995 and 1996, and was just brought under 3 per cent in 1997. Transfers from West to East Germany were enormous in this period – 3 to 4 per cent of Germany's GDP. Much of this was to pay for unemployment benefits, payments towards the pension system, and employment subsidies. Only a part was to finance the direct costs of infrastructural investment in the East. A large proportion of the costs resulted from political decisions surrounding unification – the choice of exchange rate between the Deutsche Mark and the East German mark, the immediate extension of West German labour market institutions (unions, bargaining structures, unemployment benefit system, pensions) and pressure to achieve rapid convergence of East and West German wages. Some of the fiscal indiscipline resulted from the autonomy given to the Treuhand foundation in privatising East German enterprises, which resulted in its being able to incur state borrowing without political control. Kohl, as Chancellor, contributed by allowing concessionary expenditures favouring particular interests and groups in the country.

The authors' view is that many of these changes in Germany were incidental to reunification and the costs of reconstructing East Germany, implicitly that many of these costs were the results of political choices and could have been easily avoided by wiser policy choices. However, observing Germany from (relatively) afar, the overall impression gained, the arguments of von Hagen and Strauch notwithstanding, is that reunification was the root cause of high government expenditure and borrowing. Without it, Germany would have faced none of these fiscal problems. It is deeply ironic that German views dominated the formulation of the Maastricht criteria and the Stability and Growth Pact, and that Germany has led the insistence on fiscal probity in Euroland, while at the same time Germany has a very strong case, based on the costs of reunification (a very large investment project which will yield future returns), for borrowing more heavily now and meeting a smaller proportion of the costs from current tax revenue. In a recent article, cited by von Hagen and Strauch, Marcus Miller and I have argued that the Maastricht criteria and the Stability and Growth Pact are slowing the process of East Germany's transition and possibly threatening its stability.

France appeared to be proceeding smoothly towards EMU, meeting all the criteria, until the early 1990s. The franc had weathered the assaults of currency speculation in the ERM in 1992 and 1993. The debt and deficit were well inside the limits. Inflation and interest rates were low. In the French case, fiscal retrenchment became necessary in the run-up to EMU because the fiscal position deteriorated sharply between 1991 and 1992 when GDP growth collapsed and unemployment began to rise further, reaching 12.3 per cent in 1993. Bazen and Girardin examine the balance of tax increases and cuts in transfers and in other elements of government expenditures that made up the fiscal retrenchment, and consider whether these are likely to constitute a lasting change, when compared with successful and unsuccessful policy changes in other countries. The evidence on this appears mixed. They explore whether the fall in consumers' expenditure and rise in savings rates between 1991 and 1993 (and later changes between 1993 and 1997) could be explained by Ricardian effects: expectations of higher future taxes to meet interest and repayments on an increased national debt. They look for effects of fiscal stance on consumption in France. Again, there appear to be various effects, not all pointing the same way. The overall picture is not entirely clear. The authors' summary is that fiscal retrenchment does not seem to have stimulated consumption in France, presumably as a consequence of the likely impermanence of the fiscal changes.

Bazen and Girardin offer an interesting and unusual perspective on the French labour market, which they argue is much more flexible and dynamic than is widely believed. They point to the high rates of gross job flows (creation and destruction), the fall in the share of wages in GDP, which they attribute to a revival of employer influence in wage bargaining, and the low rate of wage inflation. This does of course leave as a puzzle the persistently high rate of unemployment. They do not, however, discuss at any length the influence of social security benefits and employment protection legislation. Another important player which is left off-stage is the exchange rate. Table 5.1 gives data on the persistently strengthening effective exchange rate, and the reader is bound to wonder to what extent the fall in GDP growth and the rise in unemployment have followed from a strengthening real effective exchange rate associated with the *franc fort* policy.

All three chapters comment on the problems of persistently high unemployment and the dangers of looming pension contributions. The first increases the costs of social security payments – particularly in France and Germany where the systems are generous – and reduces GDP and tax revenues. The second points to future problems in meeting the terms of the

Stability and Growth Pact while honouring current pension obligations. It is clear that both of these will lead to pressure to weaken the Stability and Growth Pact. Indeed this pressure is already emerging, with the German government now leading the fray, and arguing that if the European Central Bank will not follow a more expansionary policy, then Euroland member governments will have to use a more vigorous fiscal stimulus to growth, even if this implies borrowing beyond SGP limits. While there is general agreement that high unemployment is a severe problem, there is less agreement on how to reduce it. The moves towards shorter working weeks in France and elsewhere are not encouraging. Neither does the political economy of labour market policy, as analysed for example in many papers by Gilles St Paul, offer comfort. While EMU seems to have made a positive start in the first months of 1999, there are growing dangers ahead, and it will be interesting to observe how they are met.

7 The UK and EMU

Michael Artis

1 INTRODUCTION

What is the proper role of an economist in a debate about such a politically charged decision as that of the potential entry of the UK into EMU? Fortunately economics itself provides a discipline-neutral framework of analysis in the form of the cost-benefit approach. That approach allows 'non-economic' factors to be admitted. If, as many probably think, the balance of purely economic factors is negative or uncertain, it may still be quite reasonable to see positive political benefits justifying entry. It still remains important to examine the economic factors carefully and to think of ways in which costs can be minimised.

This paper proceeds in that spirit. First, we recall the cost-benefit framework explicitly, as it was put forward by Krugman (1990), building on the insights afforded by the conventional economic theory of optimum currency areas. In the following section, we recognise in the 'Chancellor's Five Tests', some of these same considerations and we go on to spell out how they apply to the UK. One of the Chancellor's 'Five Tests' appears to appeal to a special interest group, the City of London. In the next section we ask whether this is a proper entry in the national calculus and what developments might sustain it. Then we consider the way forward, reviewing three scenarios, a 'Canada scenario', in which the UK does not join EMU; a 'join now' scenario and a 'join later' scenario. The paper argues that the latter is the most realistic scenario and discusses some things that need to be done to ensure its successful implementation.

2 OPTIMUM CURRENCY AREA THEORY

Traditionally, it is the theory of optimal currency areas that has been used as a guide by economists in making sense of these issues. As is well known, the lineage of authorship in this area goes back to Mundell (1961), McKinnon (1963) and Kenen (1969). Much more recently Krugman (1990) set out the theory in terms of a cost-benefit framework, which has the added benefit that it can also be made, heuristically, to encompass costs and benefits not accounted for in traditional economic analysis. Figure 7.1 reproduces Krugman's suggestion.

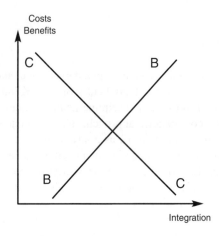

Figure 7.1 Costs and benefits of monetary union

The figure analyses the situation of a country contemplating a currency union with a partner or partner-group of countries. Along the horizontal axis is a measure of 'integration' – perhaps the economists' traditional measure $(X_{ij} + M_{ij}) / 2Y_i$ where X_{ij}, M_{ij} denote, respectively, exports from i to j and imports to i from j and Y_i is a measure of economic activity in country i. Along the vertical are measured costs and benefits to i from the currency union with j. The upward slope of the benefit line (BB) suggests that benefits rise with the amount of intra-trade, essentially because the currency union arrangement offers the prospect of freedom from exchange costs. To these, nowadays, observers might add the competitive advantages of increased 'transparency' of relative prices, the locational-efficiency benefits of a fixed exchange rate and, in the European context, the preservation of the gains from '1992'. The extent of intra-trade is a plausible measure of the potential extent of all these benefits. Other benefits, not related to the extent of intra-trade, can be accommodated simply by shifts in the BB schedule.

The CC schedule is drawn as downward-sloping in the figure. This reflects the view that the value of an independent monetary policy and flexible exchange rate (the loss of which is the 'cost' of currency union) declines with the openness of an economy. The reason for this (McKinnon, 1963) is that the larger the share of tradable goods in the consumer basket the less money illusion there will be in wage-setting behaviour and the less powerful, therefore, the effect of nominal exchange rate changes on the real exchange rate. The value of an independent monetary policy, however, is seen in this approach as stemming from its use as a stabilisation tool. If a great deal of stabilisation needs to be done, then the CC schedule should be relatively high. If there is little need, then the schedule should be relatively low – other things equal. How much stabilisation needs to be done depends on the size, nature and frequency of asymmetric shocks. Where there is a high degree of asymmetry in demand shocks, with which monetary policy might be particularly good at coping, then the CC schedule should be conceived of as cutting the BB curve relatively far to the right; if the degree of asymmetry is low, then the reverse should hold.[1] The traditional approach also stresses that a high degree of labour mobility or in more contemporary terms 'labour market flexibility' constitute alternative ways of solving the problem: in the first instance, labour would migrate from the country suffering the 'bad' shock to the one suffering the 'good' shock; in the second case, labour market flexibility would help absorb the shock by inducing a relative fall in real wages in the country suffering the bad shock. Further, a federal fiscal arrangement could offer an alternative 'buffering' function, with fiscal transfers going from the country with the good shock to the one with the bad shock.

The figure says, obviously, that a currency union yields net benefits when, for given CC and BB schedules, the degree of integration exceeds that corresponding to the intersection of the two schedules, since then benefits exceed costs. It is obvious that the framework can accommodate a variety of circumstances; in particular, perhaps, it suggests that a high level of intra-trade may not always be a good indicator of the optimality of a currency union. This will depend also on how symmetric are the shocks hitting the candidate countries.

The OCA approach has come in for a variety of criticisms that must be mentioned. First, it omits any serious mention of inflation, yet counter-inflationary properties appear to be a leading criterion for the practical desirability of a currency union. The Treaty of Maastricht lists criteria, for example, which can be read as simply a variety of ways of measuring 'counter-inflationary commitment'. Second, it treats as exogenous what might be endogenous – namely, the asymmetry (or otherwise) of shocks. Third, it proffers a framework which promises to deliver a quantitative verdict in a common numeraire – a figure of net benefit or net cost, which it cannot in fact provide. These criticisms may not be as damning as they sound. First, counter-inflationary commitment can simply be added in where appropriate. Second, the issue of endogeneity can be tested for – we note below the 'state of the art' in this respect and we conclude that a clear result has not yet been established. Third, while it is not possible to measure a net benefit or cost, it is possible to quantify quite a lot and thus to make informative comparisons between countries.

3 HOW DO THE OCA CRITERIA APPLY TO EMU AND THE UK?

The UK government's 'five tests' (HM Treasury, 1997) are as follows:

- Whether there can be sustainable convergence between Britain and the economies of a single currency.
- Whether there is sufficient flexibility to cope with economic change.
- The effect on investment.
- The impact on our financial services industry.
- Whether it is good for employment.

Of these tests, the first two are clearly related to the OCA approach. The third and fifth tests have no clear economic theory framework in which they can be answered if they are not already covered under the first two heads, and we shall set them on one side here. The fourth test is something we discuss a little further later on.

Where does the UK stand in relation to quantitative measures of OCA criteria, supplemented where appropriate by an inflation criterion? In this section we refer to studies based on measures of asymmetry of shocks and to more comprehensive studies of the application of the OCA criteria. In all these the UK appears as a less obvious candidate than some other countries for membership of a European Monetary Union. But this conclusion is not the same as saying 'the UK should not join'. We do not measure all the benefits (nor all the costs). The tests are not pass/fail.

3.1 Asymmetric Shocks

Possibly the most elusive of the OCA criteria is that pertaining to asymmetric shocks. Two methods, broadly, have been pursued to identify such shocks. The first, pioneered by Bayoumi and Eichengreen (1993), attempts to isolate shocks from a 'structural' VAR. The second, of which an example is Artis and Zhang (1997), attempts to isolate the business cycle and thence views measures of business cycle synchronisation as corresponding to the desired identification of the symmetry of shocks. Both methods have advantages and disadvantages.

Table 7.1: Shock correlations with Germany, 1960–95

	Supply	Demand
EU15 (EU)	0.37	0.57
Germany (BD)	1.00	1.00
France (FR)	0.40	0.28
Denmark (DK)	0.46	0.25
UK	0.24	0.14
Italy (IT)	0.25	0.29
Netherlands (NL)	0.34	0.18
Belgium (BG)	0.53	0.28
Austria (OE)	0.39	0.32
Spain (ES)	0.24	−0.03
Portugal (PT)	0.20	0.16
Greece (GR)	0.04	0.09
US	−0.01	−0.22
Canada (CN)	0.19	0.03
Norway (NW)	0.24	0.22
Sweden (SD)	0.19	0.19
Finland (FL)	0.19	0.02

IMF-codes of countries are given in parentheses and are
used as labels in some of the subsequent graphs

According to the former method, the initiating shock is separated from the transmission process which, incorporating some policy response, mediates the passage of the shock through the economy. This separation, however, can only be achieved at the cost of imposing some restrictions on the estimation of the VAR. Bayoumi and Eichengreen (1993) chose restrictions which correspond to the basic assumptions of the simplest neo-classical model: in particular, only 'real' ('supply') shocks have a long-run impact on output; nominal ('demand') shocks are restricted to have a zero long-run effect. In Table 7.1 here, for all the EU economies (Luxembourg being merged with Belgium) together with the US and Canada, we report a replication of the Bayoumi–Eichengreen exercise for an updated sample period.

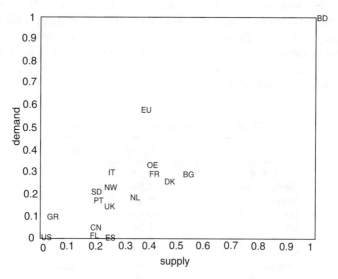

Figure 7.2   Shock correlations with Germany, 1960–95

As in the original Bayoumi–Eichengreen paper, we report the value of the correlations of the shocks with those affecting the German economy, on the assumption that Germany should be regarded as the 'centre' of the EMU. The cross-correlations are also reported, graphically, in Figure 7.2. The general run of positive correlations is lower than in the sample period originally studied by Bayoumi and Eichengreen but it remains true, as in the original study, that a core and a periphery can be identified.[2] France, Denmark, Austria and Belgium are clearly in the core, the Netherlands and Italy being less obviously well identified. The UK appears to be less strongly attached and to that extent belongs to a 'peripheral group', along with the Scandinavian and Iberian countries.

3.2 Asynchronous Business Cycles

The alternative approach, focusing on business cycle correlations, has fostered quite a large literature on business cycle affiliation and whether there now exists a 'European Business cycle'; this literature encompasses a number of technical issues. Among them are issues as to the most appropriate way to identify cycles, and the correspondence of the synchronisation (or otherwise) of cycles to the notion of symmetric (or otherwise) shocks. In particular, if the cycle itself is conceived as the outcome of a 'shock plus transmission process', then policies which are idiosyncratic before EMU may both create idiosyncratic shocks and affect the transmission process, perhaps producing the impression of wider divergence in underlying stochastic experience than is really warranted or than will appear in the common monetary policy framework of an EMU. On the other hand, differences in the transmission process between countries – whether related to underlying behavioural relationships or to the policy transmission mechanism – could imply different cyclical responses even to identical shocks (see Dornbusch *et al.*, 1998).

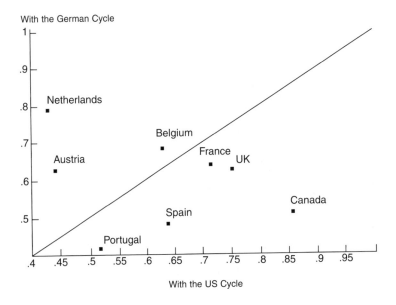

Figure 7.3A   Correlations of business cycle components, 1965:5–1979:3

Table 7.2 and Figure 7.3 (A and B) reproduce and extend the findings reported in Artis and Zhang (1997). The popular Hodrick-Prescott filter has been used to isolate the cyclical component. The dampening parameter in this filter can be set at different levels (zero corresponding to the linear trend case) and in this case is set to 50,000. Results are reported for a pre-ERM (1965:5–1979:3) and an ERM (1979:4–1997:6) period, as in the original study. The extended period results largely confirm the findings of that original study. In particular, in the pre-ERM period, there is a broadly defined 'world business cycle': cross-correlations with Germany and the US are relatively similar; after it, Germany emerges as an alternative 'attractor' for most of the European economies with the notable exception of the UK. Whereas the cross-correlations of the ERM countries with Germany generally increase between the periods, that for the UK falls sharply; and, while the UK's 'affiliation' with the US cycle remains strong, that of the ERM countries declines.

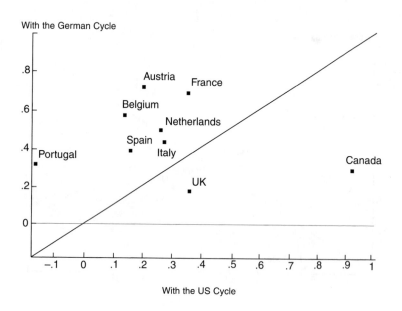

Figure 7.3B   Correlations of business cycle components, 1979:4–1997:6

Table 7.2 The US and Germany as benchmarks

	Pre-ERM		ERM Period	
	Germany	*USA*	*Germany*	*USA*
Canada	0.51	0.86	0.26	0.92
France	0.65	0.72	0.69	0.34
Italy	0.37	0.58	0.43	0.30
NL	0.79	0.43	0.48	0.31
Austria	0.63	0.44	0.73	0.22
Belgium	0.69	0.63	0.56	0.18
Spain	0.48	0.64	0.38	0.17
Portugal	0.41	0.52	0.30	−0.18
UK	0.64	0.75	0.16	0.35

3.3 Endogeneity of the Shock Criterion?

The suggestion that a 'European' cycle may have emerged in the ERM period is consistent with the hypothesis that the criterion may be 'endogenous'. The ERM may be viewed as a 'trial EMU' in this regard. Frankel and Rose (1997, 1998) have been the most eloquent advocates of this view. At first blush, as Krugman (1990) has stressed, the formation of a currency union has ambiguous effects on the asymmetry of shocks between the member states. If the union stimulates more inter-industry trade, it may stimulate more specialisation producing a propensity to greater asymmetry; alternatively, the new trade generated may be predominantly intra-industry trade, leading to greater symmetry. The replacement of idiosyncratic monetary policies by a common monetary policy, on the other hand, eliminates one source of business cycle difference (idiosyncratic policy shocks), although transmission mechanism differences may still lead to wide, possibly even bigger, business cycle differences.

Frankel and Rose (1998) provide an econometric test of the proposition that increasing levels of bilateral trade are associated with a reduction in asynchronous business cycles, obtaining a positive answer. The result has been questioned by Imbs (1998), however, on the grounds that the correlation of trade and business cycle synchronicity fails to control adequately for third factors that influence both variables. It is also an open question how far currency union will promote further trade and, to the extent it does so, whether the additional trade creation will be of a comparative-advantage type or of the intra-industry type.[3] Thus the issue is far from closed. An important question-mark has been raised about the validity of pre-union evidence on stochastic experiences, but no clearly unambiguous answers have yet been obtained.

3.4 Overall OCA Assessments

Overall assessments of the optimality of EMU for its potential members virtually always place the UK in an 'outsider' category.

Bayoumi and Eichengreen (1996) drew up an informal review of the major heads of assessment suggested by OCA theory, carefully referencing the relevant quantitative studies of these various factors for the European case. In a later study, Bayoumi and Eichengreen (1997) computed an OCA index, based on the contribution of OCA factors to the determination of bilateral exchange rates. The variables involved included: a measure of business cycle synchronisation; a measure of export composition; and measures of country size and output-weighted trade intensity. Using this approach they classified a group of countries as 'convergent' and most ripe for monetary union, another group as 'converging' and a third one as having shown little sign of convergence. The identification of these categories, and their membership overlaps quite strongly with the categories subsequently identified by Artis and Zhang (1998a, b) as 'the core' and the 'Southern' and the 'Northern' periphery. (The anomalies are that Bayoumi and Eichengreen place Ireland in the category corresponding to the core and France in the category corresponding to the Northern periphery group). The UK in all three studies appears in the 'Northern periphery' group. For good or ill, the Artis–Zhang studies come as close to a comprehensive formal assessment of the optimality of EMU, and the UK's position in relation to it, as any others.[4] Thus we proceed unblushingly to discuss those studies (albeit briefly) here.

Both studies use cluster analysis techniques, the first those of hard clustering, the later one those of 'fuzzy' or soft clustering. In each case, Germany is taken to be the 'centre' country, variables being measured, as appropriate, with respect to Germany. Data are taken for the period 1979:4–1995:10, on a monthly basis, for all EU countries (Luxembourg not separately distinguished) with, in the first study, the addition of the US, Canada, Japan and two European non-EU countries, Switzerland and Norway, as controls. The variables used are the following six: (i) the differential between a country's inflation rate and that in Germany, (ii) the volatility of a country's real bilateral DM exchange rate, (iii) the synchroni-

sation of a country's business cycle *vis-à-vis* Germany's, (iv) the synchronisation of a country's monetary policy (measured by the cyclical component
of its real interest rate) with Germany's, (v) the flexibility of a country's
labour market with respect to Germany's (measured by the relative ranking
of its employment protection legislation) and (vi) a country's bilateral trade
intensity with Germany. The motivation for using these variables comes
from OCA theory, with the addition of the inflation criterion (where actual
inflation is used as a proxy for counter-inflationary commitment). Hard
clustering algorithms work by minimising the distance between objects
(here, countries represented by the values of the six variables), progres-
sively forming groups or clusters by repeating the minimisation after countries join to form a group, or a country joins a pre-formed group. (In Table
7.3 'RMS' is the root mean square measure of distance at which the clusters
indicated are formed.) By construction, the groups comprise clusters of
countries which are 'like each other' in respect of their relationship to
Germany. Table 7.3 shows the results obtained, which are also represented
in Figure 7.4 as a tree diagram. Hard clustering throws away information in
the sense that every 'object' (country) has to be assigned to a cluster without

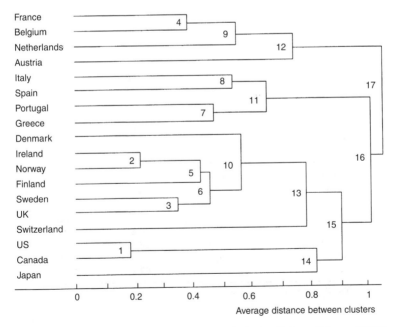

Figure 7.4   Merging process by group average clustering (Artis and Zhang, 1998a)

regard for whether it could nearly as well belong to another cluster. Fuzzy clustering remedies this defect; in this procedure 'membership coefficients' are calculated for each object (country) showing how firmly it adheres to each of the clusters nominated. Table 7.4 shows the membership coefficients computed for the 15 EU countries (Luxembourg merged with Belgium). The emboldened figures show the highest 'degree of belongingness' of a country. It can readily be seen that the fuzzy clustering results support those of the hard clustering approach. The UK is clearly in the 'Northern periphery' group, rather far away from the core group.

Table 7.3 Clusters detected under hard clustering

1.	Core Group	(France, Netherlands, Belgium, Austria)	RMS: .56
		(Denmark, Ireland, Switzerland, Sweden,	
2.	Northern periphery:	Norway, Finland, UK)	RMS: .81
3.	Southern periphery:	(Italy, Spain, Portugal, Greece)	RMS: .47
4.	North America:	(USA, Canada)	RMS: .18
5.	Japan	(Japan)	

Source: Artis and Zhang (1998a).

Table 7.4 Fuzzy clustering: membership coefficients

	Group I (Core)	Group II (Northern)	Group III (Southern)
France	**62.7**	19.9	17.4
Italy	11.6	18.5	**69.9**
Netherlands	**87.3**	7.0	5.7
Belgium	**87.9**	6.1	6.0
Denmark	22.8	**58.7**	18.5
Austria	**66.7**	16.2	17.1
Ireland	8.4	**75.8**	15.8
Spain	8.1	28.7	**63.2**
Portugal	2.1	4.9	**93.0**
Sweden	3.2	**86.8**	10.0
Finland	6.1	**82.5**	11.4
Greece	8.1	15.5	**76.4**
UK	5.3	**82.9**	11.8

Source: Artis and Zhang (1998b).

A conclusion can be drawn from this section: based on OCA analysis, with all its limitations, the UK is a marginal candidate for EMU. It is not in the core and in particular seems to have a different business cycle affiliation from that of the countries in the core. The limitations of OCA analysis, however, leave it open how far this distance from the core simply reflects the fact that the UK has been outside the reaches of the apprenticeship for EMU, the ERM, for most of the time; or whether, on the contrary, its absence from the ERM and its reluctance to participate in EMU jointly constitute a 'rational recognition' of the underlying OCA 'facts'. In the event the latter is nearer the truth than the former, there still remains the point that OCA analysis covers only a subset of the full range of considerations.

4 THE CITY'S INTEREST

The Chancellor's 'five tests' include a reference to the City of London's interests. That the interests of one sector of the British economy should be so elevated as to figure in a national decision in this way would seem controversial if it were not for the fact that the City of London's interests have probably been, all along, a determining factor in UK attitudes to EMU. Talani (1998) provides a thorough and provocative exposition of this idea. Given the generally positive attitude of British industry, the City's role here is reminiscent of the situation encountered by Churchill when he reviewed the enthusiasms of the City for the interwar return to gold, in contrast to the implications this had for British industry.[5] City interests have traditionally favoured a minimum of regulation and a fear that, inside EMU, such regulation would be encountered, is a motive for keeping out; by the same token, if indeed, the EMU leads to regulation when the UK is out, the City can profit as the 'off-shore banking centre': this prospect has also been cited as a motive for staying out.

The contrary fear is that by staying out, the City will fall victim, sooner or later, to some practice designed to protect Eurozone financial activity, hence penalising the City interest. It is not clear, either, whether there is some 'first mover' advantage which the City will forego by not being at the heart of Eurozone finance. Geographical location may not be very important; although locational agglomeration economies evidently are highly significant and this seems to imply that any incentives given to alternative centres within the Eurozone can indeed work to affect the City's built-in advantage of 'already being there'.

Initial suggestions that the continental taste for (non-interest-bearing) compulsory deposits as part of the armoury of monetary policy would be transferred to the ECB seem to have proved groundless; compulsory deposit requirements are to be part of the armoury, but they will be remunerated and thus will barely constitute a pretext for a move to off-shore banking in London. This source of prospective profit to the City does not seem likely to eventuate. Equally, though, what seemed like a possibility that access to TARGET would be restricted for the UK in such a way as to inflict higher costs on UK banks doing Eurozone business has not materialised. A source of loss has thereby been avoided.

Current indications – based on survey evidence reported in the *Financial Times* – are that 'City opinion' is now markedly more friendly to the EMU option than in previous periods, perhaps reflecting that there are no immediate signs of a loss to the City in joining EMU. Nevertheless, one of the Eurozone's 'black holes' remains that of financial regulation and last resort provision (Prati and Schinasi, 1998). What is determined in this area could have repercussions for City interests. Meanwhile in the Eurozone, bank mergers are taking place designed (mainly, it seems) to bolster the ability of incumbent banks to defend their positions in the face of an expected increase in competitive pressures. One of the promises of EMU is to make a single market out of the European Financial Area; remaining outside may prove a source of weakness for British financial institutions wishing to participate in this market. Whether this is so or not, City attitudes possibly are no longer a block on participation in EMU. We can consider now the way forward.

5 EMU AND THE UK: THE ALTERNATIVES

What is the way forward for the UK? Economic analysis imposes no imperatives; the decision is a political one. Present government policy requires a positive decision in a referendum to be called in the next parliament. The alternatives canvassed seem to be variants on two alternatives: the 'Canada' solution – staying out and not trying to participate; or 'joining now', presumably without a referendum.

Contrary to some present suggestions, the 'Canada solution' is perfectly viable; while both Canada and, to take examples closer to home, Norway and Switzerland are neighbours of large common market entities and are obliged often to accept the consequences of legislation passed in those entities without the opportunity to intervene, all three countries enjoy a degree of independence in monetary affairs. The Canadian economy is not dollarised in a way that renders the Bank of Canada ineffectual. The UK economy is bigger in relation to the Eurozone than is Canada in relation to the US (16 per cent of GDP as opposed to 9 per cent). Invoicing of imports and exports in euro is likely to be more pervasive than was invoicing in the DM and invoicing in sterling will no doubt decline. But this is a long way from saying that the euro will somehow subvert sterling as a domestic currency. All the evidence we have on currency substitution suggests that local currencies are extraordinarily persistent except in cases of extreme inflation or where governments take explicit action to encourage use of a foreign currency as a substitute. This said, the expectation that the UK will join the Eurozone within a relatively short time would assist its premature replacement and current observations may be contaminated by just such an expectation; a true Canada solution would remove this incitement.

It is impossible to avoid the judgement at this point, however, that the full-hearted acceptance of the 'Canada' solution is not one that the UK can manage, if only because its political classes would find it impossible to accept. British European policy in the past has exhibited a curious cycle. New projects are viewed at first with something approaching disdain, as unworkable. But, if workable, they are seen as against the British interest and hence in the next phase there is an attempt to sabotage the initiative from within. Then, when the project finally comes to fruition, the UK first stands aside and only later participates. The cycle arises when the UK is not in charge of the agenda, when the project itself is not initiated on a British interest. It is not surprising that the transition from disdain and hostility to participation is hard to handle: it would be so even if the disdain and the hostility were justified. If the other countries in Europe are going ahead with the project after all, then, even if it would have been better for the UK had the project never been initiated in the first place, standing aside from eventual participation may not be rational policy. The point of this detour (which in part relies on Young, 1998) is to underline that on past experience the Canada option is not one the UK is likely to be able to adopt in a full-hearted way. In the end, the UK wants to 'be in Europe'.

Clearly, if a full-hearted Canada option is not realistic and participation in EMU will come about some day, there must be merit in the Join Now option. Delay means being absent from important groundwork and institution-building, possibly quite harmful to UK interests, given that participation will occur sooner or later. There are two very practical obstacles to embracing this option, however. One is the need for a referendum; the other is the fact that the UK cannot decide simply to join. The Treaty of

Maastricht sets out some requirements for participation, which the UK must meet. The requirement for a referendum seems important at two levels; first, the promise has been given and any attempt to circumvent it would be subject to severe political attack; second, the assurance that the UK is taking a full-hearted decision to participate is extremely important, not only for its own democratic merits, but also because the chances of a smooth transition to the euro may well depend on it.

While the government's current policy path, being conditional on a positive referendum, starts with an advantage in respect of being able to assist a smooth transition, it is subject to all these same obstacles and it is worth spelling them out. First, there are the obstacles in the Treaty of Maastricht. The UK can reasonably be expected to continue to meet the convergence criteria set out in the Treaty in relation to inflation, interest rates, and the fiscal criteria – and without any points being stretched, as they were in relation to the debt/GDP ratio for most of the current constituents of the Eurozone. But the Treaty also requires that the currency of a candidate country should have been in the 'normal' bands of the ERM for at least two years, should have exhibited no stress and should not have been devalued in that period. There are grounds for expecting some leeway in the interpretation placed on this clause in the Treaty. Those grounds are that neither Italy nor Finland fulfilled this criterion to the letter, since neither country's currency was in the ERM for the full two years, although the exchange rate could be judged 'stable' for this period; and that there is *some* sign that *some* governments understand the British public's (presumed) exceptional sensitivity to 'being in the ERM'. But, it seems more than likely that, at a minimum, a requirement of exchange rate stability, somehow defined, will be made. Not only is there the Treaty requirement; there is also the well-known sensitivity of certain countries to the perception that the UK is prone to 'competitive devaluation'. If there is to be an exchange rate stability requirement, possibly followed, after a favourable decision on entry, by a further period of transition before the point of fixity is reached, a question must arise as to whether there will not have to be a framework somewhat comparable to that of the 'ERM-2' to which Denmark and Greece already adhere. The Maastricht Treaty is drafted so that the insiders may not keep out any late-joiners simply by will; countries that qualify are *obliged* to join. In respect of the exchange rate criterion, however, the interpretation of the Treaty is not straightforward and the automatic protection from exclusion which is afforded to outsiders by the Treaty cannot be relied upon.

A second requirement of the Treaty, which the UK currently does not meet, is that in respect of Central Bank independence. The independence granted to the Bank of England is instrument-independence; goal-independence has been withheld. A Maastricht-compatible independence will require both forms of independence and perhaps some other changes to the legislation in addition.

Aside from meeting the Treaty's requirements, it would also be desirable for the UK to develop means of minimising the net costs of EMU participation, in the sense of finding an alternative source of stabilisation. The Chancellor's 'Five Tests' refer to labour market flexibility and it is true that more labour market flexibility could serve as a substitute. But there are objections to looking only in this direction; first, the UK already is, by most measures, the economy with the most 'flexible' labour market in Europe. Second, further labour market reforms are likely to encounter political resistance. Third, flexible labour markets are not pleasant for many participants and, especially for temporary shocks, fiscal policy intervention may be regarded as a superior solution.

What needs to be done to fiscal policy in this context may well appear inimical to the trend in fiscal policy presentation adopted by the present government. What is needed, after all, is flexibility and discretion: flexibility to match the needs of the stabilisation objective; and discretion to choose the particular type of fiscal intervention appropriate to the precise stabilisation problem at hand. For example, variations in payroll taxes (national insurance benefits) seem like a proxy for exchange rate changes, while fiscal intervention to prick an asset price bubble might need to target transactions costs. The return to centre stage of policies of the 1960s – stamp duties, 'regulator' tax changes and the ghost of SET and the REP – is an unexpected, but logically plausible, consequence of entering a monetary union with larger and more cohesive partners whose policy interests will dominate and are likely on present evidence to respond to a different business cycle rhythm.[6]

6 CONCLUSIONS

The evidence reviewed in this paper suggests no 'strong' economic case for participation in the EMU. If anything, the organising framework of the OCA approach suggests that the UK might be right to stay outside; in particular its stochastic experience is different from that of the 'core group' within the Eurozone and on these grounds the UK will need a stabilising policy instrument. Membership of EMU would remove the possibility of using monetary policy and a floating (or adjustable) exchange rate in that role. Reliance on labour-market flexibility alone is unlikely to be enough and, in the event of joining, there will be a premium on fiscal policy flexibility. The limitations of OCA analysis are several, however; and, besides the room that this gives to 'other factors', including political ones, in making the participation decision, there is always the issue of the extent to which past patterns of behaviour will continue to hold in the future. While we reject the position occupied by some analysts that the worse the problem identified the more likely it is to yield to a nice solution (the 'ever-optimistic Lucas Critique'), it has to be admitted that the power of economic analysis alone, based on past behaviour, to identify the net benefits of a participation decision is limited.

NOTES

1. The theory assumes that monetary policy is, or could be, the 'first best' stabilisation instrument and indeed that the second best such instrument (fiscal policy?) is a very poor substitute for it. But these assumptions can be questioned. Canzoneri *et al.* (1996) find that real exchange rates do not respond appropriately. Erkel-Rousse and Mélitz (1995) find monetary policy working as a stabiliser although fiscal policy is useful.
2. In their own subsequent replication of their original exercise, Bayoumi and Eichengreen (1996) noted this general decline in the correlations, attributing it in part to the impact of German unification.
3. Fontagné and Freudenberg (1998) note that not all intra-industry trade leads to greater symmetry; specifically, while intra-trade of a horizontally integrated type could be expected so to do, intra-industry trade of vertically integrated industry, an intra-trade in *varieties* or *qualities*, is more akin to trade promoted by comparative advantage and may not induce greater symmetry in shocks.
4. Of course, there are also many informative informal studies available – a good example being that of Taylor (1995).
5. 'I would rather see Finance less proud and Industry more content' (extract of letter from Churchill to Niemeyer, 22 February 1926: see Moggridge (1972).
6. It is tempting to limit the enjoyment of this spectacle to the few who now recall the 1960s by failing to define the SET (Selective Employment Tax) and REP (Regional Employment Premium)! This would not be fair, however. The SET and REP were brainchildren of Nicholas Kaldor's. His aim was to tax labour used in services and to subsidise labour used in depressed regions.

REFERENCES

Artis, M. J. and Zhang, W. (1997) 'International business cycles and the ERM: is there a European business cycle?', *International Journal of Finance and Economics*, **2**: 1–16.

Artis, M. J. and Zhang, W. (1998a) 'Core and periphery in EMU: a cluster analysis', *EUI working papers*, RSC No. 98/37.

Artis, M. J. and Zhang, W. (1998b) 'Membership of EMU: a fuzzy clustering analysis of alternative criteria', *EUI working papers*, RSC No. 98/52.

Artis, M. J. and Zhang, W. (1999) 'Further evidence on international business cycles and the ERM: is there a European business cycle?', *Oxford Economic Papers*, January, 51, 120–32.

Bayoumi, T. and Eichengreen, B. (1993) 'Shocking aspects of European Monetary Integration', in Torres, F. and Giavazzi, F. (eds) *Adjustment and Growth in the European Monetary Union*, Cambridge: Cambridge University Press.

Bayoumi, T. and Eichengreen, B. (1996) 'Operationalising the theory of Optimal Currency Areas', *CEPR Discussion Paper*, No. 1484.

Bayoumi, T. and Eichengreen, B. (1997) 'Even closer to heaven? An optimum-currency-area index for European countries', *European Economic Review*, **41**: 761–70.

Canzoneri, M., Vinals, J. and Valles, J. (1996) 'Do exchange rates move to address international macroeconomic imbalances?' *CEPR Discussion Paper*, No. 1498.

Dornbusch, R., Favero, C. and Giavazzi, F. (1998) 'Immediate challenges for the European Central Bank', *Economic Policy*, 26, April: 15–64.

Erkel-Rousse, H. and Mélitz, J. (1995) 'New empirical evidence of the costs of European monetary union', *CEPR Discussion Paper*, No. 1169.

Fontagné, L. and Freudenberg, M. (1998) 'Endogenous (a)symmetric shocks in the Monetary Union', mimeo, CEPII.

Frankel, J. and Rose, A. (1997) 'Is EMU more justifiable ex-post than ex-ante?' *European Economic Review*, **41**: 753–60.

Frankel, J. and Rose, A. (1998) 'The endogeneity of the optimum currency area criteria', *Economic Journal*, July, **108** (449): 1009–25.

HM Treasury (1997) 'UK membership of the single currency – an assessment of the Five Economic Tests', October.

House of Commons Select Committee on the Treasury and Civil Service (1998) 'Report on preparations for Stage Three of Economic and Monetary Union', vols I–III, April.

Imbs, J. (1998) 'Fluctuations, bilateral trade and the exchange rate regime', mimeo, University of Lausanne, November.

Kenen, P. B. (1969) 'The theory of optimum currency areas: an eclectic view', in Mundell, R. A. and Swoboda, A. (eds) *Problems of the International Economy*, Cambridge: Cambridge University Press.

Krugman, P. (1990). 'Policy problems of a monetary union,' in De Grauwe, P. and Papademos, L. (eds) *The European Monetary System in the 1990s*. London: Longman, pp. 48–64.

McKinnon, R. I. (1963) 'Optimum currency areas', *American Economic Review*, 53 (September) 717–25.

Moggridge, D. E. (1972) *British Monetary Policy* 1924–31, Cambridge: Cambridge University Press.

Mundell, R. A. (1961) 'A theory of optimum currency areas', *American Economic Review*, 51 (September): 657–65.

Prati, A. and Schinasi, G. (1998) 'Financial stability in EMU', IMF Working Papers (forthcoming).

Talani, L. (1998) 'Interests or expectations? The problem of credibility of the exchange rate policy: an international political economy approach. The cases of Italy and the UK and the departure from the ERM of the EMS', PhD thesis, European University Institute, June.

Taylor, C. (1995) 'EMU 2000? Prospects for European Monetary Union', *Chatham House Paper*, 1995.

Young, H. (1998) *This Blessed Plot: Britain and Europe from Churchill to Blair*, Basingstoke: Macmillan.

8 Can Britain Join the Euro? Political Opportunities and Impediments

John Curtice

The euro is as much a political as it is an economic project. After all, one of its aims is to promote the unity of Europe so that any repeat of the conflagrations that scarred the European continent in the first half of the twentieth century becomes unthinkable. And certainly so far as Britain is concerned, both past and future decisions have been and will be influenced by political as well as economic considerations. For example, the policy of 'wait and see' developed by the Conservative government under John Major was the only stance that could unite a cabinet that included some who believed in further European integration and others who believed that having your own currency was integral to the maintenance of national sovereignty. It certainly was not simply the product of concerns about differences between British and other European trade cycles.

Indeed such decisions as have been made so far about the single currency in Britain have only served to ensure that any future decision to join the euro will be heavily influenced by political as well as economic considerations. In the 1997 general election all the main political parties promised to hold a referendum in advance of any decision to join the euro. As a result, Britain cannot now join the euro unless her politicians (with perhaps some aid from her economists) can persuade her public of the wisdom of doing so. Meanwhile, the Conservative party's decision since the election to rule out joining the euro in this parliament and the next together with Labour's commitment not to hold a referendum in this parliament (barring unexpected circumstances) means that the outcome of the next general election is likely to be important as well.

In this chapter we examine some of the political constraints and opportunities that face any attempt to ensure that Britain joins the euro in the near future. Given that securing public assent will be vital to any such attempt, our starting point is to examine the state of public opinion in Britain towards the euro up to the eve of its launch in January 1999.

Against that background, we then consider the prospects for the two hurdles that the pro-single currency movement have to surmount, that is convincing the government and persuading the public.

1 PUBLIC OPINION

Between them, two valuable time series enable us to chart attitudes towards the euro in Britain. One of these series provides us with a regular annual measure of public opinion since the early 1990s. The other, while more episodic in its timing before the last general election, provides us with a more regular set of measures from 1997 to 1999.

The first series comes from SCPR's British Social Attitudes (BSA) series, conducted in the spring of each year. Since 1992 it has regularly asked its respondents whether they favoured the introduction of the single currency either in replacement of or alongside the pound, or whether instead they favoured keeping the pound as the only currency in circulation in Britain.

Table 8.1   Public attitudes towards a single currency

Here are three statements about the future of the pound in the European Union. Which comes closest to your view?

	1992 %	1993 %	1994 %	1995 %	1996 %	1997 %	1998 %
Replace the pound by a single currency	21	14	17	18	13	17	18
Use both the pound and a new European currency	21	17	18	18	16	17	22
Keep the pound as the only currency for Britain	53	66	62	62	68	61	54

Source: 1992, British Election Study; 1993–98, British Social Attitudes.

This question has revealed clear and consistent hostility towards the introduction of a single currency (see Table 8.1). Since 1992, more than half have always expressed a preference for keeping the pound as the only currency in use in Britain, while those in favour of the introduction of a

European currency in some form have never significantly exceeded two in five respondents.

Our second series comes from MORI who have been tracking attitudes on a regular basis for the City firm, Salomon Smith Barney. Its question is more straightforward, simply asking people whether they would vote in favour or against Britain becoming part of a single European currency. On all but one occasion, at least half have said they would vote against while never have more than a third been in favour (with the remainder saying they did not know) (see Table 8.2). In short, no matter how they have been asked, the answer from the British public has been a consistent 'No'.[1]

Table 8.2   Reported euro-referendum voting intentions

If there were a referendum now on whether Britain should be part of a single European Currency, how would you vote?

	In favour	Against
	%	%
November 1991	33	54
November 1994	33	56
June 1995	29	60
May 1996	23	60
November 1996	22	64
April 1997	27	54
October 1997	27	54
November 1997	30	52
January 1998	32	52
March 1998	30	54
May 1998	31	54
July 1998	33	50
September 1998	30	49
December 1998	29	53
January 1999	33	51

Source: MORI.

So securing Britain's entry into the euro looks as although it is going to be an uphill task. Britain's political parties have between them handed the final decision to a public which, on all available evidence, is unequivocally opposed to entry. It seems that a government which proposed entry might not only simply be inviting defeat in the referendum, but perhaps may also be courting defeat in a general election. Is there really any realistic prospect of securing either governmental or public backing for joining the euro in such circumstances?

2 GOVERNMENT

Two potential problems face any government that might decide to campaign for Britain's entry into the single European currency. The first, which as we saw was a problem faced by the Major government, is whether it can maintain its internal cohesion. The second, given the evidence on public opinion, is the potential threat that such a manoeuvre might pose to the government's electability in a future general election.

Europe has proved capable of inducing more splits within Britain's two main political parties than any other issue (Gamble, 1998). With a number of anti-European rebels on his own side, Edward Heath was only ever able to take Britain into the then Common Market in 1973 thanks to the support of pro-European Labour MPs who backed entry against the instructions of their whips (Jenkins, 1991). Heath's success in securing Britain's entry resulted in the decision of the controversial former Conservative minister, Enoch Powell, to leave his party and back Labour in the February 1974 general election. Meanwhile, Labour was only able to quell its divisions by arguing for a 'renegotiation' of Britain's terms of entry and the submission of the outcome to a referendum on British membership, a policy it duly pursued on its return to power in 1974. Then, by the early 1980s anti-Europeanism had swept Labour as part of its general drift at that time to the left. The resulting commitment to withdrawal from the common market was at least one of the reasons that persuaded Roy Jenkins and three other former Labour cabinet ministers to set up a new party, the SDP.

More recently, of course, it is the Conservative Party whose divisions on Europe have been exposed. Much of the pro-Europeanism that had led the party to favour Britain's entry into the Common Market in the 1970s had been based on enthusiasm for the supposed economic benefits of integration rather than any hopes for closer political integration. So as the latter moved up the Brussels agenda, scepticism increased. Arguments within Cabinet about whether Britain should join the then European Exchange Rate Mechanism resulted in rifts that contributed significantly to Margaret Thatcher's removal as Prime Minister in 1990 (Thatcher, 1993). Although John Major's negotiation of an opt-out from both monetary union and the social chapter provisions of the 1991 Maastricht Treaty enabled his party to hide its divisions during the 1992 general election, they exploded into the open following the Danes' initial rejection of the treaty in the summer of 1992 and Britain's ignominious forced withdrawal from the exchange rate mechanism on 'Black Wednesday', in September 1992. Ratification of the Maastricht Treaty was eventually only secured thanks to Liberal Democrat support (Clarke and Curtice, 1998), while divisions over Europe both within Cabinet and within the parliamentary Conservative party continued to plague the government for the remainder of its unhappy term. Even during the 1997 general election, the *Daily Telegraph* was able to identify as many as 190 Conservative candidates who had expressed their opposition to Britain joining the single currency at any time in their personal election manifestos, compared with only 57 who clearly backed the government's line of 'wait and see' (Butler and Kavanagh, 1997).

At the heart of these splits in both parties was a tension between those who favoured economic and political liberalisation, and those who placed a priority on the merits of national sovereignty and the maintenance of British identity. These competing considerations were capable of splitting both the traditional left and the right in British politics (Ludlam, 1998; Evans, 1999). For many on the right, economic liberalisation fitted in with their belief in the virtues of the market, but at the same time the potential loss of sovereignty cut across their affection for British identity. While for some on the left the European project appealed to a belief in internationalism, for others economic liberalisation threatened the ability of the British state, or indeed any state, to implement socialism. Little wonder then that traditional party politics in Britain has found Europe such a disruptive issue.

But does the election of a New Labour government that is grounded in political discipline, has abandoned its anti-European stance a decade previously and is blessed with an overwhelming Commons majority, finally herald the arrival of a government capable of avoiding divisions on a single currency? In truth, this is unlikely to be so. It looks likely that if the current Labour government does eventually back British entry it will incur division within its own ranks.

Two surveys of parliamentary Labour opinion both point in this direction. While the first has the disadvantage that it was taken during the last parliament, it has the advantage that it asked a wide range of questions about a single currency (Baker and Seawright, 1998). Although it suggested that the vast majority of Labour MPs in the last parliament were in favour of the single currency, consistently around one in five gave a sceptical response. Thus 24 per cent said that EMU was 'not realisable', 21 per cent agreed that 'the establishment of a single EU currency would signal the end of the UK as a sovereign nation' while 16 per cent said that EMU was 'not desirable'. Meanwhile no less than 42 per cent agreed that 'Britain should never permit its monetary policy to be determined by an independent European Central Bank', one of the consequences, of course, of joining the euro.

True, this same survey also found that those who had first entered parliament after 1983 were less sceptical about a single currency than were those who had been in the Commons when Labour's common market battles had been at their most intense. But our second survey, the 1997 British Representation Study, suggests that the picture it paints is still true of the much-expanded parliamentary Labour party in the current parliament. Conducted before the last election, this second survey found that while 76 per cent of those who were eventually elected in 1997 opposed the idea that the government should 'move towards a single European currency', 17 per cent were opposed.

But of course one thing that the current government enjoys which its predecessor did not is a large Commons majority. Even if 17 per cent of Labour MPs were to go so far as to vote against any single currency legislation, the government would still be able to command an overall majority even in the absence of any assistance from the largely pro-single currency Liberal Democrats. However this may well be to miss the point. What the current government does risk in backing a single currency is the public display of disagreement within its own ranks, a risk to which the current leadership is particularly averse in view of the party's experience in the 1980s, not least because it believes, not unreasonably, that division costs votes.

Still, the government might anticipate that any divisions on its own side might be mirrored by similar divisions on the Conservative side. Two former senior Cabinet ministers, Michael Heseltine and Kenneth Clarke, continue to support Britain's entry into the euro in opposition to the stance taken by their leader, William Hague. Two Conservative MEPs, John Stevens and Brendan Donnelly have also resigned from the party, in part over the issue of the euro. On the other hand, it is far from clear that there are many indians willing to follow the lead of these chiefs. Indeed, on the evidence of the British Representation Study, the current parliamentary Conservative party appears to be more united in its opposition to the euro than the parliamentary Labour party is in its enthusiasm. As many as 86 per cent of successful Conservative candidates said they were opposed to moves towards a single currency while just 9 per cent were in favour. Little wonder then that William Hague has been able to nudge his party in a more eurosceptic direction on this issue since the last general election.

Moreover, even if Labour could remain at least as united on this issue as the Conservatives any announcement of support for a single currency might still be considered electorally hazardous. Given the apparent state of public opinion, a commitment to joining a single currency would seem more likely to lose than gain the party votes. There would certainly seem to be little incentive to give such a commitment this side of the next general election.

However, voters have to take into account a myriad of considerations in deciding how to vote in a general election. The potential electoral costs of coming out in favour of a single currency would depend not just on the distribution of public opinion on the issue but also on how important the issue was to voters in deciding how to vote. And on the evidence of the last election at least we might conclude that the single currency (or indeed the issue of Europe in general, see Evans, 1999) is unlikely to switch many votes to or from the Labour camp. We can see this by undertaking analysis of the British Election Panel Study which interviewed the same respondents regularly during the course of the 1992–97 parliament, including immediately after the 1992 and 1997 elections. This design enables us to analyse how far vote switching between 1992 and 1997 was conditional on attitudes that respondents had in 1992. So, for example, we can examine whether voters who were opposed to a single currency in 1992 were less likely to switch to Labour between 1992 and 1997 than were those who were in favour of a single currency in 1992. The resulting analysis is more powerful than any examination of the association between vote choice and attitudes towards a single currency in a single cross-section survey, as any association we might find between vote switching after 1992 and attitudes towards the single currency in 1992 cannot be the result of respondents bringing their attitudes towards the single currency in line with their vote choice rather than vice versa.

From EMS to EMU

Table 8.3 Logistic model of vote switching
and attitudes towards a single currency, 1992–97

	Voted Labour 1997 versus not voted Labour
Vote 1992	
Didn't vote	−.54 (.20) **
Conservative	−.69 (.16) **
Labour	1.43 (.17) **
Liberal Democrat	−.18 (.15)
For/Against Labour 1992	.61 (.09) **
Attitude towards euro 1992	
Replace pound	.38 (.17) *
Use pound and euro	−.14 (.18)

Main entries are logistic parameter coefficients. The coefficients for attitude towards the euro are simple contrast coefficients that compare the impact of being in the stated category with being opposed to the introduction of the euro. Entries in brackets are standard errors. * significant at 5% level ** significant at 1% level

Source: British Election Panel Study 1992–97.

Table 8.3 shows the results of just such an analysis. Using logistic regression in which the dependent variable is whether or not the respondent did or did not vote Labour in 1997 (including abstained), it shows the relationship between vote choice in 1997 and three independent variables. The first is how the respondent voted in 1992; its inclusion effectively turns our model into one of vote switching between 1992 and 1997. The second is the respondent's feelings towards the Labour party in 1992 on a five-point scale that ranges from 'strongly in favour' to 'strongly against'. It is designed to take into account the possibility that those who switched to Labour between 1992 and 1997 might well have already been favourably well disposed towards the party in 1992. Our third and final variable is attitude towards the single currency in 1992, measured by answers to the same question that has been administered regularly by the British Social Attitudes survey (see Table 8.1).

The modelling shows that, after taking into account the other variables in the model, those who were in favour of replacing the pound with the euro were more likely to back Labour in 1997 than were those who were opposed to its introduction at all. However, those who favoured the use of both the pound and the single currency were not significantly different in their voting behaviour from those who were opposed to the introduction of the single currency in any form. Moreover, even the term for those in favour of replacing the pound is only just significant at the 5 per cent level. And if we introduce into the model other terms that previous research has suggested are also related to vote switching in this period (Evans, forthcoming), such as an indicator of Labour's party image, even this term becomes insignificant.[2]

So, at most, the evidence suggests that the single currency issue had only a weak impact on vote switching at the 1997 election. This is despite the fact that not only was the issue extensively discussed during the course of the 1992–97 parliament but it also became a prominent issue during the course of the 1997 campaign (Norris *et al.*, 1999). Voters were unlikely then not to vote on the basis of the issue simply out of a lack of awareness. However, at the same time, we should bear in mind that the cues voters were receiving from the parties were not strong ones. Conservative division and Labour reluctance to allow much space to open up between them and the Conservatives on the issue meant that voters who might want to have voted on the basis of the issue found that they lacked a clear choice. Certainly evidence from the British Election Study (Evans and Norris, 1999) indicates that the perceived gap between the Conservatives and Labour on Europe in general, although larger than in 1992, was still narrower than on more traditional issues such as jobs versus prices or tax and spend (Norris, 1999), while there was particular confusion about where the Conservatives stood (Evans, 1998a). If by coming out in favour of Britain's entry into a single currency Labour were to open up a substantial gap between the parties on the issue, then voters' views on the subject might well be more likely to influence their views.[3]

Moreover, any Labour government also has to bear in mind that in coming out in favour of a single currency it would be cutting across the views in particular of its traditional working-class constituency. As Table 8.4 shows, it is those in salaried occupations who are keenest on the idea of a single currency while members of the working class are least keen, a pattern which is long standing with respect to attitudes towards Europe in general (Evans, 1999). On the other hand one of the aims of the current Labour leadership is to spread the party's appeal well beyond its traditional working-class base, a base that after all is declining in size. So, supporting a policy that has a stronger appeal among middle-class voters might be considered beneficial rather than a risk. Indeed Evans (1999) suggests that even by 1997, Labour's stance on a single currency may well have been one of the factors that enabled the party to strengthen its appeal among middle-class voters.

Table 8.4   Attitudes towards a single currency by class

	Goldthorpe-Heath Class				
	Salariat	Lower non-manual	Petit bourgeois	Foremen & technicians	Working class
	%	%	%	%	%
Replace the pound by a single currency	22	15	14	13	13
Use both the pound and a new European currency	27	20	21	16	15
Keep the pound as the only currency for Britain	48	62	61	67	68

For details of the Goldthorpe-Heath class schema see Goldthorpe and Heath (1992).
Source: British Election Study 1997.

Even so, while the idea of a single currency may be relatively popular among members of the salariat, even among that group only a minority are happy to see the demise of the pound. In the end, coming out in favour of a single currency cannot be anything less than a risk for a Labour government, or indeed any government, unless public opinion on the issue changes. And of course one of the things that might help change public opinion is an attempt at persuasion by the government itself. It is to the possibility that public opinion might eventually change, and thus that a referendum might eventually produce a majority for 'Yes' that we now turn.

3 REFERENDUM

There is no doubt that much of the opposition to the idea of a single currency is deep rooted. It reflects in particular concern about its implications for British national sovereignty and the maintenance of British national identity, a concern that also influences attitudes towards Europe more generally. Thus, for example, research undertaken on the 1997 British Election Study shows that among those with a high degree of attachment to a sense of Britishness only a quarter were prepared to contemplate the introduction of a single currency (either in replacement of or alongside the pound) while nearly a half of those with a low level of attachment favoured the single currency (Curtice and Jowell, 1998). Assuaging such concerns is unlikely to be easy for any pro-currency campaign.

On the other hand opposition is not rooted in a high level of knowledge. In the spring 1998 Eurobarometer, respondents were given six statements about the euro and asked whether they were true or false (Eurobarometer, 1998).[4] Across the six items the typical British respondent got the right answer just 49 per cent of the time, no better than they were likely to do if they had guessed all the answers and the lowest figure of any of the EU states. In contrast the EU average was 65 per cent, with no less than eight of the participating countries scoring more highly than that. At least then there appears to be the possibility that opinions about the euro could change if and when knowledge about it becomes more widespread.

There is also a degree of fatalism about public attitudes towards the euro. It might not be considered desirable but nevertheless it does seem to be thought inevitable. For example in September 1998, MORI found that over four in five believe that Britain will have joined the single currency in ten years' time. Such a belief perhaps implies an acceptance that if the euro succeeds they will have to vote to join even if it offends their sense of national identity.

Indeed we can show that economic arguments about the euro do influence public attitudes and that the issue is not simply one of national identity. The 1997 British Social Attitudes survey asked its respondents about three possible economic consequences of joining the euro, that is whether they agreed or disagreed that unemployment would be higher, mortgage rates lower, and Britain would trade more successfully with Europe. At the same time it asked a question that addressed the issue of sovereignty, that is whether Britain might lose its ability to decide its own tax and spending plans. In Table 8.5 we show the results of a logistic regression in which the dependent variable is whether the respondent was in favour of the introduction of the euro either alongside or in place of the pound, while attitudes towards these four possible consequences are the independent variables. It shows that while our 'national sovereignty' item was clearly correlated with attitudes towards the euro independently of the three economic items, two of the economic items were also significantly correlated, with the item on trade the most strongly so of any item. The one issue, at that time at least, that did not appear to have any bearing on voters' attitudes towards the euro was the level of mortgage rates. Indeed very few people, that is just 9 per cent of the total sample, identified this as a potential advantage of the euro at all. Whether the differential that opened up between sterling and euro interest rates when the euro was launched in January 1999 will persuade people otherwise remains to be seen.

From EMS to EMU

Table 8.5 Logistic model of attitudes towards the euro

	Introduce euro v. not introduce
Trade more successfully	.85 (.09) **
Lose ability to decide tax and spending plans	−.47 (.06) **
Unemployment become higher	−.43 (.08) **
Lower mortgages	.14 (.09)

Main entries are logistic parameter coefficients. Entries in brackets are associated standard errors. In the dependent variable those who favoured the introduction of the euro and the scrapping of the pound have been combined with those who favour its introduction alongside the pound, and this combined group is compared with those who opposed the introduction of the euro. Each of the independent variables was measured on a five-point scale from 'strongly agree' to 'strongly disagree' and all are treated as interval level variables. ** significant at 1% level

Source: British Social Attitudes Survey 1997.

Indeed in practice, as Tables 8.1 and 8.2 show, while the British public may have been consistent so far in its opposition to the euro, the degree of opposition has varied from time to time. In Table 8.1 we can see that opposition peaked in 1993 and again in 1996, while on the most recently available reading in the BSA series, opposition has fallen back to what it was in 1992. Table 8.2 also shows a peak of opposition in 1996, and provides a wealth of evidence to suggest that attitudes towards the euro became somewhat warmer in 1997 and 1998 although there was, however, a slight reversal of that trend just weeks before the euro was actually launched.

So public opinion towards the euro does then appear capable of changing. But how might we account for that change? And what clues does it provide as to what may be required to achieve the large swing of opinion that would be needed to produce a Yes vote in a referendum? We approach these questions by combining an informal analysis of the trend data in Tables 8.1 and 8.2, with evidence from cross-sectional analysis of what are the correlates of attitudes towards the euro.

A number of hypotheses suggest themselves in examining the data in Tables 8.1 and 8.2. First we should note that hostility towards the euro peaked in the wake of unfavourable publicity in Britain about Europe. Thus the high level of opposition recorded in 1993 was found in fieldwork that was undertaken just six months after 'Black Wednesday' when Britain was forced out of the European Exchange Rate Mechanism.

Meanwhile the high level of opposition in 1996 developed in the wake of the BSE crisis that resulted in the banning of British beef from EU markets and the temporary withdrawal of co-operation with the EU by the British government. In short, it appears that bad news from Europe produces hostility to the euro, and we might surmise that good news from Europe might reduce hostility.

Cross-sectional analysis certainly confirms that attitudes towards the single currency are related to broader attitudes towards Europe. Thus, for example, in the 1997 British Social Attitudes survey, no less than a quarter of those who wanted to keep the pound as the only currency for Britain also favoured Britain's withdrawal from the EU. In contrast only 3 per cent of those who favoured the replacement of the pound by a single currency wanted to withdraw from the EU. Moreover, as Evans (1998b) notes, the relationship between attitudes towards the EU and attitudes towards the single currency has strengthened in recent years. As Figure 8.1 illustrates using Eurobarometer data, we can also show that support for Britain's EU membership reached a low point in 1996 and has still not fully recovered to the level of the early nineties (see also Evans, 1998b).

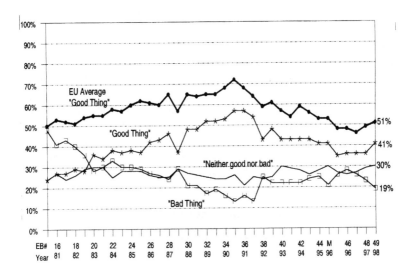

Figure 8.1   Support for EU membership (Eurobarometer, 1998)

From EMS to EMU

A second proposition that comes to mind in looking at the data in Tables 8.1 and 8.2 is that attitudes may be influenced by the position adopted by the incumbent government. Certainly opinion became less favourable to the euro under the increasingly eurosceptic Conservative administration led by John Major while it has become somewhat more favourable under the current Labour government, which has indicated a willingness to recommend joining the euro should the government (ever) come to the conclusion that the economic circumstances were right. This might suggest that public opinion might swing yet further if the government explicitly stated that it was now convinced of the case for joining the euro.

Two pieces of evidence certainly suggest that what governments, or indeed political parties in general, say can have an influence on attitudes towards the euro. The first comes from looking at how attitudes towards the euro have changed over time among different groups of party identifiers. As Table 8.6 shows, in 1992 Conservative and Labour identifiers had very similar views on the euro. But by 1997, attitudes towards the euro were more antagonistic among Conservative identifiers than they were among their Labour counterparts. Meanwhile Evans (1999) has noted that attitudes of Labour and Conservative voters towards Europe in general have varied in line with the changes in official party policy, with Labour voters being less pro-European than Conservative voters up to and including the 1987 election, while by 1997 they had become more pro-European. In part of course this pattern could be the result of voters changing their party identification so that it conforms with the parties' positions on a single currency; but given that we have already demonstrated that relatively few voters changed their vote on the basis of their attitudes towards a single currency, it looks likely that the opening up of a gap between Conservative and Labour identifiers on this issue also reflects the fact that they were influenced by the changing messages they were receiving from their party leaderships.

Table 8.6   Attitudes towards the euro by party identification,
1992 and 1997

	% saying keep pound as only currency Party Identification				
	Con	*Lab*	*LDem*	*Other*	*None*
1992	56	56	39	50	53
1997	68	57	52	49	68

Source: British Election Study 1992 and 1997.

The second piece of evidence comes from looking at the trend in attitudes towards the euro across the EU in recent months. According to the Eurobarometer, between the autumn of 1997 and the spring of 1998, when the launch date for the euro was announced, there was a nine point rise across all 15 EU countries as a whole in support for the creation of a single currency (Eurobarometer, 1998). The fact that the euro moved from an aspiration to a reality appears to have had a significant impact on public attitudes, a point to which we shall return. But support for the euro rose by noticeably less than the EU average in the three countries, the United Kingdom (+5 per cent), Sweden (+5 per cent) and Denmark (+2 per cent), where the government had decided to opt out of the single currency. One explanation for this pattern at least, is that the lack of advocacy of the merits of the euro by these three national governments meant that the announcement of the launch of the euro had less impact on public opinion in these three countries.

Still, even if we accept that governments may well be capable of exercising some influence on public opinion, the power of governments to persuade and thereby enjoy success in the referendum ballot box should not be exaggerated. In part of course, we might anticipate that the persuasive power of the government would depend on its current level of popularity. An unpopular government might be expected to be less influential than a popular one, a thesis that appears to be confirmed by the fact that the vote in favour of devolution was significantly higher in both Scotland and Wales in 1997 when referendums were held early in the lifetime of a newly elected government, than it was in 1979 when they were held in the dying days of a divided administration.

Yet the 1997 Welsh referendum also indicates that the persuasive power of a popular government may well not be a sufficient condition to deliver a Yes vote. The Yes majority in the principality comprised just 0.6 per cent of the votes cast. Meanwhile, both survey evidence and the geography of the result both suggest that success for the Yes camp depended on differential abstention by those opposed to devolution. Moreover, this outcome occurred despite the fact that opinion poll evidence on attitudes towards devolution in Wales was far more favourable to the Yes camp than are the figures for attitudes towards the euro in Tables 8.1 and 8.2. In short, a government would be ill advised to assume that it could expect to win a euro referendum simply by holding it in the honeymoon of a second term. It is likely to have to use its persuasive powers over a more extended period than that (Curtice, 1999).[5]

The third potential influence suggested by Tables 8.1 and 8.2 is the media. After all, the period between 1992 and 1997 was not only marked by an increasingly eurosceptic government, but also an increasingly eurosceptic press (Seymour-Ure, 1997). More than one newspaper went so far as to publish the names of candidates from all parties who were believed to be opposed to the introduction of single currency, and indeed *The Times* actually opted to endorse a vote for whichever candidate was locally the most opposed to a single currency rather than back any particular party. Moreover, the rise in anti-single currency feeling identified by MORI between September and December 1998 was laid by some commentators at the door of some newspapers' attacks a few weeks earlier on the possibility that the next stage of European integration would be further tax harmonisation.

Table 8.7   Attitudes towards single currency by newspaper readership

	% favour keep pound as only currency in Britain
Eurosceptic	
Sun	78
Other Tabloid	63
Quality	47
Europhile	
Mirror	59
Quality	27
Other newspaper	58
Do not read newspaper	59

Eurosceptic, Other tabloid: *Express, Mail, Star.* Quality: *Telegraph, The Times.* Europhile, Quality: *Financial Times, Guardian, Independent.*

Source: British Election Study 1997.

Yet the influence of newspapers on the attitudes of their readers towards the single currency should not be exaggerated. Even a simple cross-sectional analysis of the relationship between which newspaper a respondent reads and their attitude towards a single currency demonstrates this. In such an analysis, of course, we might be picking up the impact of newspapers' euro stances on their choice of newspaper as well as any influence that newspapers may have on the readers' views about the euro. Even so, as Table 8.7 shows, readers of the europhile *Mirror* are less keen on scrapping the pound than are readers of the two eurosceptic quality papers, *The Times* and *Daily Telegraph*, while they barely differ in their views from readers of tabloid eurosceptic newspapers other than the *Sun*. Meanwhile the difference between the attitudes of *Mirror* readers and those of europhile quality readers is greater than the difference between the attitudes of *Mirror* readers and those of *Sun* readers. A similar point can also be made about the differences among readers of eurosceptic newspapers.

A look at what happened during the last general election campaign points to the same conclusion. Despite the eurosceptic tone of much of the press, the British Election Campaign Study found that the proportion wanting to keep the pound as the only currency for Britain after polling day was, at 59 per cent, four points lower than it was before polling day. Moreover those reading a eurosceptic newspaper did not significantly differ in how their attitudes moved during the campaign from those reading a europhile newspaper.

In short, despite the fears of some commentators and the hopes of others, the stance taken by particular newspapers towards the euro is unlikely to be crucial in determining the outcome of the referendum. That is not to say that the collective message broadcast by the media does not matter; we have already suggested that bad news about and from Europe can change attitudes. But it is the news itself that seems to matter rather than the slant put on it by one newspaper rather than another.

4 CONCLUSION

Some clear and important implications flow from our analysis if it is indeed the case that the current Labour government is minded to join the euro in the not too distant future. We have seen that the political barriers to securing entry are considerable. The British public, in whose hands the final decision has been placed, has until now at least consistently expressed scepticism about the merits of joining. Moreover, if that scepticism is to be turned into acquiescence (if not enthusiasm), our analysis implies that the government needs to adopt a long-term strategy to achieve it.

The centrepiece of that strategy does not simply consist of winning over the *Sun* or any of the rest of the eurosceptic press. Their influence as persuaders is too weak. Neither does it involve simply springing a referendum on an unprepared public in the immediate wake of a second election victory. An election honeymoon cannot be relied upon to change the public's mind. Rather the strategy needs to be based on strong, risk-taking leadership, combined with effective news management of the media as whole.

We have seen that the position adopted by government is capable of influencing public opinion. A decision to advocate entry into the euro could be expected to pay dividends. But given the consistency and longevity of the public's scepticism towards the euro it is dangerous to assume that sufficient dividends will be reaped in a short period of time. Neither is the government's indication to date that it would be willing to argue for entry into the euro when the economic conditions are right likely to have much persuasive power.[6] Rather a sustained campaign of advocacy is likely to be required in which the public's fears about the impact of the euro on national sovereignty are counterbalanced by positive arguments about its economic merits. In other words, even if the government's aim is simply to win a referendum after the next election, it may well need to declare its position before that election.

Yet we have seen that that step could bring its own problems. It risks internal division and, by opening up further the gap between the two main parties on the issue, could well render it a more important influence on voting behaviour than it appears to have been in 1997. How might these dangers be minimised? By, we would suggest, declaring the government's position as early as possible. If some division is inevitable, the earlier it appears the greater the chance that media interest in it will have abated by the time of the election, and may in any case be counteracted by the appearance of divisions within the Conservative party. And if the euro does become an issue at the next election, an early declaration of the government's position increases its chances of reducing the level of scepticism, and thus the danger that the issue will be a vote loser by the time the election is called.

At the same time it needs to be recognised that ministerial advocacy will, on its own, not be enough. We have seen that bad news from Europe, news that is disseminated by all the media, and not just by its eurosceptic bastions, can fuel the British sceptical mood about the euro. The British government will need help from its European partners to ensure that the integration agenda does not proceed at so fast a pace that public fears about where it might all lead are given apparent credence. Equally, news of how European money is being put into Britain is needed, not another disaster such as the banning of British beef.

But the most important good news of all could be the performance of the euro itself. If in its early months it retains, or even gains in value (not least against sterling), maintains a lower interest rate than in Britain, and the European Central Bank avoids stoking either inflation or unemployment, the euro itself will become a good news story. Certainly polling taken in the early weeks after its launch suggested that the fact that the euro was now in existence might be beginning to influence attitudes. As seen in Table 8.2, in January 1999 MORI found that support for the euro had returned to its all-time peak, while a poll undertaken in February by ICM put support for the euro even higher, at 36 per cent. If indeed, the actual launch of the euro had made something of a favourable impact on British public opinion, then a first crucial step to overcoming the political barriers to entry may already have been taken. Whether the government will follow it up in the manner we have suggested remains however to be seen.

NOTES

1. The European Union's own Eurobarometer surveys also affirm this conclusion. For example, in its spring 1998 survey, just 34 per cent of those in the UK were in favour of the proposition, 'There has to be one single currency, the euro.'
2. Thus, for example, if we introduce whether or not the respondent believed that Labour was or was not capable of strong government, this term proves to be strongly correlated with vote switching while attitude towards a single currency become insignificant. Note however that here we are using perception of the Labour party in 1997, so our analysis may in part be picking up the influence of vote choice on perceptions of the Labour party.
3. For further evidence of the impact of party repositioning on issues on the level of issue voting in general, see also Sanders (1999). We should also bear in mind that some voters' euroscepticism helped persuade them to vote for the Referendum party in 1997, including some voters who might otherwise have been expected to vote Labour (Heath *et al.* 1998).
4. The six items were as follows:
   The euro will be used to pay for goods and services in all participating countries (True)
   Most of the countries of the EU will take part in the euro (True)
   Once there is a euro, there will be a European Central Bank (True)
   The euro will be worth the same whatever the participating member states (True)
   Notes and coins in euros will be introduced in 2002 (True)
   The euro will still need to be changed into the currency of another participating Member State to pay for goods and services in that Member State (False)

5. Equally, the outcome of the Scottish referendum on devolution cautions against any expectation that an indication that a majority of British business supports joining the euro would ensure a majority vote in favour. Surveys of business opinion in Scotland in the years before the referendum had repeatedly found a majority of Scottish businesses feared the economic consequences of devolution.

6. On 23 February 1999, the Prime Minister announced a national changeover plan, designed to indicate what preparations were required to make it possible for Britain to enter the euro, and in so doing announced his willingness to campaign in favour of entry in the event of a referendum being held. Yet he still drew back from advocating entry.

REFERENCES

Baker, D. and Seawright, D. (1998) ' A "rosy" map of Europe? Labour parliamentarians and European integration' in Baker, D. and Seawright, D. (eds) *Britain For and Against Europe: British Politics and the Question of European Integration*, Oxford: Clarendon.

Butler, D. and Kavanagh, D. (1997) *The British General Election of 1997*, London: Macmillan.

Clarke, S. and Curtice, J. (1998) 'The Liberal Democrats and European integration' in Baker, D. and Seawright, D. (eds) *Britain For and Against Europe: British Politics and the Question of European Integration*, Oxford: Clarendon.

Curtice, J. (1999) 'Is Scotland a nation and Wales not? Why the two Referendum results were so different', in Taylor, B. and Thomson, K. (eds) *Scotland and Wales: Nations Again?*, Cardiff: University of Wales Press.

Curtice, J. and Jowell, R. (1998) 'Is there really a demand for constitutional reform?', *Scottish Affairs: Special Issue on Understanding Constitutional Change*, pp. 61–93.

Eurobarometer (1998) *Eurobarometer No. 49 Report*, Brussels: European Commission.

Evans, G. (1998a) 'Euroscepticism and Conservative electoral support: how an asset became a liability', *British Journal of Political Science*, **28**: 573–90.

Evans, G. (1998b) 'How Britain views the EU' in Jowell, R., Curtice, J., Park, A., Brook, L., Thomson, K. and Bryson, C. (eds) *British – and European – Social Attitudes: the 15th. Report: How Britain Differs*, Aldershot: Ashgate.

Evans, G. (1999) 'Europe: a new electoral cleavage? in Evans, G. and Norris, P. (eds) *Critical Elections: British Parties and Voters in Long-Term Perspective*, London: Sage.

Evans, G. (forthcoming) 'Image and economics in the decline of the Conservative Party 1992–95', *Political Studies*.

Evans, G. and Norris, P. (1999) (eds) *Critical Elections: British Parties and Voters in Long-Term Perspective*, London: Sage.

Gamble, A. (1998) 'The European issue in British politics', in Baker, D and Seawright, D. (eds) *Britain For and Against Europe: British Politics and the Question of European Integration*, Oxford: Clarendon.

Heath, A., Jowell, R., Taylor, B. and Thomson, K. (1998) 'Eurosecpticism and the Referendum Party', in Denver, D., Fisher, J., Cowley, P. and Pattie, C. (eds) *British Election and Parties Review Volume 8: the 1997 General Election*, London: Frank Cass.

Jenkins, R. (1991) *A Life at the Centre*, London: Macmillan.

Ludlam, S. (1998) 'The cauldron: Conservative parliamentarians and European integration' in Baker, D. and Seawright, D. (eds) *Britain For and Against Europe: British Politics and the Question of European Integration*, Oxford: Clarendon.

Norris, P. (1999) 'New politicians? Changes in party competition at Westminster' in Evans, G. and Norris, P. (eds) *Critical Elections: British Parties and Voters in Long-Term Perspective*, London: Sage.

Norris, P., Curtice, J., Sanders, D., Scammell, M. and Semetko, H. (1999) *On Message: Communicating the Campaign*, London: Sage.

Thatcher, M. (1993) *The Downing Street Years*, London: HarperCollins.

Sanders, D. (1999) 'The impact of Left-Right ideology', in Evans, G. and Norris, P. (eds) *Critical Elections: British Parties and Voters in Long-Term Perspective*, London: Sage.

Seymour-Ure, C. (1997) 'Newspapers: editorial opinion in the national press', *Parliamentary Affairs*, **50**: 586–608.

Discussion of Chapters 7 and 8

Philip Stephens

These chapters rightly identify the question of whether Britain will join the euro as essentially a political rather than an economic issue. As Mike Artis states, 'economic analysis imposes no imperatives'.

For all the supposed faith invested by Gordon Brown, the chancellor, in the Treasury's 'five economic tests' for participation, it is apparent at the highest level that the present government has made the decision in principle to join. The outstanding question is when it will publicly admit to this private position. The timing of entry into the euro may be dictated by whether there is sufficient economic convergence between the British economy and that of the Eurozone. But the particular tests devised by the Treasury are designed in such a way as to meet what is seen as an overriding political imperative. As one senior Treasury official has been heard to remark, the tests are there first to make membership possible and only second to make it plausible.

My comments on these chapters start from a position of neutrality on whether Britain should join. They seek rather to illuminate some of the political and economic issues.

Tony Blair's administration believes that framing the question in essentially economic terms will make it easier to win the referendum it has promised before sterling is abolished. The Government's position is that while there are some constitutional implications, this is essentially an issue about the nation's economic prosperity. Since its last major policy statement on EMU in October 1997 – when it ruled out joining in this parliament but said it must be ready to join early in the next – the government's strategy has been to encourage an air of inevitability about eventual participation.

The pledge that it will do so only if it is 'unambiguously' in the nation's interest is logically flawed. There are no such certainties in economics. Calculation of the costs and benefits of membership have to be weighed against the hypothetical costs and benefits of remaining outside. Independence of action in setting monetary policy, for example, has to be set against the potential risks of limited access to the single market and of a damagingly volatile exchange rate.

By contrast, the political calculation made by Mr Blair is much clearer. He has set as one of the most important goals of his premiership the return of Britain to the mainstream of European politics and influence. He knows, and privately admits, that this is impossible if Britain remains indefinitely outside the euro.

There is, as Artis says, a Canada option. This would involve Britain accepting the framework of rules for the single market established by its partners while maintaining a degree of autonomy in monetary policy. The impact would be felt in the political as well as the economic sphere. Over time Britain's voice would be weaker across the range of European policy. It might start with exclusion from a new G3 forum for economic policy co-ordination but would gradually extend to foreign policy and defence. It would have to accept also a diminished status in the hierarchy in Washington – a deal of its present influence in US policymaking rests on the presumption that it is able to influence the European debate. There are arguments to be made in favour of such a retreat from past grandeur, but as Artis notes, they are not yet palatable to the British political classes. The opportunity to dance on the world stage is still one of the more compelling motives for a career in politics.

The Conservatives, of course, intend to frame the debate in political/ constitutional rather than economic terms. Their opposition to participation is based on the transfer of sovereignty involved – EMU is a leap in the direction of a 'European superstate'. In this context, a single currency is to be seen as a pernicious assault on the democratic underpinnings of the nation state. The potency of this argument within a nation which is by and large suspicious of the European Union's ambitions has been demonstrated in recent months by the ease with which opponents of EMU have seized upon alleged plans by the Bonn government to harmonise taxes. William Hague's party, however, refuses to accept the long-term consequences of remaining permanently outside EMU, preferring to pretend that, even in the guise of Canada, Britain could sustain a starring role on the world stage.

John Curtice in Chapter 8 correctly identifies the major shift in public opinion necessary for the government to win a referendum on this issue – particularly if opponents succeed in creating the impression that the euro is the precursor to economic rule from Brussels and harmonisation of taxation at higher continental European levels. As Curtice shows, there have been consistent majorities of between 55 and 65 per cent in favour of keeping the pound. Less than a third of voters have typically indicated a willingness to substitute the euro.

From that it follows that Mr Blair cannot risk a short referendum campaign. If, as seems likely, the government intends to hold such a vote immediately after the next election (the present thinking in Whitehall presupposes a general election in spring 2001 and a referendum in September of that year – the model for Scotland in 1997) it will need to step up its advocacy of participation well before then.

Pro-European ministers are arguing within government for a formulation which advances the present public position from 'prepare and decide' to 'the government intends to join providing that... ' These ministers would also like an indicative timeframe for the referendum – say an expressed intention to hold a referendum by the autumn of 2002 – a few months after the last possible date for the general election.

The prospect of turning round public opinion may not be quite as daunting as it appears at first sight. Beneath the quantitative polling there is evidence that public distaste for the euro is matched by a sense that Britain has to live in the world as it is. This has been a constant undercurrent in attitudes towards the EU – we don't like it but we can't opt out. The present polling evidence is based overwhelmingly on the period before the euro became a reality. The fact that it has been launched without immediate catastrophe may greatly reinforce the air of inevitability about British participation. This point is made by the polls themselves. While most people oppose entry a significant majority think Britain will eventually join – 80 per cent according to a Gallup poll in the *Telegraph* at end 1998.

The likely components of a campaign by the government to capitalise on that air of inevitability are threefold. The first is to continue to emphasise the economic 'benefits' as it has done by signing the manifesto of European socialist parties ahead of the elections to the Strasbourg parliament in June 1998. The second is to rely on business – particularly the large multinational corporations – to promote the supposed gains, a process which the government hopes to accelerate with the publication of its National Changeover Plan. The third is to cast opponents of EMU as opponents of the European Union itself. The low politics here is a strategy which says that a Conservative government would eventually withdraw entirely from the European enterprise.

Opponents of the euro will respond by attacking the transfer of national sovereignty involved in giving up sterling and by emphasising that joining will mark the beginning of a slide to European government.

This is an argument that the Blair Government can win. But it demands of the proponents of EMU a greater honesty and a franker espousal of the single currency than they have hitherto been prepared to offer. The most depressing (and potentially dangerous) outcome would be a decision by Britain to join because it seemed 'inevitable'. The refusal of successive British governments to own up to the implications of European integration and to freely acknowledge the trade-off between sovereignty and political influence or economic prosperity has been at the root of the nation's unhappy relationship with its continental partners from the moment it joined in 1973.

Discussion of Chapters 7 and 8

Martin Weale

These two chapters, by Curtice and Artis, look at aspects of EMU membership. Curtice addresses the question 'Will we, won't we?' while Artis asks 'Should we, shouldn't we?' In these comments I focus mainly on Chapter 7 (Artis), but would first like to offer one or two general comments on Chapter 8 (Curtice). Whether a plebiscite on EMU membership can be won may depend on the question asked. 'Do you support the government's recommendation?' is a very different question from 'Do you want to join?' Second, it is impossible to fail to notice that in Germany public opinion became favourable only shortly before the euro became a reality. Does this suggest that the existence of the euro on the Continent may make the British less sceptical? But now to the economic issues.

It is widely acknowledged, and Artis provides further evidence in this respect, that the timing of the cycle in the UK is different from that in much of the continent, raising the question whether EMU membership would suit the UK. But in Table 1 the author also shows that the UK's situation is more closely related to Germany's than is Spain and is similar to that of Portugal. Both of these have joined EMU, although it remains to be seen with what consequences.

However, we also see, in Table 2, that during the ERM period the correlations of business cycles in continental countries increased, compared with the pre-ERM period. The pre-ERM period includes both the fixed exchange rate system, which ended in 1972 and the currency snake of the mid-1970s. During the ERM period the UK had the highest business cycle correlation of any European country with the United States, although with a correlation of 0.16 against Germany and 0.35 against the United States the picture is rather more of the UK 'doing its own thing'.

How does one proceed from this historical observation that the UK business cycle is not correlated with Germany's, to reach conclusions about whether membership of the Eurozone would work? I must confess it is not obvious. If ERM membership led to a convergence of continental business cycles might not the greater straitjacket of Eurozone membership lead to a faster convergence of the UK business cycle with the Eurozone? The chapter does not attempt to provide a satisfactory account of why the

UK business cycle should be distinct from everyone else's, although there is a suggestion that it may be to do with bilateral trade. (Where, one wonders, does this leave the Irish Republic which is left out of Tables 7.1 and 7.2?). There is no point in worrying about lack of convergence if euro membership would rapidly steer the UK into line with the existing euro area.

But given the present state of the European economy there is a separate question about the use of Germany as a reference point. The analysis assumes that the ECB is a replacement for the Bundesbank. What we actually see is that, while Germany is slipping into depression, France and some of the other peripheral countries are growing fairly rapidly and the ECB seems unwilling to cut interest rates any further. It looks as though the first recessionary victim of a euro interest rate policy may turn out to be Germany itself. The exercises would be clearer if they were presented as correlations with a European business cycle calculated by aggregating the various economies in the Eurozone. This may give a rather different picture of how the UK would fit in.

That said, it is difficult to disagree with the point that, if the UK joins the Euro-area, active use of fiscal policy will be needed to replace use of a national monetary policy. Indeed, the most obvious policy instrument would be to mimic the effects of changes in the domestic interest rate by means of a tax on credit: the rate of this tax could be varied every month in exactly the same way that the interest is varied at present. It is often said that credit controls 'do not work'. An enforcement mechanism would be legislation which said that any creditor wanting to collect a debt through the courts would have to demonstrate that the tax had been paid. With this in place it should be possible on the one hand to retain the flexibility offered by an independent monetary policy while at the same time participating in the benefits of a fixed exchange rate. I am unsure whether this tax would be replaced by a credit subsidy if the UK needed interest rates lower than those in the rest of the Euro-area. But half a loaf is better than no bread.

9 On the Conduct of Monetary Policy in an Asymmetric Euroland

Paul De Grauwe, Hans Dewachter and Yunus Aksoy

1 INTRODUCTION

The institutional environment in which monetary policies are conducted in Euroland is by now well established. The European System of Central Banks (ESCB) is solely responsible for the conduct of monetary policy. Its mandate is to maintain price stability. Other objectives, such as output stabilisation, can be pursued by the ESCB provided these do not interfere with the primary objective of price stability. This institutional structure creates the possibility of conflicts about macroeconomic policies in Euroland.

First, it is unclear how much stabilisation the ESCB will want to perform. The other branches of government who could take upon them the task of output stabilisation in Euroland remain organised at the national level. Co-ordinating their actions is likely to be difficult.[1] As a result, national governments may want to shift much (some will say too much) of the stabilisation task onto the ESCB. This response is understandable because the ESCB will be the only institution with the means to undertake such responsibility at the level of Euroland. It is equally understandable that the ESCB is likely to resist these efforts by national governments. Conflicts between the ESCB and national governments are, therefore, almost inevitable.

A second source of conflicts is internal to the operation of the ESCB. The Governing Council, which is the main decision-making body of the ESCB, consists of seventeen members. Six of these are the ECB-Board members and eleven are the governors of the eleven national banks. Although the mandate of all the seventeen members of the Governing Council is to pursue euro-wide objectives, it is also clear that the eleven national governors, especially, will be influenced in their policy decisions by local economic conditions. And the latter are unlikely to be uniformly the same. Differences in national economic conditions will arise from two sources. First, asymmetric shocks will occur occasionally. Second, the economic and financial structures remain very different between Euroland countries so that the same shock, including interest rate changes decided by the Governing Council, will be transmitted differently across Euroland. This then is likely to create different views about the appropriate monetary policy within the Governing Council, even if the members of the Council have the same preferences concerning inflation and output stabilisation.

In this chapter we analyse the potential for conflict within the Governing Council arising from the asymmetry of shocks and different transmission mechanisms. We study different decision rules and ask the question how these different rules deal with these asymmetries and the ensuing policy conflicts. The remainder of the chapter is structured as follows. In section 2 we analyse the degree of asymmetry that prevails between the different member states of the EMU. The implications of these asymmetries for the optimal (desired) monetary policy are discussed. Section 3 proceeds by analysing the aggregation problem, which has to be undertaken in the Governing Council. Different voting procedures will lead to different schemes for aggregating these national demands. We will consider several types of voting procedures. The implications of these alternative-voting schemes will be discussed in section 4. More specifically, we assess the degree of macroeconomic stabilisation and the effectiveness of monetary policy under each of these different voting procedures. Finally, section 5 summarises the most important findings.

2 SOURCES OF ASYMMETRY AND MONETARY POLICY IMPLICATIONS

In this section we analyse the sources of asymmetry in Euroland and we derive the monetary policy implications.

2.1 Asymmetries in Euroland

Obviously, if all the member states were identical, each of them would opt for the same monetary policy and conflicts would not arise. The scope for conflicts arises from the structural differences (asymmetries) between member countries. We consider three types of asymmetries, which may trigger differences in the desired monetary policies: (i) countries may be hit by asymmetric shocks, (ii) the structure of the economies (for example labour markets) may differ so that the same shocks are transmitted differently, (iii) countries may have different preferences (different weights attached to the policy objectives). Each of these three sources of asymmetry could generate differences in the desired monetary policies of the member states and therefore induce conflicts within the ESCB.

2.1.1 Asymmetric shocks

Numerous studies have documented the degree of asymmetry that is likely to persist in EMU. For instance, Bayoumi and Eichengreen (1992) using a Blanchard-Quah decomposition find that both supply and demand shocks affect the core-countries (Belgium, France, Germany and the Netherlands) differently than the peripheral countries (Ireland, Italy, Portugal and Spain). Bayoumi and Prasad (1995), using panel data techniques, decompose output variability into aggregate (EMU-wide) shocks, country-specific and industry specific shocks. Their conclusion is that of the 70 per cent explained variability of output, more than half is due to the latter two types of shocks. Since they also show that European countries are more regionally diversified in most of the sectors than the US, strongly different reactions to shocks, be they country-specific or industry-specific, may be expected. These results are broadly confirmed by other studies, for example Artis and Zhang (1995), Beine (1997). Recent empirical evidence suggests that the asymmetry in shocks tends to be concentrated at the high end of the frequency of output movements, while the co-movements of output shocks over longer cycles tend to be high. In a recent paper, Croux *et al.* (1998) corroborate this view. Using dynamic factor models they construct a measure based on the co-spectrum, the cohesion. Results indicate that the cohesion in output across the EMU countries is highest for the low frequency components, almost as high as the cohesion of the US states but that cohesion decreases strongly (more strongly than in the USA) from the business cycle onwards to the higher frequencies. In addition, some evidence of core-periphery dichotomy is present. While the cohesion of the core is similar to the cohesion of the US, suggesting that the core is close to a real monetary union, cohesion of the periphery is lower. Therefore output correlations seem to be more diffuse and more dispersed across countries at the high frequencies. Thus the co-movements in the economic indicators suggest that in the long run the monetary policies desired by member states will be more or less alike but that at the higher frequencies, starting with the business cycle, substantial discord about these monetary policies may be present.

2.1.2 Transmission of shocks

Even if asymmetries in shocks would be unimportant, there is still the possibility that symmetric shocks are transmitted differently throughout the national economies. Empirical evidence on the importance of significantly different transmission processes is mixed, however. Taking again as a reference Bayoumi and Eichengreen (1992), the impulse response functions of the countries differ considerably in the dynamic response to a (demand or supply) shock. Bayoumi and Eichengreen find a clear core-periphery pattern in the output adjustment to shocks. Shocks are not only larger in the periphery but they also take more time before the system converges to the (new) steady state. The results of Dornbusch *et al.* (1998) point in the same direction. The more recent literature focuses on the size and the transmission of one particular type of shock, that is a monetary one. More particularly, the discussion revolves around the question of whether or not significant differences exist in the size and the adjustment period to a change in the interest rate. Gerlach and Smets (1995), using a trivariate VAR in output prices and interest rates, find some differences among the core countries in EMU but conclude that these differences are not important. On the other hand, Ramaswamy and Sloek (1998), using a somewhat different identification scheme and a larger data set find significant differences both in the size and in the adjustment speed of the reactions to an interest rate shock. They argue that EMU can be divided into a group of countries with a smaller impact factor and faster adjustment of the economy (Austria, Belgium, Finland, Germany and the Netherlands) and another group (Denmark, France, Italy, Portugal, Spain and Sweden) for which both the direct impact and the adjustment period are about twice as large as in the first group of countries. Here a core-periphery pattern as suggested by Bayoumi and Eichengreen (1992) is also found for a specific monetary policy shock. De Grauwe *et al.* (1998) come to qualitatively similar conclusions as Ramaswamy and Sloek (1998). They find that impact factors as well as adjustment speeds differ considerably across countries. A clear core-periphery classification was, however, not recovered. Thus, although there seems to be evidence of significant differences in the transmission processes, there does not (yet) exist a consensus on either the size or the timing of responses to shocks.

It should be stressed here that all the empirical studies surveyed are (by necessity) based on data from the pre-EMU era. Given the fundamental change in the monetary regime, it is unclear whether these results can be extrapolated into the future. Asymmetries in Euroland may very well be quite different from those observed before 1999. This still leaves open the question of whether monetary union will reduce the degree of asymmetries in Euroland. Economists disagree on this issue, some claiming that asymmetries will decline (see European Commission, 1990), others that they will increase (see Krugman, 1991).

2.1.3 Different preferences

Although the Maastricht convergence programme undoubtedly has also led to a convergence of policy preferences among central bankers in Europe, it is unclear how robust this convergence is. It is not inconceivable that differences in the weights to be given to price stability versus output stabilisation will emerge again, thereby exacerbating policy conflicts. Empirical evidence about these policy preferences is difficult, if not impossible to obtain. We will therefore make different alternative assumptions about the degree of convergence of these preferences.

2.2 Monetary Policy Implications

From the point of view of the individual country, the optimal monetary policy is the policy that maximises the country's objectives. We follow Rudebusch and Svensson (1998) and Svensson (1998a) by modelling the optimal monetary policy as a linear feedback interest rate rule. Details on the state space representation can also be found in De Grauwe *et al.* (1998). We thus follow a large literature which models the behaviour of the central bank policy by means of Taylor rules. As shown by Clarida *et al.* (1997) and Taylor (1993), among others, the interest rate policies of the central banks of the major economic powers are captured very well by these Taylor rules, especially since the 1980s when central bank independence increased significantly. We start by assuming some linear state space representation for the economic state X_t:

$$X_t = AX_{t-1} + Bi_t + v_t. \tag{1}$$

The economic state is some vector with output gap, inflation and past interest rate variables. More formally we define the state to depend on n lags of the output gap and inflation level while also the past n interest rates are included:

$$X_t = [\pi_t, \cdots, \pi_{t-n}, y_t, \cdots, y_{t-n}, i_{t-1}, \cdots, i_{t-n}].$$

These lags are assumed to be sufficient to grasp the linear dynamics of the state variable X_t. The dynamics of X can be decomposed into an autonomous part, a first order vector autoregression with matrix A and a part which can be attributed to monetary policy. The vector B measures the direct impact of changes in the interest rate on the economic state. The autonomous part, as represented by the matrix A, measures the transmission of shocks and interest rate changes into the output gap and inflation. The matrix B is constructed in such a way that changes in the interest rate only have a direct effect on the output gap. The effects on inflation then come from the indirect effect of the output gap on inflation. Note that by using simple linear feedback rules for the interest rate instrument, that is, $i_t = fX_t$, the central bank can alter the dynamics of the economic state. The dynamics then become: $X_t = MX_{t-1}$, with $M = A + Bf$.

Optimal linear feedback rules are then constructed such that they minimise an intertemporal loss function defined on the economic state itself, $L_t = E[Y'KY]$, with $Y'_t = [\bar{\pi}_t, y_t, \Delta i_t]$. In De Grauwe *et al.* (1998), following Rudebusch and Svensson (1998), it is shown that for a given weight matrix K, the optimal linear feedback rule is given as:

$$i_t = -(R + B'VB)^{-1} (U' + B'VA) X_t \tag{2}$$

where the matrix V is defined by:

$$V = Q + Uf + f'U' + f'Rf + M'VM, \tag{3}$$

$$Q = C'_X KC_X, \quad U = C'_X KC_i \text{ and } R = C'_i KC_i$$

and defining $e_{n:m}$ as a vector with $1/12$ on the entries from position n till m and e_m as a vector containing a 1 on the *m-th* position and zeros elsewhere, the matrices C_X and C_i are defined as:

$$Y_t = \begin{bmatrix} \bar{\pi}_t \\ y_t \\ i_t - i_{t-1} \end{bmatrix} = C_X X_t + C_i i_t, \text{ where } C_X = \begin{bmatrix} e_{1:12} \\ e_{n+1} \\ -e_{n+m+1} \end{bmatrix} \text{ and } C_i = \begin{bmatrix} 0 \\ 0 \\ 1 \end{bmatrix}. \tag{4}$$

Table 9.1   Optimal feedback rules ($\lambda = 1$, $\gamma = 0.5$)

	Aus	Bel	Fin	Fra	Ger	Ire	Ita	Lux	Net	Por	Spa
	interest rate response to inflation										
π_t	.052	.092	.075	.112	.077	.030	.0141	.088	.049	.111	.008
$\pi_t{-}1$	.045	.071	.070	.060	.059	.023	.0106	.069	.038	.080	.007
$\pi_t{-}2$	.043	.075	.059	.077	.059	.021	.087	.063	.036	.087	.007
$\pi_t{-}3$	.036	.085	.060	.047	.048	.017	.067	.056	.039	.060	.007
$\pi_t{-}4$	.041	.057	.051	.047	.043	.015	.055	.053	.031	.062	.006
$\pi_t{-}5$	.036	.061	.043	.040	.038	.014	.059	.045	.034	.064	.006
$\pi_t{-}6$	.034	.056	.031	.016	.035	.011	.061	.035	.010	.051	.005
$\pi_t{-}7$	.024	.054	.020	.015	.033	.014	.047	.031	.015	.033	.004
$\pi_t{-}8$	.023	.047	.018	.007	.026	.011	.044	.017	.012	.033	.003
$\pi_t{-}9$	.014	.023	.018	−.004	.018	.007	.022	.011	.006	.020	.002
$\pi_t{-}10$	.009	.012	.004	−.004	.008	.003	.001	.005	.006	.014	.001
	interest rate response to output										
y_t	.432	.277	.581	.388	.486	.236	.279	−.353	.155	.393	.164
$y_t{-}1$	.308	.246	.258	.185	.239	.135	.180	−.181	.091	−.009	.059
$y_t{-}2$	.197	.130	.116	.057	.059	.068	.126	−.145	.054	.059	.032
$y_t{-}3$	−.033	.035	−.032	−.017	−.010	.036	.058	−.003	.039	−.052	.032
$y_t{-}4$	−.059	.070	−.067	−.012	−.016	.006	−.032	.028	.045	.066	.011
$y_t{-}5$	−.048	.015	−.163	−.060	−.022	−.030	−.030	.000	.004	−.023	−.012
$y_t{-}6$	−.093	−.050	−.069	−.094	−.015	−.071	−.029	.054	.012	.049	.016
$y_t{-}7$	−.010	−.037	−.056	−.080	−.038	−.021	.001	.054	.025	−.011	−.012
$y_t{-}8$	.000	−.037	−.061	−.064	−.085	−.004	−.028	.124	−.002	.059	−.005
$y_t{-}9$	.018	−.110	−.013	−.024	−.011	−.014	−.009	.041	−.007	−.010	.007
$y_t{-}10$	.028	−.032	.008	.021	−.030	.015	−.018	.019	.009	.065	.002
	interest rate response to past interest rates										
$i_t{-}1$	.746	.604	.772	.857	.706	.794	.732	.702	.829	.675	.962
$i_t{-}2$	−.038	−.060	−.020	−.008	−.034	−.017	−.028	−.034	−.011	−.041	−.001
$i_t{-}3$	−.036	−.056	−.019	−.007	−.032	−.015	−.025	−.032	−.010	−.037	−.001
$i_t{-}4$	−.033	−.051	−.017	−.006	−.029	−.013	−.023	−.028	−.009	−.034	−.001
$i_t{-}5$	−.030	−.046	−.015	−.005	−.026	−.012	−.020	−.025	−.008	−.029	−.001
$i_t{-}6$	−.026	−.040	−.012	−.005	−.022	−.010	−.017	−.022	−.006	−.025	−.001
$i_t{-}7$	−.022	−.034	−.010	−.004	−.018	−.008	−.014	−.018	−.005	−.020	.000
$i_t{-}8$	−.017	−.027	−.008	−.003	−.015	−.006	−.011	−.014	−.004	−.016	.000
$i_t{-}9$	−.013	−.020	−.006	−.002	−.011	−.004	−.008	−.010	−.003	−.011	.000
$i_t{-}10$	−.009	−.013	−.004	−.001	−.007	−.003	−.005	−.007	−.002	−.007	.000
$i_t{-}11$	−.004	−.007	−.002	−.001	−.004	−.001	−.003	−.003	−.001	−.003	.000

As can be inferred from equation (2) the optimal interest rate rule is conditional on (i) the current state of the economy X_t, (ii) the propagation of shocks in the system, as measured by the matrix A and (iii) the preferences of the country over the three objectives through the matrix K. If any of these three components differs across countries, desired interest rate policy (as measured by the interest rate rule) will also differ across countries.

The optimal feedback rules can be computed for each of the EMU members. Using the estimation results from De Grauwe *et al.* (1998), we present in Table 9.1 the optimal linear feedback rules (for the set of preferences $K_{11} = 1$, $K_{22} = 1$ and $K_{33} = .5$) for each of the EMU member states. As can be inferred from this table, optimal interest rate rules differ across countries. Note that the size of the coefficients as well as the differences across feedback rules is in line with the findings of Clarida *et al.* (1997) who also find significant differences in the observed Taylor rules of the central banks of France and Germany. Moreover, in line with the findings of others, for instance Peersman and Smets (1998), we find that the output coefficient is much larger than the coefficient on inflation. Note that a larger coefficient on the output gap is not equivalent to a larger weight on output stabilisation. Whatever the preferences over output- or inflation-stabilisation, the weight on the output variable will remain relatively large because of the fact that inflation stabilisation can only be attained by output stabilisation.

3 VOTING PROCEDURES

The monetary policy decisions will be taken by the Governing Council of the ESCB which consists of seventeen representatives. Six members represent the ECB board and will probably take a euro-wide view. The other eleven members are the governors of the national banks and are appointed by each of the individual member states. There is up till now no clear prescription about the procedures to be followed in the decision process. These procedures will be at the discretion of the Council itself. As a result, one can argue that the ESCB has target and instrument independence. In other words, the ESCB sets itself goals for inflation and possibly output stabilisation, designs its own strategy to meet these goals and moreover is the only one responsible for the design of the voting procedures in the governing council as well.

To evaluate the effects of the decision procedures on the conduct of monetary policy we distinguish three procedures. The first one is denoted a nationalistic rule. In this case each of the seventeen members of the Council determines the optimal interest rate rule based on the loss function of the country he or she represents. Thus the optimal interest rate rule for the representative of country j is:

$$d_{j,t} = i_{j,t} = -(R_j + B'_j V_j B_j)^{-1} (U'_j + B'_j V_j A_j) X_{j,t}, j = 1, ..., 11. \qquad (5)$$

The second rule is labelled the consensus rule. In this rule each representative takes a euro-wide perspective, that is, he or she takes into account the macroeconomic situation of the whole union. We model this by assuming that such a representative would form the desired interest rate (rule) as a weighted average of the desired interest rates of the individual countries:

$$d_{EMU,t} = \sum_{j=1}^{11} w_j d_{j,t}. \qquad (6)$$

The weights, w_j, $j=1, ..11$, represent the weight assigned to each country in the general loss function.[2] Equation (6) can be interpreted as a short cut to a euro-wide optimal policy rule. As Gerlach and Schnabel (1998) show, the weighted average of euro interest rates can be replicated well by a simple Taylor-rule on euro aggregates of inflation and output. Therefore, we can interpret equation (6) as an approximation to an optimal linear interest rate rule for the euro as a whole.

The third rule is called the ESCB-rule. This is a combination of the previous two rules. More precisely, when this rule applies, we assume that the members of the ECB Board take a euro-wide perspective, that is they apply equation (6) while the eleven national governors take a nationalistic perspective, that is they apply equation (5).

In all three cases we assume that the decision is taken by majority voting. Since the conditions of the median voter theorem apply, we select the desired interest rate of the representative located in the middle of the distribution of the desired interest rates. It is clear that other voting rules could be analysed. In particular, the Governing Council may want to avoid applying majority voting so as to base its decisions on a broader consensual basis. We leave this to further research.[3]

Before discussing the results, it is useful to point out that that the short cut to a euro-wide optimal policy rule represented by equation (6) can be given another interesting interpretation. One can write the following:

$$d_{EMU,t} = \sum_{j=1}^{11} w_j d_{j,t} = f_t^E X_t^E, \qquad (6)$$

where X^E denotes the appropriately weighted average of the economic states of the different member countries and thus represents the euro-wide economic state:

$$X_t^E = \sum_{j=1}^{11} w_j X_t^j,$$

and f_t^E denotes the euro-wide linear feedback rule. The k-th element in the feedback rule, $f_{t,k}^E$, is defined as:

$$f_{t,k}^E = \frac{\sum_{j=1}^{11} w_j X_{t,k}^j f_k^j}{\sum_{j=1}^{11} w_j X_{t,k}^j} \qquad \text{for all } k.$$

In this interpretation the euro-wide representatives take European aggregated economic conditions, that is, X_t^E, as the basis for the linear feedback rule. However, in their response to this economic state they aggregate the optimal responses of the individual countries, f^i, using a weighted average which not only takes into account the size of the country, w_j, but also the particular economic conditions of that country, X_t^j. Economic responses are thus weighted using the severity of the economic situation in the country multiplied by the size of the country. Obviously, these weights will vary through time with the variation in the economic conditions.

4 THE EFFECTIVENESS OF MONETARY POLICY

In this section we assess how the asymmetries discussed earlier affect the effectiveness of the monetary policies in Euroland. We use the optimal interest rate rules as described in section 2. In addition, we use the estimated variance–covariance matrix of the output equations to obtain a measure of the asymmetries of shocks. We then simulate the model under the different decision rules discussed in the previous section. As was stressed earlier, this procedure makes the desired interest rate dependent on the shocks, the transmission process and the preferences of the authorities. We first ask the question how well the optimal interest rate of each country is correlated with the interest rate decided by the Governing Council. A lack of correlation can then be interpreted as a source of potential conflicts between the member states. We then analyse how well the economies are stabilised under the three different decision rules.

4.1 Correlation Between Desires and Outcomes

We simulated the decided interest rates in Euroland, assuming that infla-tion shocks are equal across all countries of Euroland and output shocks retain the covariance structure observed over the period 1979–94 (the sample period for which the optimal feedback rule was calculated). Table 9. 2 lists the correlations between the desired interest rate of each of the countries and the actual (decided) interest rate. Several results stand out. First, the correlation of the ECB-desired (euro-wide) interest rate with the actual decided interest rate is more than 99 per cent, irrespective of the assumptions about the preferences of the representatives . This means that most of the time the ECB-desired interest rate is also the outcome. This result is due to the fact that the ECB Board takes an aggregate view of the desired interest rate and then votes in unison on this. This ensures that most of the time the ECB Board's desire is very close to the median voters' desire. As a result, there will be no opposition (most of the time) capable of outvoting the ECB Board. The interesting thing is that this result is obtained even though the ECB Board only controls six out of seventeen votes. Second, it appears from Table 9.2 that the correlation coefficients of the large countries, France, Germany, Italy and Spain, are large, while they are much smaller for the smaller countries (with the exception of the Netherlands). Thus, the large countries find themselves more in harmony with the interest rate decisions taken in Frankfurt than the small countries. This result is due to the fact that the ECB Board's weighting gives a high weight to large countries. As a result, the ECB Board's desires, which prevail most of the time, come closer to the desires of the larger countries than to those of the small countries. Third, we observe that under the nationalistic rule the large countries do not fare as well anymore. When everybody votes nationalistically (including the ECB Board) the implicit weight the large countries obtain drops significantly. Fourth, the greater is the preference to stabilise output (as measured by the parameter λ) the smaller the correlation coefficients become. The reason is that most of the asymmetries come from the output equations. Thus, a greater desire to stabilise output amplifies the effect of asymmetries on the optimal interest rate of each country. Thus, too much ambition to stabilise output is likely to exacerbate tensions and conflicts in Euroland.

Table 9.2 Correlation of desired and decided interest rates ($\lambda = 1$, $\gamma = .5$) in per cent

	Aus	Bel	Fin	Fra	Ger	Ire	Ita	Lux	Net	Por	Spa	ESCB
Corr. between decided and desired interest rates, $\lambda = 1, \gamma = .5$												
ESCB Rule	57	56	56	91	88	69	75	28	91	34	92	99.8
Nationalistic	34	59	55	84	66	59	60	60	77	38	89	na
Corr. between decided and desired interest rates, $\lambda = 1, \gamma = .25$												
ESCB Rule	57	49	68	92	90	79	82	46	89	35	95	99.95
Nationalistic	62	56	51	80	74	73	66	37	88	40	87	na
Corr. between decided and desired interest rates, $\lambda = .2, \gamma = .5$												
ESCB Rule	87	85	75	95	95	93	87	80	96	55	90	99.94
Nationalistic	82	83	63	86	79	91	76	73	95	38	98	na
Corr. between decided and desired interest rates, $\lambda = 5, \gamma = .5$												
ESCB Rule	30	29	4	83	84	40	65	10	69	35	86	99.5
Nationalistic	49	45	47	58	56	52	43	26	80	26	69	na

The fact that the ECB Board has such great influence over the Governing Council can be due to two factors. The first one is related to the set-up of the ESCB itself. Six of the members of the Governing Council are ECB Board representatives, who take a euro-wide perspective. This implies that in order to have a successful opposition, at least nine countries should find themselves at one side of the proposed interest rate. A second factor has to do with the degree of asymmetry. Since the proposal of the ECB is a weighted average of desired interest rates, the distribution of desired interest rates would need to be extremely skewed to generate successful opposition. Which of the two factors is responsible for the control of the ECB over the Governing Council? In order to answer this question, we performed simulations with a Governing Council consisting of only two ECB Board representatives (that is, Germany and France), keeping the economic structures and shocks as in the previous simulations. It turns out that the correlation between the desired interest rate of this reduced ECB Board and the decided interest rates decreases only marginally to about 97 per cent. Therefore, even with only two representatives, the ECB Board would still be able to dominate the Governing Council. Thus, it turns out that the asymmetries are simply not strong enough to break the grip of the ECB Board on the Governing Council. If, however, the ECB Board loses its grip over its own representatives and if these take a nationalistic perspective, country-specific conditions will dominate the ESCB monetary policy. In this case the larger countries see their influence on the ESCB policy reduced. This is due to the fact that in this scenario large countries have only 2 of the 17 votes, while under the ESCB-rule the fact that the ECB Board takes a weighted average of national variables guarantees a larger weight for large countries.

4.2 Macroeconomic Stabilisation

In our framework, monetary policy is directed towards the stabilisation of the economy and more precisely the stabilisation of inflation, the output gap and interest rate movements. How well does the ESCB-rule perform relative to the nationalistic rule? In order to answer this question we substituted the simulated inflation, output and interest rates into the loss functions of each country. The realised losses give us a measure of the relative success in stabilising inflation, output and interest rate (for more detail, see De Grauwe *et al.*, 1998). Table 9.3 presents the results under the alternative voting procedures. We show the simulation results for the preference set $\lambda = 1$, $\gamma = 0.5$.

In order to give some perspective to the realised losses, we also provide the results of a benchmark case, which assumes that each country implements its own monetary policy (its own nationally desired interest rate). This also assumes that each country remains outside the monetary union. Obviously, the degree of macroeconomic stabilisation obtained in this benchmark case overestimates the possibilities of each country to stabilise output and inflation on its own. For example, we disregard the effects on the exchange rate when a country follows an autonomous national monetary

Table 9.3   Loss functions

	Aus	Bel	Fin	Fra	Ger	Ire	Ita	Lux	Net	Por	Spa
					$\lambda = 1,\ \gamma = 0.5$						
Benchmark											
π	.0004	.0007	.0159	.0219	.0244	.0436	.0333	.0378	.0402	.1192	.0915
y	.1393	.1170	.1208	.0696	.0761	.1341	.1131	.1874	.0795	1.1041	.1006
R	.0097	.0047	.0092	.0027	.0024	.0043	.0024	.0110	.0012	.0518	.0010
Loss	.1446	.1200	.1413	.0929	.1017	.1799	.1476	.2307	.1202	1.2492	.1926
Av. loss	.2473										
ESCB Rule											
π	.0004	.0005	.0168	.0242	.0252	.0324	.0335	.0379	.0400	.0961	.0935
y	.1462	.1252	.1246	.0805	.0764	.1586	.1145	.1925	.0799	1.1737	.1006
EMU R	.0024	.0024	.0024	.0024	.0024	.0024	.0024	.0024	.0024	.0024	.0024
Loss	.1478	.1269	.1427	.1059	.1032	.1921	.1492	.2316	.1211	1.271	.1954
Av. loss	.2534										
Nationalistic											
π	.0006	.0007	.0261	.0350	.0357	.0450	.0558	.0660	.0673	.1208	.1195
y	.1963	.1194	.1512	.0698	.0695	.1348	.1220	.1698	.0777	1.1275	.0975
EMU R	.0022	.0022	.0022	.0022	.0022	.0022	.0022	.0022	.0022	.0022	.0022
Loss	.1981	.1212	.1784	.1059	.1063	.1808	.1789	.2369	.1461	1.2494	.2181
Av. loss	.2654										

policy. The benchmark case only serves as an optimistic point of reference to assess the effectiveness of the euro-wide monetary policy. Some results of Table 9.3 are noteworthy. First, and not surprisingly, the centralised monetary policy in a monetary union is generally less effective in stabilising output compared to the benchmark case. This can be seen from the fact that the losses associated with the variability of output are always higher under monetary union than under the benchmark case of no monetary union. The reverse side of this coin is that the losses associated with interest rate variability are generally lower in a monetary union than in the benchmark case of no monetary union. The interpretation is the following. In the absence of a monetary union, countries use their interest rates more actively to stabilise output. In contrast, in a monetary union most output asymmetries are averaged out, so that the interest rate, which applies to the whole union, reacts less to output shocks. Second, for most of the countries, inflation variability in the monetary union does not seem to differ much from the inflation variability obtained in the benchmark case of absence of monetary union. Thus, the move to a monetary union does not reduce the capacity to stabilise inflation. Third, turning to the nationalistic case, we observe an average increase in the realised losses relative to the ESCB-rule. This decrease in effectiveness of monetary policy can be observed by comparing the entries for inflation and output stabilisation. Especially the increase in the inflation variability is noteworthy, rendering the nationalistic case inferior to the ESCB-rule. This result obtains despite the fact that the interest rate variability (which is a part of the loss) is lower in the nationalistic case as compared to the ESCB-rule. As suggested earlier, the decrease in the interest rate variability reflects the fact that the averaging process implicit in a monetary union makes the interest rate less sensitive to and therefore also less effective for (asymmetric) output and inflation shocks. This seems to be more of a problem in the nationalistic case than when the ESCB-rule applies.

5 CONCLUSION

The conduct of monetary policies in Euroland will be complicated by the diversity of economic conditions in the member states. In this paper we analysed some of this complexity using a simple model in which the participants use optimal interest rate rules based on national and euro-wide information.

Our main results can be summarised as follows. First, if majority voting is used in the Governing Council of the ESCB, the desired interest rate of the ECB Board prevails most of the time (at least if its six members in the Governing Council vote in unison). This result is due mainly to the fact that the asymmetries in shocks and in the transmission process are not strong enough to create coalitions that can override the desires of a unified ECB Board.

Second, not all countries are equally happy with the decisions of the Governing Council. We found that the small countries are often put in a position in which the interest rate decided by the Governing Council correlates badly with their desired interest rates. Such a situation can create tensions within the Governing Council. It could also lead to a situation in which the Governing Council will avoid the systematic use of majority voting.

Third, a decision mode in which the ECB Board sets the optimal interest rate using information on euro-wide aggregates (inflation, output) stabilises these variables better not only at the aggregate but also at the national level, than a decision mode where everybody only looks at his or her own national variables.

ACKNOWLEDGEMENTS

We would like to thank Paul Bergin, Mathias Brueckner, Matt Canzoneri, Casper de Vries, Marie Donnay, Daniel Gros, Hanno Lustig, Patrick Minford, Manfred Neumann, Andy Rose, Mark Salmon, Lars Svensson, Jurgen von Hagen and participants at conferences and seminars in Trouville (Denmark), Rotterdam, Berkeley, Harvard, Bielefeld, Bonn (ZEI), Leuven, CEPR Barcelona and AIEA New York for useful comments on an earlier draft of this paper. They do not share any responsibility for remaining errors.

NOTES

1. The Stability and Growth pact may be seen as one way to co-ordinate the budgetary policies of the member countries, see for instance Allsopp and Vines (1998) or Allsopp *et al.* (1998 a,b).
2. See Brueckner (1997) for a theoretical analysis of this issue. In the simulations we take the capital share (renormalised so as to add up to 1) of every central bank in the ECB as the weight for the country. These weights are assumed to be a function of the country's population and GDP as a fraction of the aggregate EMU population and GDP. The weights are for Austria 0.0299, Belgium 0.0366, Finland 0.0177, France 0.2138, Germany 0.3093, Ireland 0.0106, Italy 0.1896, Luxemburg 0.0019, the Netherlands 0.0542, Portugal 0.0244 and Spain 0.1119.
3. Issues related to the effects of the constitution of the ECB on macroeconomic performance can also be found in Von Hagen (1995, 1998) and Von Hagen and Sueppel (1994).

REFERENCES

Allsopp, C. and Vines, D. (1998) 'The assessment: macroeconomic policy after EMU', *Oxford Economic Review*, **14**(3): 1–23.
Allsopp, C., McKibbin, W. and Vines, D. (1998a) 'The stability and growth pact in Europe: some empirical issues', unpublished manuscript, Institute of Economics and Statistics, Oxford University.
Allsopp, C., McKibbin, W. and Vines, D. (1998b) 'Fiscal consolidation in Europe: is the stability and growth pact the solution to a prisoner's dilemma?', unpublished manuscript, Institute of Economics and Statistics, Oxford University.

Artis, M. and Zhang, W. (1995) 'International business cycles and the ERM: is there a European business cycle', CEPR discussion paper, No. 1191.

Bayoumi, T. and Eichengreen, B. (1992) 'Shocking aspects of European Monetary Unification', CEPR discussion paper, No. 643, May.

Bayoumi, T. and Prasad, E. (1995) 'Currency Unions, economic fluctuations and adjustment: some empirical evidence, CEPR discussion paper, No. 1172, May.

Beine, M. (1997) 'Union Monetaire Europeene et Theorie des Zones Monetaires Optimales', PhD dissertation, ULB, Brussels.

Brueckner, M. (1997) 'Voting and decisions in the ESCB', EUI working papers, No. 97/29, European University Institute, Florence.

Christiano, L. J., Eichenbaum, M. and Evans, C. (1994) 'The effects of monetary policy shocks: some evidence from the flow of funds', NBER working paper No 4699.

Clarida, R., Gali, J. and Gertler, M. (1997) 'Monetary policy rules in practice: some international evidence', CEPR discussion paper, No. 1750.

Croux C., Forni, M. and Reichlin, L. (1998) 'A measure for economic indicators', unpublished manuscript, ECARE, Brussels.

De Grauwe, P., Dewachter, H. and Aksoy, Y. (1998) 'The European Central Bank: decision rules and macroeconomic performance', CES discussion paper Series 98.34, Catholic University of Leuven.

Dornbusch, R., Favero, C. and Giavazzi, F. (1998) 'Immediate challenges for the European Central Bank', *Economic Policy*, **26**: 15–52, April.

Eichengreen, B. (1997) *European Monetary Unification: theory, practice and analysis*, Cambridge, MA: MIT Press.

European Commission (1990) 'One market, one money', *European Economy*, 44.

Frankel, J. and Rose, A. (1996) 'The endogeneity of the Optimum Currency Area criteria', NBER discussion paper, No. 5700.

Gerlach, S. and Schnabel, G. (1998) 'The Taylor Rule and average interest rates in the EMU-11 area: A Note', mimeo, Bank for International Settlements.

Gerlach, S. and Smets, F. (1995) 'The Monetary Transmission Mechanism: evidence from the G-7 countries, discussion paper, Bank for International Settlements.

Giovannetti, G. and Marimon, R. (1998) 'An EMU with different transmission mechanisms', CEPR discussion paper, No. 2016, November.

Krugman, P. (1991) *Geography and Trade*, Cambridge, MA: MIT Press.

Peersman, G. and Smets, F. (1998) 'The Taylor Rule: a useful monetary policy guide for the ESCB', mimeo, University of Gent.

Ramaswamy, R. and Sloek, T. (1998) 'The real effects of monetary policy in the European Union: what are the differences?', *IMF Staff Papers*, forthcoming.

Rudebusch, G. D. and Svensson, L. E. O. (1998) 'Policy rules for inflation targeting', paper prepared for NBER Conference on Monetary Policy Rules.

Svensson, L. E. O. (1998a) 'Inflation targeting as a monetary policy rule', IIES seminar paper, No. 646.

Svensson, L. E. O. (1998b) 'Open-economy inflation targeting', *Journal of International Economics*, forthcoming.

Taylor, J. (1993) 'Discretion versus policy rules in practice', *Carnegie-Rochester Conference on Public Policy*, **39**: 195–214.

von Hagen, J. (1995) 'Inflation and monetary targeting in Germany', in Leiderman, L. and Svensson, L. (eds) *Inflation Targets*, London: Centre for Economic Policy Research, pp. 107–21.

von Hagen, J. (1998) 'The composition of bank councils for monetary unions', unpublished manuscript, ZEI, University of Bonn.

von Hagen, J. and Sueppel R. (1994) 'Central Bank constitutions for federal monetary unions', *European Economic Review*, **38**: 774–82.

Discussion of Chapter 9

Andrew Haldane

The chapter by De Grauwe, Dewachter and Aksoy is neat, technically accomplished and, most of all, important. Important to the 'ins' – the Euro-11 countries already embarking down the monetary union road and who might want some gauge of the likely welfare costs they will incur along the way. It is important too for the 'pre-ins' – which would include the UK, Sweden and Denmark – considering the potential costs to participation, as and when it occurs. Finally, the chapter is also important to 'ECB-watchers' – those scribblers charged with monitoring and guessing the policy actions of the ECB. ECB-watching is an industry that has already grown in recent months and will doubtless grow further in future. I will come back to it below.

The chapter has three parts: (i) it derives optimal feedback rules for each of the Euro-11 individually; (ii) it considers various voting strategies for the ECB governing council; and (iii), by combining (i) and (ii), it calculates the proximate welfare cost for each country of being part of the union, under various ECB voting strategies. My comments will be directed at these three sections in turn.

DERIVING OPTIMAL FEEDBACK RULES

The first section of the chapter seeks to derive a counterfactual against which ECB policymaking can be set – the optimal monetary feedback rule for each of the Euro-11 countries. This involves taking a model, some shocks and an objective function. The plausibility of the counterfactual depends on the plausibility of these choices.

On the *model*, the authors use what is increasingly becoming the workhorse Rudebusch/Svensson AD/AS framework. But this is a restrictive model in several respects. It is essentially a backward-looking, closed economy model. This may be a legitimate characterisation of the US, which was the focus of Rudesbusch and Svensson's work. But it is rather less appropriate for the small, open economies of many of the Euro-11.

So how might generalisations of the model alter the chapter's conclusions? Perhaps the two most important omissions from the model would be: the absence of foreign variables and the real exchange rate from the AD relationship; and the absence of an inflation expectations term from the AS relationship. The inclusion of, for example, a foreign demand term in the AD relation would tend to increase the degree of cross-country output comovement, arising as a result of trade spillovers. So omitting these terms from the model would tend to lead to an *overstatement* of asymmetric demand shocks. Likewise, the inclusion of an inflation expectations term in the supply curve would tend to enhance the degree of cross-country inflation co-movement, to the extent that inflation expectations across the Euro-area are increasingly being anchored on a single nominal endpoint. Again, the omission of this term would tend to lead to an *overstatement*, this time of asymmetric supply shocks. So taken together, the rather restrictive choice of model would tend to exaggerate the differences between disturbances afflicting the Euro-11 countries. Correspondingly, the differences between their optimal feedback rules would also tend to be exaggerated.[1]

Turning to the *objective function* used in the exercise, this has standard arguments with which I would not quibble. But it is questionable whether the fully optimal rule is, as a practical matter, the most convincing counterfactual. There are at least two reasons why the derived optimal rules would be inoperable for each of the Euro-11. First, the derived optimal rules are complicated beasts and hence potentially non-monitorable/verifiable. That raises time-consistency questions about the plausibility of committing to such rules in practice. Second, the linear feedback rules are conditioned on current-period values of the states. Most of the macro data available to central banks tends, however, to come with a (sometimes substantial) lag. That too would tend to render the rules inoperable. These practical problems may not affect welfare comparisons between the country-specific optimal rule and the ECB rule. But they do call for a non-too-literal reading of the Euro-11 feedback rules by themselves.

ECB VOTING STRATEGIES

The authors consider a range of possible models of ECB decision-making. The voting model they posit is a median voter model. And they assume that the voting preferences of the individual governing council members take one of three forms (consensus, the ESCB rule, or nationalistic). This seems a reasonable array of voting possibilities. The taxonomy does, however, raise as many questions as it answers. Will the ECB board be the

ones making the initial policy proposal? Will they indeed vote as a bloc? If
they do not, will they necessarily vote along nationalistic lines? Will the
ECB board members behave differently than the NCB governors? (There
is some evidence of such differential voting behaviour between Fed board
governors and regional presidents in the US (Tootell, 1996). Might NCB
governors themselves vote as a bloc, forming effective cross-country
coalitions to nullify the power of the ECB board? More generally, what
potential is there for strategic behaviour among governing council
members? Simulations of these variants would be an interesting topic for
future research.

The answers to all of the above questions are of course that we do not
know; it is too early to tell. What is worse, however, is that we are very
unlikely to find out in the near future. There are no current plans for the
ECB to publish minutes of Governing Council meetings. Nor will there be
any public record of voting patterns. This opacity of ECB decision-making
means only one thing – that ECB-watching will flourish!

This is an unfortunate set of circumstances. If central banks were clear
and transparent about their preferences, voting procedures and intentions,
the rewards to ECB-watching would be zero. ECB-watchers would be
driven instead into more economically efficient employment – perhaps
road sweeping, or working in central banks. Uncertainties about the ECB's
decision-making procedures, as well as raising political-economy concerns
and increasing risk premia at the short-end of the yield curve, will also
heighten inefficiencies in labour allocation.

THE WELFARE COSTS OF AN ESCB RULE

The welfare costs for individual countries of adhering to the ECB rule,
under various voting procedures, are tackled in the last part of the chapter.
It is striking here that there is such a high degree of correlation, for most
countries, between actual ECB-set interest rates and the individually
desired level of rates. Reflecting this, the welfare losses associated with
adherence to the ESCB rule are on the whole not enormous. Table 9.4
provides some estimates of percentage losses of welfare for a selection of
countries derived from the authors' estimates, for a given (common) set of
taste parameters across countries.

There are, however, several reasons why these welfare estimates may be
a significant understatement of the true welfare costs of adhering to an
ESCB-like rule. First, there is the choice of asymmetric shocks. The authors

Table 9.4   Welfare losses (%) from pursuing ESCB rule

Germany	Netherlands	France	Italy	Spain	Ireland
1.5	0.75	14	1.1	14.5	6.8

assume that all inflation (supply) shocks are perfectly symmetric under the monetary union. I do not find this assumption plausible. There are myriad reasons why asymmetric supply shocks may survive the creation of a monetary union – NAIRU shifts, differential terms of trade shocks, indirect tax shocks and so on. Although, for Lucas critique reasons, we may not take too literally pre-regime empirical evidence, this does point decisively towards a large and significant degree of supply shock asymmetry (for example Bayoumi and Eichengreen (1994), perhaps for some of the reasons outlined above. To assume these asymmetries disappeared on 1 January 1999, is, for me, a bridge too far.

Second, the estimates in Table 9.4 assume a common set of preferences (over inflation, output and interest rate smoothing) among all eleven NCB governors and the six ECB board members. But if we allowed for a degree of diffusion across voting preferences – potentially between all seventeen members of the Governing Council – then we would expect the resulting welfare losses to be (potentially significantly) larger. How much larger is an empirical issue and would be interesting in itself.

Third, the authors' simulations rule out the possibility of state-dependence in governing council members' preferences. For example, a large adverse shock in one country may not just result in that country's NCB governor arguing for a softer monetary stance for given preferences. It may itself cause a switch in inflation/output preferences. The perceived welfare costs of a failure to adjust policy to accommodate that shock would be raised correspondingly. In this event, the welfare losses calculated by the authors are potentially a very significant understatement. Again, future research might seek to quantity those welfare losses. Interestingly, recent empirical evidence in the US suggests that FOMC voting behaviour is dependent on, and influenced by, the outside preferences of the general public regarding inflation and output, in addition to the usual array of macroeconomic variables (Tootell, 1999). Despite its different statutory make-up, there is no reason to expect the ECB Governing Council to be immune to similar such influences.

Finally, there is a silver lining to this otherwise dark cloud. Asymmetric shocks, differential propagation mechanisms and differential tastes are indeed potential sources of welfare cost when operating within a monetary union. But it does not follow from this that removing one of these distortions by themselves will necessarily be welfare-enhancing. This is only true in a partial equilibrium. In a general equilibrium setting, where we are beginning from a position of second-best (or, more probably, worse), the eradication of one set of potential frictions is potentially welfare-depleting. One set of frictions may be counterbalancing another set of frictions elsewhere in the economy (for example Bridgen and Nolan, 1998). Disturbing that balance of distortions may make matters worse.

This second-best line of argumentation applies to the current situation in the UK. Some have, for example, argued that the UK should not join EMU until its monetary transmission mechanism is better aligned with that in Europe. To do otherwise would store up potential asymmetric costs in the event of even symmetric disturbances. But in a general equilibrium setting, this is a *non-sequitur*. This is a point forgotten by most economists – and lost on all politicians.

NOTE

1. Full simulations of a richer model would of course be needed to establish this result for sure.

REFERENCES

Bayoumi, T. and Eichengreen, B. (1994) 'One money or many? Analysing the prospects for monetary unification in various parts of the world', *Princeton Studies in International Finance,* No. 76, September.
Brigden, A. and Nolan, C. (1998) 'Monetary stabilisation policy in a monetary union: some simple analytics', mimeo, Bank of England.
Tootell, G. M. B. (1996) 'Appointment procedures and FOMC voting behaviour', *Southern Economic Journal,* **63**: 91–204.
Tootell, G. M. B. (1999) 'Whose monetary policy is it anyway?' *Journal of Monetary Economics,* **43**: 217–35.

10 The Relationship Between the European Central Bank and the National Central Banks within the Eurosystem

Robert Pringle and Matthew Turner

1 INTRODUCTION

> It is crucial that the European System of Central Banks develops into a truly European organization with a European outlook. Regional or national monetary policy in EMU cannot and will not exist. All monetary policy decisions and actions will have to be based on Euro-area wide analyses and considerations. (Willem Duisenberg, President of ECB, 1999)

Even before the launch of the euro, the relationship between the European Central Bank (ECB) and Europe's politicians hit the headlines. There was the tussle over the appointment of the president, when France promoted the claims of its candidate, and, later, calls by Germany's new Social Democrat government for lower interest rates. Less discussed, but possibly more important in practice, is the relationship between the new monetary authority and the existing national central banks (NCBs), which together as the European System of Central Banks (ESCB) devise and implement policy.

This chapter sets out to examine this relationship, from the legal basics as written in the Maastricht Treaty, to how it might work in practice. In particular, we discuss four critiques that have been made of the current setup. The appendix notes the legal basics covering the relationship between the NCBs and the ECB and in particular the framework set out in the Maastricht treaty and the ECB statute.

2 POLICY ISSUES: IS THE EUROSYSTEM'S STRUCTURE WELL DESIGNED?

There are four main strands in the criticisms that have been made of the design of the Eurosystem arising especially from the crucial relationship between the NCBs and ECB and their respective tasks. These have to do with (a) possible weaknesses in the conduct of monetary policy; (b) an alleged lack of clarity about the lender of last resort (LLR) function – in a panic, who would do what? (c) decentralization of banking supervision and the absence of a clear role for the ECB; and (d) the alleged excessive costs of some NCBs and of the entire Eurosystem with its 55,000 employees. We shall examine each of these in turn.

2.1 The governance structure of the ECB may distort the Community's monetary policy

The most wide-ranging critique that we are aware of is in the CEPR paper (Begg *et al.* 1998).[1] The authors argue that the ECB's executive board is small and weak compared with the NCBs not only because of the voting structure but also because NCBs are in daily contact with the financial markets. Its centre should be strengthened in relation to national central banks whose governors will otherwise retain too much power.

Expanding on this theme, the authors state that while Messrs Tietmeyer, Trichet *et al.* remain as governors of their national central banks but simultaneously control the ECB council, national perspectives are likely to persist. The study identifies three dangers as arising from the 'weakness' of the centre: inertia in policy formulation; slow transition to a truly European mentality; and conflict between interests organised on national lines. For example, a governor from a country where the economy is overheating is likely to support higher interest rates; a governor from a country hard hit by a banking crisis is likely to argue for a liquidity injection.

The authors recommend that existing treaties should be redrawn to give the executive board a built-in majority on the governing council, with the NCBs in a permanent minority; and that different member countries be grouped together for voting purposes. As this cannot be expected to happen quickly, in the short run they appear to recommend that national governors move house to Frankfurt:

it is undesirable to perpetuate a situation in which many of those perceived as Europe's leading central bankers continue to be based in national central banks.

The dangers identified in this analysis certainly need to be guarded against, and the members of the Governing Council are doubtless aware of them.

We offer two comments. First, the Executive Board appears in practice to be turning out to be much stronger than expected (indeed, this came as a shock to some NCBs). As they will doubtless take a common position on policy issues, the six only need to gather the support of three governors to prevail if it should come to a vote on any specific issue.

Second, the CEPR study seems to us to underestimate the role of peer-group pressure. As indicated in the quotation from Duisenberg cited in the previous section, members of the ECB and ESCB's Governing Council are mandated to adopt a pan-Euro perspective: they must 'act in a personal capacity with a responsibility for the entire Euro-area'. Begg *et al.* assume they will follow (narrowly defined) national interests. Yet if one of the NCB governors were to advocate a given monetary policy purely on grounds of national self-interest, he would be out of order. He would have to argue that conditions in his country were such that they endangered pursuit of stability at the euro-wide level. Such an argument is really only open to Germany and France to make, because of their weight in the Euro-area; and even they would need to be careful how to present such an argument.

The fact that the Eurosystem has started with an interest rate lower than would be predicted by averaging the (assumed) preferences of NCB governors if they were to follow narrow national interests suggests that the voting structure in the ECB governing council will not present an insurmountable obstacle to the development of a truly euro-wide mentality. Moreover, the underlying problem of reconciling the different economic conditions of different regions and countries with a single monetary policy and interest rate – largely at present a centre versus periphery issue – cannot be alleviated or solved by changes in governance or voting arrangements.

If the dangers for monetary policy arising from the governance structure of the ECB have been exaggerated, we suggest there are also significant benefits to be derived from it. By involving each governor individually in the debate within the Governing Council and giving each the same voting power, each is fated to become an ambassador for the policy decided collectively. He may 'lose' on one occasion (that is, accept an interest rate above or below what he would regard as suitable for his country) but would defend it not only because he may expect to 'win' on another occasion but because any particular interest rate decision in itself is only one element in an overall project that is supported by his government and people as being in their national interest, and sanctioned by international treaty. This is the line that Maurice O'Connell, Governor of the Central Bank of Ireland, takes in answering critics who say that the Euro-area interest rate is inappropriate to the conditions of the Irish economy which is in danger of overheating.

Moreover, so long as confidentiality of voting and debates is respected, an individual governor will have little incentive to vote on narrow national lines. Some observers have assumed that national governments will quickly learn how each member of the Governing Council voted on each occasion. Presumably they expect that at least some governors will immediately inform their respective finance ministers of the debates in the governing council. We doubt this. On the contrary, we expect NCB governors will be very cautious in what they release about the confidential debates in the ECB – especially to their own governments.

More generally, and without going here into the debate about whether or not the ECB should publish its minutes and if so how promptly, it is surely essential that discussion among policy-makers must be as open as possible, and this would be inhibited by the release or selective 'leaking' of information from policy meetings (the minutes of the Fed's FOMC, often taken as a model, are severely edited). This links up with the broader issue of maintaining the political legitimacy of the ECB, to which we return below.

Of course, governors will doubtless draw on their understanding of economic conditions in their countries in the general contributions they make to the council's deliberations. But they will also be aware of the need to place this in a euro-wide context. So we would expect their research departments to raise their level of Euro-area economic expertise, precisely so that the governors are not put at a disadvantage in debating issues with the Executive Board.

Asked recently whether there were any plans to transfer more decision-making to the centre, Duisenberg (1999) replied:

> No. By virtue of the Treaty establishing the European Community, all decision-making powers have already been vested in the ECB. They are exercised by the decision-making bodies of the ECB, that is, the Governing Council and Executive Board.

On balance, the provisions of the Treaty provide an adequate base for an effective relationship, which will clearly evolve over time.

2.2 Lack of clarity about its lender of last resort role will inhibit the ECB's response to a banking or payments system crisis

On the lender of last resort, the most well-known critique has come from the IMF (1998). In its 1998 capital markets report, the Fund argued that this issue was pressing because the first years of monetary union may bring 'several tendencies for systemic risk to increase temporarily'. The Maastricht treaty does not allocate the LLR role to the ECB or NCBs. NCBs lose the right to create liquidity to support failing banks or contain a more generalised panic, leading the IMF to observe that 'there is no provider of emergency liquidity in the event of a crisis'.

According to the report, the ECB, designed as a monetary-policy-making body, lacked the tools to assess bank creditworthiness and so to distinguish between insolvent and illiquid banks. The report also suggested that the ECB lacked the necessary information-sharing arrangements with EU financial supervisors to allow it to make well-informed decisions in a crisis. In practice, therefore, the ECB would rely heavily on advice from the national central bank or banks involved and the initiative for using the LLR weapon would come 'from below', that is, from the national level.

The CEPR paper also discusses the LLR issue. Its views appear to be similar to those of the Fund:

> No secure mechanism exists for creating liquidity in a crisis, and there remain flaws in proposals for dealing with insolvency during a large banking collapse. (p. xii)

On this issue, we have sympathy with the criticisms made by the Fund and CEPR. Banking and financial markets are likely to change rapidly in the near term, partly as a result of the elimination of exchange risk in the Euro-area, partly for other reasons. There is likely to be a shift towards a greater role for securities markets, as well as (within banking) the emergence of 'super-regional' banks. There will be greater possibilities of disintermediation as threats to the banks' traditionally dominating role in the system increase. Thus even though there has not been much need for classic LLR operations in continental Europe in the past, this is no guarantee that they will not occur in future.

There are as many varieties of LLR operations as there are banking systems, but among these two are especially well known. First, the Federal Reserve model; second, the Bundesbank model. In Germany there appears to be an understanding that the main banks would stand together in a crisis; although this does not amount to a system of cross-guarantees between banks, there has not been any need for a formal assignment of LLR responsibility and that is why it appears that the Bundesbank has been opposed to the ECB having that role. Critics have alleged that, if there were to be a need for a LLR operation in the early years of EMU, it may be too late to start thinking about who should bear the responsibility for it. Certainly, it is questionable whether the approach that has been followed in Germany is 'exportable' to the whole Euro-area at a time of rapid financial market change. However, we should add that we believe in practice the ECB would act as a LLR, because it would have no option, 'all bets would be off'.

Indeed, perhaps partly in response to criticisms, we understand that Eurozone central bankers have now set rules to counter an incipient panic, defining who would do what in a crisis. But in traditional central banking fashion, there is no intention to make these internal arrangements public: 'constructive ambiguity' remains the order of the day. All we would add is that markets have yet to be convinced that these arrangements would work effectively in practice.

2.3 Decentralised banking supervision undermines the authority of the ECB, may inhibit its response to a crisis and means the EU does not have an effective supervisory system

This criticism seems premature. At present, monetary policy and banking supervisory functions are separated in one-half of the EU countries and combined in the other half. The general trend is towards separation and towards a greater role for the government, which bears the ultimate cost of bank rescues. According to Goodhart and Schoenmaker (1993), the question of the appropriate design needs to be viewed in the context of the banking system or systems concerned. At present, as noted above, banking in the EU remains essentially national, with only 4.2 per cent of the assets and 6.2 per cent of the liabilities of the banks in the five largest countries cross-border (White, 1998). The system of home country control is appropriate to this situation. What is essential is close co-operation between national supervisory authorities, and between them and the NCBs, and the ability of the ECB to obtain all the information it requires. The supervisory committee of the ESCB, which includes the Bank of England and UK FSA, seems appropriate to this task. Given the sensitivity of some EU central banks to potential conflicts of interest when a central bank also acts as a supervisor, it was inevitable that the ECB should not be given specific responsibilities in this area other than those specified in the Maastricht treaty summarised in the previous section.

Karel Lannoo of the Centre for European Policy Studies in Brussels (Lannoo, 1998) concludes after a careful review of the evidence that 'For the time being, the current framework for prudential control requires no major adaptations… Keeping bank supervisory powers at the local level and limiting ECB functions to monetary policy is part of a general trend and fits with the home country control principles of the single market'. Lannoo makes the suggestion, however, that the ECB should act as a clearing house for co-operation agreements between national supervisors at EU and international levels, and 'make sure that every bank or conglomerate operating in Europe has a lead supervisor'. Duisenberg himself sums up the ECB's role as follows (Duisenberg, 1999):

> For the time being, banking supervision remains a matter of national responsibility. The Treaty on European Union contains provisions which enable the council of the European finance ministers to assign more responsibilities in this field to the ECB. If and when more really pan-European financial institutions were to emerge, it cannot be ruled out that the organization of banking supervision would also evolve in the direction of more centralization.

2.4 The system is burdened by excessive costs

Central Banking calculates that the operating costs of the EU central banks in 1997 were about 4.6 billion euros ($5.29 billion). The Federal Reserve System's operating costs were then $3.0 billion. On the face of it, there is significant scope for economies in the ESCB. However, during the process of creating an appropriate legal and operating framework for the launch of the euro, it was inevitable that the national central banks would be left to carry on very much as before in matters that did not concern monetary policy and that did not interfere with the work of the ECB. It was too much to expect the statutes and tasks of each of the NCBs to be harmonised at the same time as creating the framework for a single currency; and, in fact, they remain very diverse, reflecting long histories and differing national traditions.

Thus the huge differences in staffing levels (see Figure 10.1) between the NCBs will continue for the foreseeable future, reflecting these differing tasks. Indeed, some central banks are expanding, especially those like the

Bank of Italy which did not have responsibility for reserve management. Thus the Bank of France, the Land central banks and the Bank of Italy will continue to carry out activities that for many observers are far removed from the core activities of a modern central bank.

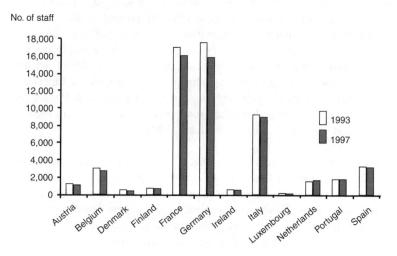

Figure 10.1   Staff numbers at EU-11 central banks

However, as Sirkka Hamalainen, the ECB executive director in charge of market operations has indicated, while decision-making is already centralised, implementation of monetary policy (at present decentralised) may also gradually become more centralised in the major centres. Over time it is natural to expect that they will shed some of these tasks and slim their large labour forces. Indeed, as Figure 10.1 shows, they have already made some progress on the latter front: total staffing of the Euro-11 central banks fell by nearly 10 per cent between 1993 and 1997, with especially large cuts from the Bundesbank, reducing staffing numbers by nearly 2000 since 1993. Most of the NCBs plan to reduce staff totals further.

What of the longer-term future? Here we believe much can be learned from the experience of the US. There, all reserve banks are involved in monetary policy and in the payments system. But beyond that each has tended to specialise, to find a niche for itself in a specific field, and recently the Washington Board has deliberately encouraged this on efficiency grounds. Thus one district Fed might specialise in cheque processing, another in processing savings bonds. Much of this has occurred in a natural way because of the location of the reserve bank concerned. The Boston Fed's research focuses on New England, the New York Fed specialises in financial markets and associated commentary on international affairs and market place changes. It takes prime responsibility for derivative markets because the banks it examines tend to be those most active in these markets. It would be natural to expect a similar evolution over time in the Eurosystem.

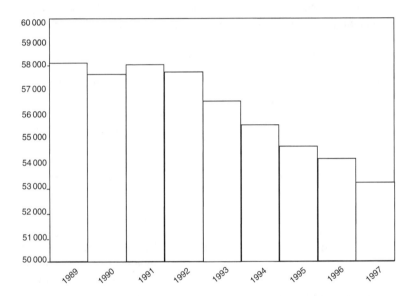

Figure 10.2   Staff numbers in the Eurosystem

3 CONCLUSIONS

The following are the main conclusions from the above analysis:

1. As is widely recognised, the ECB and ESCB have established positions that are unique in the world of central banking and indeed in constitu-

tional history – with the independence not only of the ECB but of each NCB guaranteed by international treaty and community law.

2. What is not as widely recognised is that all the constituent NCBs have also experienced a significant accretion of power versus their respective governments, not only in the area of monetary policy but as regards the control and management of external reserves.

3. However, they exercise this power only by virtue of their membership in a supranational organisation, the ESCB, whose governing bodies take all policy decisions in the fields reserved for them.

4. Meanwhile, they are allowed to continue to conduct the wide range of operations that they have been accustomed to carry out within each country as well as implementing the policy decisions of the central governing bodies.

5. We agree with critics who warn against potential policy problems of the ESCB arising from the built-in majority for the NCB governors, lack of clarity about the LLR role, and decentralisation of responsibility for supervision. But we do not think these arise from fundamental design faults. They constitute challenges that can be met by good policy and management. We believe the executive directors and senior management of the ECB are aware of them and able to take appropriate action to offset their influence.

6. There is a potentially serious defect in the absence of any provision about the assignment of a LLR function given the rapid changes expected to take place in the Euro-area financial market. The ECB should make clear that it stands ready to assume the role, even although it will wish to maintain the tradition of central bankers' 'constructive ambiguity' in refraining from specifying in advance the circumstances under which it would undertake LLR operations.

7. In conclusion, we would emphasise an aspect of the role of the NCB's governors that seems to us not to have yet received the attention it deserves – their function as ambassadors for the Eurosystem, including the euro itself and the ECB's policies. Far from being in conflict with the Frankfurt head office, it seems to us that the NCBs have no choice but to be a prime channel for securing the acceptability of the ECB's policies to the EU population. The biggest threat to the euro and the ESCB arises not out of any faults with the 'internal' design of the system but with the absence of a mechanism for political accountability.

In America, the Federal Reserve is politically vulnerable – Congress can alter its responsibilities very quickly if it has a mind to, despite the tradition of independence – and the Fed Chairman is well aware of this every time he gives testimony to a congressional committee. The ECB has no such political vulnerability, and no formal mechanism or 'traditional channels' (that is, channels sanctified by use and acceptability) for ensuring its sensitivity to the wishes of the people and the broad acceptability of its policies. No central bank can operate in the long term in an environment that is not in tune with the public interest. We do not suggest that the ECB is out of touch with public opinion at this early stage. The point is that there is no accepted mechanism for ensuring its continued political legitimacy.

Appendix I: The Legal Basics

1 THE EUROPEAN SYSTEM OF CENTRAL BANKS

The framers of the Maastricht Treaty were faced with the task of devising institutions to replace Europe's multitude of central banks. Their solution was the ESCB, an organisation comprising the existing NCBs (article 1.2 of the statute[2]) but also a new institution, the ECB.

Although all EU NCBs are members of the ESCB, the term is commonly used to describe the ECB and only those NCBs whose countries have adopted the euro, that is, not including the Bank of England, Sveriges Riksbank, Denmark's National Bank and Bank of Greece. To avoid confusion, the ECB itself refers to the ECB and the euro-adopting NCBs as the 'Eurosystem'.

1.1 The decision-making bodies of the ESCB and ECB

The statute of the ESCB seems clear enough: the decision-making bodies of the ECB are in charge of the whole system. According to Article 8:

> General principle
> The ESCB shall be governed by the decision-making bodies of the ECB.

Those decision-making bodies are the Governing Council, the Executive Board (a sub-set of the Governing Council), and the General Council. Of these, it is the Governing Council and its Executive Board that wield the power.

1.2 The Governing Council

Article 12.1 of the Statute gives the Governing Council two main roles:

> The Governing Council shall adopt the guidelines and make the decisions necessary to ensure the performance of the tasks entrusted to the ESCB under this Treaty and this Statute.

The Governing Council shall formulate the monetary policy of the Community including, as appropriate, decisions relating to intermediate monetary objectives, key interest rates and the supply of reserves in the ESCB, and shall establish the necessary guidelines for their implementation.

Under the tasks assigned to it, the General Council will:

adopt Rules of Procedure which determine the internal organisation of the ECB and its decision-making bodies

exercise the advisory functions referred to in Article 4

take the decisions referred to in Article 6 [deciding how the ESCB shall be represented in the field of international co-operation]

1.3 Membership of the Governing Council

This important body is where the NCBs and the ECB come together. Of its 17-members 11 are the Governors of the NCBs participating in monetary union (Article 10.1), and six form the Executive Board. (Article 11.1). The Executive Board is responsible for the day-to-day running of the ECB, and includes the president of the ECB, the vice-president and four other members. The president chairs Governing Council meetings (or in his absence the vice-president) (Article 13.1).

For most decisions the Governing Council operates on a simple majority, one-person, one-vote. However, for various issues where who owns the ECB matters, the Executive Board members receive no vote, and the NCB governors vote according to the size of their shareholdings.

In total, the Treaty and Statute contain six different ways in which Governing Council votes should be undertaken (see Appendix II). As with many European institutions, the rationale behind the ECB's numerous voting arrangements appears to be national sensitivities over certain key issues.

1.4 Governing Council and the national central banks (NCBs)

That the NCBs are to play a substantial role in the ESCB is without doubt. Duisenberg has noted four reasons why a strong NCB element was desirable (Duisenberg, 1998a).

It allows the ESCB to rely on the NCB's infrastructure and operational experience.
It allows the ESCB to take account of local markets' historical differences.
It gives the ESCB credibility through keeping the same people at the helm of
monetary policy as before EMU.
It helps keep overheads to a minimum.

However, the general theme of the Statute is that all policy-making will be
done at the centre by the Governing Council, while the NCBs will have to
implement those decisions. Here the treaty gives them a potentially extensive role, in Article 9.2:

> The ECB shall ensure that the tasks conferred upon the ESCB under Article
> 105(2), (3) and (5) of this Treaty[3] are implemented either by its own activities
> pursuant to this Statute or through the national central banks pursuant to Articles
> 12.1 and 14.

and Article 12.1:

> The Executive Board shall implement monetary policy in accordance with the
> guidelines and decisions laid down by the Governing Council. In doing so the
> Executive Board shall give the necessary instructions to national central banks.
>
> To the extent deemed possible and appropriate and without prejudice to the
> provisions of this Article, the ECB shall have recourse to the national central
> banks to carry out operations which form part of the tasks of the ESCB.

The Governing Council has confirmed that monetary policy implementation will be decentralised. But the statute (Article 14.3) also makes clear
the NCBs' role is to do what they are told by the ECB.

> The national central banks are an integral part of the ESCB and shall act in
> accordance with the guidelines and instructions of the ECB.

1.5 Ensuring NCB compliance with the Governing Council's decisions

It is the Governing Council which is given the task of ensuring the NCBs
follow the instructions from the ECB (Article 14.3):

The Governing Council shall take the necessary steps to ensure compliance with the guidelines and instructions of the ECB, and shall require that any necessary information be given to it.

Some academics have questioned the enforcement procedure if the NCBs refuse to comply with the Governing Council's requests. The Statute places the 'necessary steps' the Governing Council shall take to ensure compliance with the ECB's instructions in the hands of the European Court of Justice. Article 35.6:

The Court of Justice shall have jurisdiction in disputes concerning the fulfillment by a national central bank of obligations under this Statute. If the ECB considers that a national central bank has failed to fulfill an obligation under this Statute, it shall deliver a reasoned opinion on the matter after giving the national central bank concerned the opportunity to submit its observations. If the national central bank concerned does not comply with the opinion within the period laid down by the ECB, the latter may bring the matter before the Court of Justice.

2 NATIONAL CENTRAL BANK INDEPENDENCE ('LEGAL CONVERGENCE')

The ability of the NCB governors to take a 'community' view on monetary policy, as opposed to a 'parochial view' is strengthened by the institutional and legal changes required by the Maastricht Treaty.

2.1 Legislative changes

Member States were required to ensure that their national legislation and the Statutes of their NCBs were compatible with the Treaty and the Statute of the ESCB by the date of the ESCB's establishment.

This has brought many changes for the NCBs. Most obviously, national governments have lost any of their rights to interfere with the conduct of monetary policy. Moreover, many of the rights previously exercised by third parties, for example government, were declared incompatible with the Treaty. This included the right to give instructions to the NCB; to approve, suspend, annul or defer their decisions; to participate in the decision-making bodies with a right to vote, or to be consulted (*ex ante*) on an NCB's decisions.

Of equal importance are the safeguards against pressure being applied to the individual governors on how they vote. The statutes of the NCBs have to ensure that governors of NCBs have a minimum term of office of five years, that a governor may not be dismissed (for reasons other than those mentioned in Article 14.2 of the Statute); that other members of the decision-making bodies of NCBs involved in ESCB related tasks have the same security of tenure as governor; and that no conflict of interest will arise between the duties of members of boards of NCBs *vis-à-vis* their respective NCBs and other functions they may perform and which may jeopardise their personal independence.

2.2 National laws

Countries' national laws that affected their NCBs operations were also changed, including the right to print bank notes and the ownership of official gold and foreign exchange holdings.

2.3 Harmonisation of statutes

Despite the extensive legal changes the NCBs have made, each institution retains a separate structure. Although there is no need for NCBs' statutes to be harmonised, the EMI (1997) has said that where they perform ESCB tasks, and especially when the primary competence lies at central level, 'it would be desirable to avoid the statutes of NCBs containing different provisions on the same issues'.

3 MONETARY POLICY

3.1 Formulating monetary policy

Duisenberg (1998b) has ensured there is little doubt that the ECB formulates monetary policy at the centre, although its application is decentralised through the NCBs.

> The set of monetary policy instruments and procedures being prepared by the EMI will ensure that the Governing Council of the ECB and – for the day-to-day management – the ECB Executive Board are in a position to control the

overall stance of monetary policy at all times, in conformity with the decision-making framework of the ESCB. Decisions will thus always be taken at the ECB level, whereas implementation will, to the extent deemed possible and appropriate, be executed in a decentralised manner by the participating national central banks.

Decisions on interest rates are taken by the Governing Council (Article 12.1) on the basis of one-member, one-vote.

The Governing Council shall formulate the monetary policy of the Community including, as appropriate, decisions relating to intermediate monetary objectives, key interest rates and the supply of reserves in the ESCB, and shall establish the necessary guidelines for their implementation.

3.2 Implementing monetary policy

Implementation of monetary policy is down to the Executive Board, subject to a framework established by the Governing Council (Article 12.1).

The Executive Board shall implement monetary policy in accordance with the guidelines and decisions laid down by the Governing Council. In doing so the Executive Board shall give the necessary instructions to national central banks.

The Governing Council has said the technical resources of the NCBs will have a prominent role in implementing monetary policy. The ECB will conduct open market operations through weekly tenders for two-week repo, and monthly tenders for three-month repo. In both cases bids by credit institutions will be made to their local NCB (that is, the country in which they are based) by 9:30am CET on the day of the tender. The ECB will allocate the funds centrally, but depending on the legal framework, the counterparty will either repo or pledge eligible securities to its local NCB.

Similarly, credit institutions will have access to overnight deposit and collateralised marginal lending facilities with their local NCBs. However, the deposit facility lending rate and the marginal lending facility rate will be determined by the ECB.

Each credit institution must keep minimum reserves at the NCB of the country in which it is located, but the ECB will determine the details of the system, including the ratio of reserves, which it has set at two per cent of the relevant liability base.

4 RESERVE ASSETS

4.1 Transfer of reserve assets from NCBs to ECB

The issue of the ownership, control and use of national foreign reserve assets has naturally been a contentious one. With most academic studies suggesting the NCBs collectively hold more reserves than they will 'need' after EMU, who will be able to authorise the disposal of any 'excess' reserves has become a crucial point.

4.2 Foreign reserves call-up

The statute allows the Governing Council to call-up up to euro 50 billion of reserve assets (Article 30.1) from the NCBs on establishment of the ECB and at later dates. This is by a *simple majority on a weighted vote*, hence votes representing 50 per cent of the ECB's capital are needed to adopt the motion. The president, vice-president and other Executive Board members have no say in this decision.

Initially, the Governing Council has chosen to call up nearly euro 40 billion. This is the maximum allowable amount of euro 50 billion scaled downwards to take account of the fact that the UK, Sweden, Denmark and Greece are not joining in the first wave of entrants. The implication is that when those countries join in the future their contribution to reserves will bring the total up to the euro 50 billion limit.

The NCBs have supplied the foreign reserves in proportion to their share in the subscribed capital of the ECB. Although the NCBs are free to supply the reserve assets in whatever form they wish, except their own currencies, ECUs, IMF reserve positions and SDRs, the ECB has full right to hold and manage the reserves once they are transferred to it. For its first decision on foreign reserves the Governing Council decided to take 15 per cent of the euro 40 billion in gold and the rest in foreign currencies. However, the Governing Council has confirmed that subsequently the share of gold is allowed to fluctuate as market prices move.

4.3 Further calls

However, the initial call-up is not the end of the matter. The NCBs retain large reserves of gold and foreign exchange. Who controls these?

The treaty allows the ECB to make further calls above the euro 50 billion limit, through the Governing Council, again by a simple majority on a weighted vote. The limits and conditions to further calls are set by the Council of Ministers in accordance with the procedure laid down in Article 42, that is, by a qualified majority and after consulting the ECB, the Commission and the European Parliament.

Therefore, as Jean-Claude Trichet, the Bank of France governor, has stated (1997/8), 'This means that in case of need all the foreign currency and gold reserves of the participating countries could be called in principle and transferred to the ECB; so it is not wrong, as far as the treaty is concerned, to assert that all the NCBs' assets are at the disposal of the ESCB.'

Certainly, the publication of the Eurosystem's weekly statement supports this view – it lists all the foreign exchange and gold holdings of the NCBs as assets of the Eurosystem. This amounted to a huge 100 billion euros of gold and 230 billion euros of foreign exchange assets.

4.4 NCBs retaining foreign reserve assets

The NCBs retain some control over their remaining assets. The Statute allows them to use these in fulfillment of their obligations towards international organisations (Article 31.1).

However, other foreign reserve transactions (for example buying or selling of assets, loaning gold) over a certain limit shall be subject to approval by the ECB (Article 31.2). This approval will be by a single-vote, simple-majority, that is, 17 Governing Council members will receive one vote, and nine votes are needed to adopt a resolution.

The limit above which foreign exchange transactions need approval is set by the Governing Council, again operating on a single-vote, simple-majority basis (Article 31.3). A very low limit would severely restrict the NCBs' freedom to sell or buy foreign exchange, including gold. So far only one country is known to have altered its reserves, by the comparatively small sum of nine million euros.

5 REGULATION

At present, one-half of the EU national central banks are responsible for regulation of their country's financial sector. In the other half regulation is undertaken by a separate body, such as Britain's Financial Services Authority.

As it stands, the creation of the ECB should have little effect on this. Banking regulation is to remain decentralised, with each national authority (whether central bank or other) keeping control of its own financial system.

5.1 Treaty provisions

However, the Maastricht Treaty does give the ECB a role in supervision, and one which potentially allows it a greater say in the future. Article 105.5 states:

> The ESCB shall contribute to the smooth conduct of policies pursued by the competent authorities relating to the prudential supervision of credit institutions and the stability of the financial system.

Article 105.6 adds:

> The Council may, acting unanimously on a proposal from the Commission and after consulting the ECB and after receiving the assent of the European Parliament, confer upon the ECB specific tasks concerning policies relating to the prudential supervision of credit institutions and other financial institutions with the exception of insurance undertakings.

Article 25.1 of the ECB statute states:

> The ECB may offer advice and be consulted by the Council, the Commission and the competent authorities of the member states on the scope and implementation of Community legislation relating to the prudential supervision of credit institutions and to the stability of the financial system.

Article 25.2 continues:

> In accordance with any decision of the Council under Article 105(6) of this Treaty, the ECB may perform specific tasks concerning policies relating to the prudential supervision of credit institutions and other financial institutions with the exception of insurance undertakings.

Appendix II: Voting Methods in the Governing Council

1 SINGLE-VOTE, SIMPLE-MAJORITY

The most common method is the single-vote, simple-majority as outlined in Article 10.2:

> Subject to Article 10.3 and 11.4 each member of the Governing Council shall have one vote. Save as otherwise provided for in this statute, the Governing Council shall act by simple majority. In the event of a tie the President shall have the casting vote.

Here each of the 17 members of the Governing Council has one vote, and nine are required to adopt a decision.

2 SINGLE-VOTE, TWO-THIRDS MAJORITY

Under Article 14.4 and Article 20 the Statute requires that two-thirds of the votes are in favour for a resolution to be adopted. For example, Article 14.4:

> National central banks may perform functions other than those specified in this Statute unless the Governing Council finds, by a majority of two thirds of the votes cast, that these interfere with the objectives and tasks of the ESCB. Such functions shall be performed on the responsibility and liability of national central banks and shall not be regarded as being part of the functions of the ESCB.

With all 17 members present this would be 12 votes.

3 WEIGHTED VOTES, SIMPLE-MAJORITY

There are also weighted votes, described in Article 10.3:

> For any decisions to be taken under Articles 28, 29, 30, 32, 33 and 51, the votes in the Governing Council shall be weighted according to the national central

banks' shares in the subscribed capital of the ECB. The weight of the votes of the members of the Executive Board shall be zero.

For this only the eleven NCB governors receive a vote, and these votes will be weighted in the proportions listed in the table below. So for example, Germany and France together have more than enough to pass a decision.

Table 10.1   Share of weighted votes

NCB	% share	NCB	% share
Germany	31.0	Austria	3.0
France	21.3	Portugal	2.4
Italy	18.9	Finland	1.8
Spain	11.3	Ireland	1.1
Netherlands	5.4	Luxembourg	0.2
Belgium	3.6		

4 WEIGHTED VOTES, QUALIFIED-MAJORITY

For certain weighted votes a *qualified-majority* is required. This is defined in Article 10.3:

> A decision requiring a qualified majority shall be adopted if the votes cast in favour represent at least two-thirds of the subscribed capital of the ECB and represent at least half the shareholders.

Examples of qualified majority voting include Article 28, which refers to the ECB's capital subscription and Article 32 which deals with the distribution of the ESCB's profits. Under this method France and Germany would not have enough votes to adopt a resolution on their own.

5 SINGLE-VOTE, SIMPLE-MAJORITY (WITHOUT EXECUTIVE BOARD)

Article 11.3 requires another voting type. It says the Governing Council shall fix pay and conditions of ECB staff on a proposal from a committee established by the Governing Council and the Council of Ministers. The article goes on to say

> The members of the Executive Board shall not have the right to vote on matters referred to in this paragraph.

So here, the eleven NCB governors have one vote each, and a simple majority of 6 is required.

6 SINGLE-VOTE, UNANIMOUS

Finally, there is one other voting type in the Statute. Article 41.1 outlines the process by which the ECB's Statute can be altered.

> In accordance with Article 106(5) of this Treaty, Articles 5.1, 5.2, 5.3, 17, 18, 19.1, 22, 23, 24, 26, 32.3, 32.4, 32.2, 32.6, 33.1(a) and 36 of this Statute may be amended by the Council, acting either by a qualified majority on a recommendation from the ECB and after consulting the Commission, or unanimously on a proposal from the Commission and after consulting the ECB. In either case the assent of the European Parliament shall be required.

Article 41.2 notes:

> A recommendation made by the ECB under this Article shall require a unanimous decision by the Governing Council.

This would require all 17 members to vote to recommend a change in the Statutes.

The different voting methods are summarised in Table 10.2 below.

Table 10.2 Voting methods in Governing Council

Voting method	No. of voters	Weighted?	Victory post	Applies to
Single-vote, simple-majority	Six executive board + 11 NCB governors	No	Nine votes*	Everything else
Single-vote, simple-majority, without Executive Board	11 NCB governors	No	Six votes*	Article 11.3 on ECB staff pay and conditions
Single-vote, two-thirds majority	Six executive board + 11 NCB governors	No	12 votes*	Article 14.4 and Article 20
Single-vote, unanimous	Six executive board + 11 NCB governors	No	17 votes*	Article 41.1
Weighted votes, simple-majority	11 NCB governors	Yes, by capital shares of ECB	Votes representing 50% of capital share	Articles 28, 29, 30, 32, 33 and 51
Weighted votes, qualified-majority	11 NCB governors	Yes, by capital shares of ECB	Votes representing two-thirds of capital share and at least six governors*	Some votes in Articles 28 and 32

* Assuming all able to vote do so.

NOTES

1. This paper was published in October 1998, well before some of the details of the proceedings of the ECB were decided. The authors may well have changed their view in light of later information. We cite the study because it clearly delineates some of the major issues to do with the role of the NCBs.
2. This and all subsequent references to articles are articles of the Protocol annexed to the Treaty of Maastricht on the Statute of the European System of Central Banks and of the European Central Bank.
3. The tasks referred to are those listed above, namely monetary policy, foreign-exchange policy and ensuring a smooth payments system.

REFERENCES

Begg, D., De Grauwe, P., Giavazzi, F., Uhlig, H. and Wyplosz, C. (1998) *The ECB: Safe at any speed?*, London: Centre for Economic Policy Research.

Duisenberg, W. F. (1998a) Speech to the World Economic Forum, Davos, 30 January.

Duisenberg, W. F. (1998b) Speech given to the Royal Institute of International Affairs, London, 27 November.

Duisenberg, W. F. (1999) Interview with the Editor, *Central Banking*, **9**(3): 21–32.

European Central Bank (1998) *The Single Monetary Policy in Stage Three*, September, Frankfurt.

EMI (1997) *General Documentation on ESCB Monetary Policy Instruments and Procedures*, Frankfurt.

Goodhart, C. and Schoenmaker, D. (1993) 'Institutional separation between supervisory and monetary agencies', Financial Markets Group, London School of Economics.

IMF (1998) *International Capital Markets*, Washington DC, September, pp. 104–10

Lannoo, K. (1998) 'What role for the ECB?' *The Financial Regulator*, **3**(2), London.

Trichet, J-C. Interview with the Editor, *Central Banking*, **8**(3): 12–22 (1997/8).

White, W. R. (1998) 'The coming transformation of continental European banking', *BIS working papers*, No. 54.

Discussion of Chapter 10

Joseph Bisignano

Before I get to the substance of my remarks on the chapter by Pringle and Turner I want to make a couple of comments on the historical position in which we find ourselves. It is my view an enormous accomplishment that a large piece of Europe has established a single central bank, when countries in Europe continue to retain much of what goes with sovereignty. By my political yardstick, the fact that this has occurred is little short of a political miracle. There is no equivalent institution for fiscal or structural policy in Europe. The new institution has as one of its foundation stones that of independence, a responsibility which weighs heavy on the shoulders of the ECB policymakers. This independence was granted, I believe, because of the considerable success European central banks acting in a co-ordinated manner achieved, seen in the convergence to low inflation and interest rates in Europe. The establishment of a European System of Central Banks is an enormous institutional, as well as economic policy, accomplishment. And it succeeded because of the success of co-operation among central bankers who shared similar views regarding the contribution low inflation could make to the attainment of economic growth and stability in Europe. The need for further co-operation and the search for shared views on how best to promote financial and economic stability will continue. But note what has already been established: national central banks are now making monetary policy within the framework of a single institution with a single currency.

The interesting chapter by Pringle and Turner raises several concerns over this new structure, namely, (1) that the governance structure of the ECB may distort the Community's monetary policy; (2) that the lack of clarity regarding the role of lender of last resort will inhibit the ECB's response to a banking or payments system crisis; (3) that decentralised banking supervision undermines the authority of the ECB, and may inhibit its response to a crisis, implying that the EU does not have an effective supervisory system, and (4) that the system is burdened by excessive costs.

Of these four concerns the last is the easiest to address, simply by stating that the national central banks are well aware of this problem and have for some time been attempting to reduce costs, for example, by reducing the number of regional branches. As some central banks have found, this can be a sensitive political issue. And as with any consolidation, it will be necessary and desirable to re-examine resource allocations. Like the US Federal Reserve System it may be advantageous for the national central banks to specialise in certain activities. However, it is also obvious that there may be some competition among ECB member countries for certain activities. This may arise as a result of the increasing consolidation in the financial services industry and the desire of several countries to become dominant financial centres. A single currency should promote competition in financial services. Any trend towards specialisation will likely be influenced by the outcome of the increasing competition and consolidation in the financial services industry. The fact that the United Kingdom is Europe's dominant financial centre but has yet to adopt the euro could also complicate decision making on any future specialisation of central banking services.

Let me now treat the first three issues raised by Pringle and Turner by first providing a simple framework. Central banking is typically thought of as being a three-legged stool composed of monetary policy, payments systems and banking supervision. The concerns of Pringle and Turner fall onto each of the three legs. For the ECB two broad issues need to be confronted with respect to these three legs: first, how much of each of these functions will be transferred from the national central banks to the centre institution and, second, whether the function be conducted by explicit rules or with complete discretion (or a combination of the two). At first glance we observe that not all of these functions have been transferred to the new centre institution and the institution is blending both rules and discretion in the conduct of its functions.

Pringle and Turner's first concern regards the governance structure of the ECB, namely that the national central bank governors have a majority of the Governing Council. This view has earlier been expressed by Begg *et al.* (1998). However, I see this as a strength of the new central bank, not a weakness. The new institution, to gain credibility and truly exercise independence, must act as an institution reflecting the views of all constituent members. Someone once stated that they had heard of a country without a central bank but not of a central bank without a country. The ESCB will produce one monetary policy for a group of sovereign nations. This requires that the central bank be truly representative and transparent. This is best accomplished, in my opinion, by placing the burden of the decision-making on the representatives of the national central banks. Will the majority of the national central banks on the Governing Council lead to inertia in policy formulation and result in conflicts based on national interests? It is difficult to say. But the burden will be on the national central bank governors to reconcile these differences and recognise any potential dangers of inertia in decision-making. Only in this manner will the new institution be able to confront possible criticism from the participating national publics and their elected representatives. To have at the outset a central bank with more voting power at the centre than with the participating central banks could, I believe, expose the institution to criticism of a lack of representation. We should also recall that it is only recently that some central banks have received true monetary policy independence.

Pringle and Turner agree with critics of the ECB regarding the lack of clarity of the lender of last resort (LLR) function. There are two aspects to this question: formal and informal. The formal aspect relates to the exercise of a lender of last resort function in times of liquidity crisis. The new central bank can exercise this function under the aegis of its role in protecting the stability of the payments system, a function explicitly given to the ECB. Here there is no lack of clarity. Should greater clarity be given with regard to how the LLR function will be exercised? This concerns the informal aspect of LLR. It is often expressed that central banks can helpfully reduce the dangers of moral hazard by maintaining a degree of 'constructive ambiguity' in the exercise of its safety net role. Those who argue that greater clarity should be given to the lender of last resort role need to identify how this clarity can be increased without increasing moral hazard and without inducing undesirable risk-taking by financial intermediaries.

Consider now the third leg of the stool, banking supervision. The new ECB is criticised for its decentralisation of responsibility for supervision. This criticism appears to imply that it is well accepted that the central bank must necessarily have banking supervision as one of its functions in order to assure the stability of the financial system. Independent of my own views, there is no such agreement. Looking at the two ends of the spectrum we observe the Bank of Canada and the Banca d'Italia. The Bank of Canada has no responsibility for prudential regulation and supervision. Indeed, it has little formal role in financial market surveillance and no role in operating the large value funds transfer system in Canada. The Banca d'Italia, in contrast, has extensive responsibilities in the regulation and supervision of banks and non-banks. In between these two we have a wide variety of arrangements. In the Netherlands the model is close to that in Italy, while in a number of other countries the structure is much closer to that in Canada. In some cases, such as in France, the central bank and the supervisory authorities remain legally separate but the administrative and co-operative links are very close. And recently we have seen some central banks lose their bank supervisory role. In both the United Kingdom and Australia the supervisory function has been given to a global financial regulator/supervisor, reflecting in part the desire that financial oversight be conducted along functional rather than institutional lines.

The above argument does not imply that there do not exist potential co-ordination and information problems in the supervision of European financial intermediaries. The ECB is likely well aware of these potential difficulties. Here again we are dealing with the desired transfer and the practical difficulties involved in the transfer of responsibilities for financial/monetary policy from the constituent members to the centre. This is no doubt a difficult task, given differences in legal, political and financial structure. The competition in finance that a single currency will give rise to makes this concern real if not immediate.

REFERENCE

Begg, D., De Grauwe, P., Giavazzi, F., Uhlig, H. and Wyplosz, C. (1998) *The ECB: Safe at any Speed?* London: Centre for Economic Policy Research.

11 The Emergence of International Currencies: Will the Euro be Used Internationally?

Paul Mizen

1 INTRODUCTION

The countries of the European Union have embarked on a major new monetary arrangement. For eleven of the member states of the EU (hereafter the EU-11), exchange rates have been locked since 1 January 1999 as the precursor to the replacement of national notes and coin in 2002. The euro is now a tradable currency on international exchanges and the question that many people are asking is: how influential will the euro be internationally? Undoubtedly, the euro will be a major currency. It will be the largest home currency since the population group is well in excess of the United States and has a combined purchasing power measured by the GDP of the participating states of some 8 trillion US dollars (measured at the end of 1997). The market for securities and loans denominated in euro will be the deepest and the most liquid of all international markets. It is also likely that many countries will hold significant stocks of euros as official reserves.

So will the euro be an 'international currency'? Certain currencies such as the US dollar, the Japanese yen and the Deutsche Mark have attained a higher status than others because they have been used beyond their own borders as international currencies. These are generally accepted as a means of exchange for transactions between third parties, as assets in private sector portfolios or in official reserves (McKinnon, 1969; Swoboda, 1969; Black, 1990; Tavlas and Ozeki, 1992; Hartmann, 1996; Gebhard, 1998; Tavlas, 1998). Arguably, the euro could take on this role in place of the Deutsche Mark (Gebhard, 1998) or even the dollar (Portes and Rey, 1998).

In this chapter we consider whether the euro will become an international currency by considering how its use might be adopted in a transactions vehicle role. We start by examining the evidence from existing currencies, we then consider what the theory tells us about the emergence of international currencies before making an assessment of whether the euro possesses the necessary characteristics to enable it to attain the status of an international currency.

2 CHARACTERISTICS OF INTERNATIONAL CURRENCIES

In this section we will draw attention to some defining features of international currencies using the examples of the US dollar, the Deutsche Mark, and also to some degree the yen, during the postwar period to illustrate our points.

Robert Mundell points out that international moneys have been closely associated in world history with *political supremacy and power* (Mundell, 1998). First, an economic superpower has a large market, defined both in terms of its size and its scope, and this gives good reason for the superpower currency to be adopted by those that trade with them directly, in import or export markets. It also encourages those with excess balances of international currency to accept payments or invoicing in the international currency even for third party trades. The argument is based on the liquidity of the market for the currency, the ready acceptability of the medium of exchange, and network externalities that accrue to users of the currency.

Second, international currencies are *economically stable*. Mundell notes that the pound lost its position as top currency to the dollar when its stability (convertibility) was questioned, not when the size of US GDP outgrew the British output. Low inflation and predictability of prices reduce the costs of writing contracts in the stable currency for export and import trades. The third and fourth characteristics of international currencies follow from the second: the *political stability* of the nation state issuing the international money, and a basis for a *fallback value* are vital. Political instability can cause a flight from the currency – and examples abound in the twentieth century of countries that have shown political weakness, resorted to unchecked money creation and have experienced subsequent inflation. If the purchasing power of money could be eroded through inflation, the holder would have no assurance that the money would not become worthless at some date as a medium of exchange and its acceptability would decline. An inherent value to the currency is then a necessary characteristic that protects the holder from irresponsible governments or central bankers. Points two, three and four all point to instability as the precursor to the demise of a currency's status as an acceptable

medium of exchange, unit of account or store of value. Stability is a necessary feature of an international currency.

International currencies take on a special significance as vehicles for
international trade in goods and services, foreign exchange transactions
and official transactions, (see Chrystal 1977, 1984; Page, 1977, 1981;
Chrystal *et al.* 1983; Black, 1990; Mizen and Pentecost, 1994, 1996;
Milner *et al.* 1996, 1998; Rey 1997a, b; Artis *et al.* 1998; Portes and Rey,
1998). The result follows in large part from the observation by Grassman
(1973) that exporters of manufactured goods tend to invoice in their own
currency rather than in a foreign currency (to transfer the exchange risk to
the buyer). Third currency invoicing is only viable as an option when the
benefits exceed the costs. Currencies that have this property are regarded
as transactions vehicles. They are often used in the following cases:

1. Export and import trades between industrialised and developing countries are usually invoiced in the industrialised country's currency or a
   vehicle currency.
2. Inflationary currencies are not generally used for invoicing, and again a
   vehicle currency will typically be used instead – this can be a natural
   extension of the currency substitution phenomenon, by which domestic
   trade is conducted through a foreign currency medium.
3. Trades in most primary commodities (for example oil) are conducted
   predominantly in dollars.

International currencies readily take on this role as the third party currency
through which many other trades are conducted. The total transaction cost
of two trades (measured by the sum of the bid-ask spreads) is lower through
two trades with an exotic and a vehicle currency on one side of the transaction, than through one trade between two exotics. Bessembinder (1994) and
Hartmann (1996) have shown that as predictable volumes of trade increase
the bid-ask spread declines due to economies of scale in market making.
This gives rise to the observation that certain international moneys become
the 'money of the money markets' (Chrystal, 1977).

The total volume of foreign exchange trading vastly exceeds the total
world trade in goods and services. Foreign exchange deals that are directly
related to trades are a small fraction of the total, since foreign exchange
markets can be put to many other uses. Traders or financial institutions
taking short-term positions in the markets will increase the total volume of
transactions in the foreign exchange market. The foreign exchange market
is also used for the reduction of risk, that is, hedging activity, as a means of

insurance through financial derivative products, and portfolio management practices by pension funds, dealers and so on. A single transaction for trade in goods and services can give rise to a substantial number of other foreign exchange deals as the dealers receiving the currency may hedge or pass on the currency several times to rearrange their portfolios.

Activities in the foreign exchange market also involve official bodies such as central banks that intervene on behalf of their governments to manage the exchange rate. In the extreme this can involve the purchase or sale of domestic currency through the adjustment of foreign currency reserves to enforce a fixed exchange rate. Alternatively, in a floating exchange rate regime the central bank can intervene to prevent the rate from moving too far from an acceptable central rate, the strategy of 'leaning against the wind'. Since the volumes of currency involved are often large and the interventions need to take immediate effect, international currencies are used to intervene in thick markets located in the main financial centres.

The evidence on the characteristics of the currencies that have already developed an international status is illustrated in the post-war period by the US dollar, the Deutsche Mark and partially the Japanese yen. The extensive network advantages of the dollar can be clearly illustrated by measures of network size such as the size of GDP, the depth of the capital market or the population (see McKinnon, 1969; Swoboda, 1969). Consider Table 11.1. Today, the population size of the United States is 263 million, more than the combined total of Germany and Japan. The size of the US GDP was $7.3 trillion in 1995 and had risen to about $8.5 trillion in 1997, making it easily the largest single currency domain by the scale of output of the issuing country. The Bank for International Settlements reported that the total of bonds, commercial paper, treasury bills and international bonds outstanding in the US capital market was over $11 trillion and the market capitalisation of the stock market was a further $7 trillion, of which $12.2 billion was traded daily. By any standard this puts the value of the domestic market and the market for financial instruments traded in US dollars well ahead of the values in any other single currency. This confers large network externalities on users of the US dollar by lowering the transactions costs for traders importing from or exporting to the US, but it also lowers the transactions costs for third-party transactors from other countries.

The emergence of the Deutsche Mark and the yen has been due to the commitment of their monetary authorities to maintain the quality of the currency. Neither currency had a strong pre-war following nor was the scale of domestic operations sufficient to confer network benefits on users. Only since the 1970s have these countries appeared to have sufficiently

Table 11.1 EU, North America and Japan: selected indicators of the size of the capital markets, 1995

	Population (in millions)	GDP	Total reserves minus gold	Stock market capitalisation	Debt securities Public	Debt securities Private	Debt securities Total	Bank assets	Bonds, equities, and bank assets	Bonds, equities, and bank assets (% of GDP)
EU-15	371.8	8 427.6	376.3	3 778.5	4 809.9	3 863.5	8 673.4	14 818.0	27 269.9	323.58
EU-11	289.0	6 804.9	284.5	2 119.4	3 903.8	3 088.6	6 992.4	11 971.6	21 083.4	309.83
United States	263.0	7 253.8	74.8	6 857.6	6 728.0	4 322.6	11 050.6	5 000.0	22 908.2	315.81
Japan	125.2	5 134.3	183.3	3 667.3	3 447.7	1 877.1	5 324.8	7 382.2	16 374.2	318.92
Germany	81.6	2 412.5	85.0	577.4	893.6	1 284.5	2 178.1	3 752.4	6 507.8	269.76
United Kingdom	58.3	1 105.1	42.0	1 407.74	429.9	396.3	826.2	2 424.4	4 658.3	421.53

Data in $billion unless otherwise stated.
Source: IMF.

large economies to support network externalities based on size. Both the Deutsche Mark and the yen built their post-war reputations on the basis of their determination to avoid inflation. The level of inflation has been remarkably low in Germany and Japan since the mid-1970s and almost exactly half on average relative to the US over the period. Likewise, the variability of prices has been lower compared to the US, reducing the uncertainty surrounding the quality of the currency.

The dollar, Deutsche Mark and yen are used as vehicle currencies in many trades that do not involve domestic residents on either side of the transaction. Table 11.2 shows the currency of denomination of exports (imports) of certain industrialised countries over the period 1992–96. According to Grassman's law we should expect the invoicing to be done in the seller's currency, since the exchange rate risk is then borne by the buyer, Grassman (1973). The large proportion of trades conducted in local currency, indicated by the values on the leading diagonal for the first three countries/currencies, upholds this point. Yet many trades are conducted in currencies other than that of the seller. This is most noticeable for the US dollar that is used to invoice more than half of the exports of Japan, and around 20 per cent of exports for the UK, France and Italy. The Deutsche Mark is also used widely in its own region to invoice exports of UK, France and Italy. The yen is little used outside of Japan, but the list of reported countries excludes the near neighbours of Japan in the far east.

A similar pattern is observed for data on the currency of denomination of imports of given industrialised countries. With the exception of Germany, the use of the US dollar dominates even the domestic currency of the exporter – showing that the advantages accruing to the user of a vehicle currency outweigh the benefits of exchange rate risk reduction. The regional and country dominance of the dollar merge, since the US is both more closed and more distant from its trading partners than either Germany or Japan. Both Germany and Japan have local spheres of influence that involve other countries that could invoice in their own currency but choose to use the Deutsche Mark or the yen. The Deutsche Mark is dominant in Europe since the proportions of imports and exports invoiced in Deutsche Mark exceeds those invoiced in the sum of all other currencies (for exports the figures are 80 per cent:20 per cent while for imports they are 60 per cent:40 per cent). For the yen about half of all Japanese exports to the South East Asian region were invoiced in yen (the remainder were largely in dollars), while one-fifth of imports were invoiced in yen.

Table 11.2　Currency denomination of exports and imports:
selected industrial countries, 1992–95 (%)

	US dollar	Deutsche Mark	Japanese yen
Exports			
United States	98.0	0.4	0.4
Germany	9.8	76.4	0.6
Japan	52.7	—	35.7
United Kingdom	22.0	5.0	0.7
France	18.6	10.6	1.0
Italy	23.0	18.0	—
Imports			
United States	88.8	3.2	3.1
Germany	18.1	53.3	1.5
Japan	70.4	2.8	22.5
United Kingdom	22.0	11.9	2.4
France	23.1	10.1	1.0
Italy	28.0	13.0	—

Source: Tavlas (1998).

Those transactions that are conducted in local currency rather than the currencies of the US, Germany or Japan are still likely to be conducted indirectly through the spot, forward and swap markets in international currencies for reasons given in Chrystal (1984). Since most currencies are quoted in US dollars (and possibly also Deutsche Mark, sterling or yen on the exchanges in Frankfurt, London and Tokyo) third-party transactions will often use one of these currencies as an intermediary in buying and selling the necessary domestic currency. Table 11.3 gives the percentage share of each currency used on one side of a transaction relative to the gross global turnover of the foreign exchange market. Clearly, the dollar, Deutsche Mark and yen dominate, with the pound sterling as a fourth contender, probably due to the fact that London has the largest global market for foreign exchange. Survey results indicate that London has the largest global turnover in foreign exchange, summing to more than the combined total of US, German and Japanese markets. It is easier to quote the rates of the two currencies in terms of a common third currency (for example the dollar), and to exploit the depth of the market for each currency versus the dollar, than to attempt to make a direct exchange, a point developed further in the next section.

Table 11.3 Use of selected currencies on one side of transaction as a percentage of global gross foreign exchange market turnover (percentage shares)

Currency	April 1992	April 1995	April 1998
US dollar	82	83	72
Deutsche Mark	40	37	32
Japanese yen	23	24	15

Source: Tavlas (1998), Bank of England Quarterly Bulletin (1998).
Currencies can appear on more than one side of the transaction so percentages do not sum to 100.

Average daily foreign exchange market turnover

Market	1992	1995	1998
UK	291	464	637
US	167	244	351
Japan	120	161	149
Singapore	74	65	139
Germany	55	76	94

Source: Bank of England Quarterly Bulletin (1998).

Relative shares of total net turnover by currency pair

Currency pair	1992	1995	1998
£/US$	17	11	14
US$/DM	24	22	22
US$/yen	12	17	13
£/DM	5	3	3

Source: Bank of England Quarterly Bulletin (1998).

The official use of the US dollar, Deutsche Mark and yen also clearly marks them out as international currencies. Industrialised countries have substantial holdings in dollars and in Deutsche Mark and yen to a lesser extent, estimates calculated by Gebhard (1998) suggest the figures were 60 per cent, 15 per cent and 8 per cent in 1995 for total foreign exchange reserve holdings world-wide. In developing countries shares are even more distorted towards the dollar. In Latin America for example the dollar took the lion's share as a proportion of the total reserves at 76 per cent at the end of 1995, while the Deutsche Mark and yen took the proportions 7 per cent and 4 per cent respectively. The French franc has a high share in Africa due to the CFA (African Financial Community) zone and this also explains the large number of countries using the franc as an exchange rate peg, Table 11.4. The dominant position of the Deutsche Mark and the dollar in composition of currency baskets in the emerging markets of eastern Europe is also relevant. The combined share is 100 per cent for the Czech Republic (65/35 split), Hungary (50/50 split), Slovak Republic (60/40 split) and 80 per cent for Poland (45/35 split, with 10/5/5 per cent taken by sterling, French franc and Swiss franc).

Table 11.4   Use of currencies as exchange rate pegs

	1980	1996
Total pegged of which:	72	45
US dollar	39	20
French franc	14	14
SDR	15	2
Other	4	9
	(5.6)	(14.9)

Source: Tavlas (1998).

Shares of major currencies in total foreign exchange reserves, 1975–95 (per cent)

End of period	US dollar	Deutsche Mark	Japanese yen
1980	69.7	14.7	4.2
1985	66.0	14.1	7.4
1990	56.4	19.1	9.0
1995	60.0	15.3	8.2

Source: Gebhard (1998).

3 THE EMERGENCE OF INTERNATIONAL CURRENCIES

The use of a currency internationally involves substantial use by the private and public sectors in direct transactions with the issuing country and in third party trades, where the currency acts as a vehicle. This section considers how a currency may come to be the preferred medium of exchange, unit of account, or store of value over and above other currencies that might do the function just as well.

Two innovative papers by Krugman (1980) and Chrystal (1984) propose similar models to explain the settlement of international trades and foreign exchange transactions based on the minimisation of search and exchange costs. To illustrate the point they consider three countries with separate currencies that are used to finance bilateral trade between them. If traders wishing to buy a good from country j are holding currency i and wish to minimise the costs of searching for an exchange at market prices into currency j they have two options. They could use the exchange market or they could aim to use thick, liquid markets that increase the probability of finding a suitable match, and may go via an indirect route involving a third 'vehicle' currency. Taking $p_i p_j$ as the probability of finding a dealer with currency j willing to exchange for currency i, the cost of search can be stated as the holding period defined by $1/p_i p_j$. If either currency j or currency i is a readily acceptable currency then dealers may make a direct exchange, but if it is not they may use a third currency. Hence, if $1/p_i p_k + 1/p_k p_j < 1/p_i p_j$ then the dealer will use currency k as a vehicle that is, as an indirect exchange. When there are unambiguously lower transaction costs of using a vehicle currency then Krugman shows trade between two countries will be settled in *partial indirect exchange* that is, by transactions through direct *and* indirect exchange markets. If trade between two countries is settled by indirect transactions alone, so that one direct exchange market is eliminated altogether, *total indirect exchange* occurs. However, the direction in which exchange is conducted matters. Multiple equilibria result from these scenarios so that for three currencies there are six possible cases: any currency can be the vehicle but it depends on the transactions costs as to which will actually take on the role and whether indirect trade will be total or partial.

Rey (1997a,b) has a similar relationship in the settlement of international trade, based on the framework devised by Lucas (1990) and the concept of network externalities discussed by Chrystal (1984) and Dowd and Greenaway (1993). This makes a leap forward over other models of emerging currencies and trade based on 'random matching', where trade takes place when one trader 'happens' to meet another. An example of this type of model is the Kiyotaki and Wright (1989) extension of Jones (1976), where trading strategies are endogenous and a fundamental equilibrium exists in which the good (currency) with the lowest storage cost should be chosen as the medium of exchange. Rey (1997a, b) criticises their model for the fact that money is indivisible and cannot be stored (traders can only store one unit of the money or one unit of the commodity), and the lack of an explicit supply side with flexible prices. She also notes that the Kiyotaki and Wright model does not readily extend to an open economy case and so cannot tell us about the emergence of international currencies.

Rey's paper is international, however, and involves three producers of different tradable commodities invoiced in different (national) currencies. There is a government that controls the money supply by issuing bonds through open market operations; it is required to remain solvent through a no Ponzi game condition. Consumers in each country gain utility from all three goods and have a standard intertemporal utility function, which they maximise subject to six binding cash-in-advance constraints, a budget constraint, and non-negativity conditions over money and goods. Production is described by a country-specific CRS production function in labour while transactions are conducted through profit maximising financial intermediaries with increasing returns to scale. Importantly, the transactions cost of operating through an intermediary falls with the thickness of the market. Prices are flexible and all markets clear.

The same total and partial indirect exchange conditions emerge in Rey's model as in Krugman (1980) and Chrystal (1984) and international currencies can be more efficient if sufficient traders use them. Multiple equilibria emerge again and the equilibrium selection depends on whether the transactions costs lower the cost of indirect versus direct exchange. Taking Ti/j as the transactions cost of trading between currency i and j then partial exchange occurs using currency i as a vehicle if

$$Ti/j < Tj/k: Ti/k < Tj/k \text{ and } Ti/j + Ti/k > Tj/k$$

and total indirect exchange occurs using currency i if

$$Ti/j < Tj/k: Ti/k < Tj/k \text{ and } Ti/j + Ti/k < Tj/k$$

The vital assumption that the cost of currency exchange is decreasing with the volume of trades means that heavily used currencies will emerge as international currencies, since they will then be used by others in third party transactions.

The concept of 'network externalities' on which this assumption relies, says that benefits accruing to the user of a popular currency give that currency an advantage over others. Acceptability increases giving positive externalities to the user as the domain of the currency grows, which has a double incentive effect since the growth in the network of one currency diminishes the network of another. Network advantages are likely to accrue to company pricing strategies too. Companies that price in a popular currency gain from the transparency in pricing that reveals competitiveness, while those that do not may very well face prejudice from their customers. Together the positive benefits conferred on the holder of a currency as a larger number of others make use of the currency in receipt (invoicing behaviour) and payment, causes the number of 'international' currencies to be small. It also accelerates the process of transition between the use of currencies that are waning in popularity and those that are growing. The extent of the externality relative to the transition costs of establishing new financial arrangements and networks is the main issue for the emergence of an international currency. The vital issue empirically is to determine the likelihood that a currency will experience these lower trans-actions costs relative to other currencies due to network externalities. These will depend on the size and extent of trade in goods, invoicing patterns, use of financial markets and official use of a currency, so we must return to the empirical data to determine whether a currency (in this case the euro) will be an international currency.

4 WILL THE EURO EMERGE AS A NEW INTERNATIONAL CURRENCY?

This section will consider whether the euro will be an international currency. Crucial to the analysis is the effect of the scale of the markets and the low inflation environment expected to prevail in the EU-11 area, which were central to Mundell's four features. The emergence of international currencies depends crucially on the transactions costs and network exter-nalities conferred on users of the currency and these are related to economic size and stability.

In terms of Mundell's four features, the euro appears to have the neces-sary characteristics of an international currency, see Table 11.1. It has a sizeable network (or domain) defined by the combined GDP of the EU-11 countries – this is close to US GDP at $6.8 trillion and encompasses a larger population of 289 million residents. If we consider the possibility of enlargement or the scope of the markets with which the EU trades imported or exported goods the network could extend to a much larger market. Likewise on stability the EU looks set to fulfil the criteria for an international currency. The ECB has shown that it intends to use monetary and inflation targeting to achieve low inflation and low price variability to match the performance of the Deutsche Mark, making the euro a suitable currency for pricing contracts. Mundell concurs with these views, although he is less than convinced that the euro has the political stability and fall back value to attain a true international currency status. There are reasons to disagree with his conclusions however. The euro has the political backing of its member states and that is likely to be sufficient to support it in the absence of a central state. The economic incentives for countries to 'make it work' would seem to be sufficient: one cannot otherwise explain the continuation of the European Monetary System after the disastrous experience of exchange rate targeting in the ERM during 1992–93. On the question of the fallback value, it can be pointed out that none of the inter-national currencies of the post-war period has a fallback guarantee since they are all fiat moneys built on trust. In the absence of this characteristic, a constitutional commitment to inflation control appears to have reassured wary investors that the purchasing power is not likely to be jeopardised.

If the euro does become an international currency then what will encourage its use beyond the borders of the EU-11? We advance some reasons why the transactions costs and network externalities central to the emergence of international currencies will encourage the use of the euro by residents outside the EU area.

4.1 Swoboda's International Square-root Rule

With the emergence of an internationally acceptable currency like the euro, residents of the EU-11 countries will find their diversified deposits rede-nominated into euros in 1999. Swoboda (1969) has shown, by an applica-tion of the Baumol-Tobin square-root rule, that it is more efficient to hold deposits in one currency than in many, in proportion to the needs of trade and inversely with the relevant opportunity cost. The existence of a single currency would increase efficiency by reducing the total level of balances required. The reduction in the optimal balance required overall will cause an excess stock of euros in the initial stages to be offloaded in other assets or goods. Ultimately, to offload the deposits the euros will need to be exchanged for assets and goods priced in other currencies, so a hot potato effect may cause the euro to depreciate. The economisation of liquid balances, the reduction in the costs of currency management and lower staffing levels associated with foreign exchange management for the members of the EU-11 will put them at an advantage compared to those outside the Euro-area. The excess (the difference between the original diversified deposits and the new, lower, optimal level of deposits in euros) and savings from economisation could be reallocated into less liquid interest bearing assets, earning a higher rate of return, or simply be spent on goods and services. These advantages may persuade those outside the EU-11 to hold deposits in euros rather than in domestic currency, so that they also gain from the reduction in total liquidity.

Many of the economies will be reaped in the first instance by multinational firms through more efficient foreign exchange management. Anecdotal evidence suggests that changes are already underway to ensure that they are exploited. The toolmakers Trumpf (Germany) (cited in the *Financial Times,* 17 December 1998) suggest that although conversion will involve costs of installing new software and currency management systems amounting to a one-off payment of 2 million Deutsche Marks, they will save 1 million Deutsche Marks annually from the reduction in staff costs and payments made to banks for currency conversion. If these figures are representative, a payback period of two years provides a good incentive for companies to make the conversion to handle euro deposits and price in euros rather than in national currency.

4.2 Trade Patterns, Externalities and Currency Usage

If the introduction of the euro is to have a major effect on the holdings of currency and deposits then it is likely to operate through trade patterns and invoicing behaviour. Firms that have substantial bi-directional trade with EU-11 countries may prefer to invoice in euros: survey evidence suggests that up to half of sales to the EU will be invoiced in euros and many sales outside the EU will be invoiced in euros to make pricing more transparent. The dividing line is likely to be between large companies, that will be invoiced in euros, and small- or medium-sized enterprises, that will continue to pay for goods and services in domestic currency. On 1997 direction of trade statistics, if half of exports to the rest of the EU from Euroland countries are invoiced in euros then this would amount to $540 billion of trade, while if importers from the rest of the EU insist on paying in euros this would amount to $417 billion. By holding the proceeds in euro (transactions) accounts rather than in other currencies (that will later need to be transferred back to euros at a future, uncertain exchange rate) firms will reduce their transactions costs in the foreign exchange market and their exposure to currency risk.

In an interview with the *Financial Times*, deputy head of ICI Peter Everett indicated that the euro is likely to be the normal transactions vehicle for trade between ICI and its customers and suppliers in the UK, Denmark, Sweden and Greece as well as the EU-11. While the customers may not always be invoiced in euros, suppliers are likely to be paid in euros under the 'no compulsion, no prohibition' ruling, as companies can usefully use make payments of invoices in euros to facilitate a hedging operation against the large euro takings from elsewhere in Europe. The network externalities to customers and suppliers in these countries will be large and even for countries outside of the EU such as Switzerland, which imports $58.3 billion of goods from the EU and exports $45.3 billion to the EU, the rewards for using the euro could be considerable.

4.3 Financial Markets

The size of the European capital market is about as large as the US market. Table 11.1 shows that the EU-11 area had total trade in bonds, equities and bank assets of 21 trillion dollars versus the US at 23 trillion, at the end of 1995. The market for futures and forwards is more skewed towards the US, since the derivatives trade in Europe represented only 36 per cent of the US level according to 1995 figures (Thom *et al.*, 1998).

Accounting for the total trade within Europe, the capital market will be very large, but much of this trade will fall off now that intra-EU trade has been eliminated by the single currency. However, the deeper capital market (with the lower transactions costs of operating through euros versus the dollar or the yen) may gain trade for the euro which may offset the reduction due to monetary union (Hartmann, 1996). Financial institutions that do not deal in the euro will lose credibility and therefore business. Recent estimates by Morgan Stanley Dean Witter suggested that up to $1300 billion of new money would flow into new equities in euros from fund managers alone in the next ten years. Many investors have begun to treat financial markets as if they were pan-European, even though this is some way off, by no longer conducting operations on a national level but adopting a new sectoral basis for investment. Companies now work to raise finance on a continental level in larger markets and bid-ask spreads are likely to fall in

Europe as a result. Restructuring of financial arrangements will help remove segmentation in the market and improve competition through transparency, first of all at the corporate level, but subsequently for the retail sector, and the outlook for some small traders with specialisations in niche markets is therefore bleak. The market for debt is likely to experience some redenomination into euros as banks issue debt in euro to buy back current debts in dollars (McCauley, 1997).

4.4 Official Holdings

Estimates from the *IMF International Capital Markets* suggest that around 25 per cent of EU official reserves are denominated in EU currencies, have been converted into euros since 1 January 1999 and have disappeared from the reserves of EU-11 countries altogether. Other things being equal, the countries would need to buy other currencies as reserves but the pooling of reserves will result in an excess of foreign currency in official hands that could be reduced. The reduction in reserves, due to economies of scale along the lines of the Swoboda argument outlined above, and the diminished ERM intervention obligations on the part of EMU participants, will reduce total foreign exchange reserve requirements. The stock of EU currencies used as reserves in the EU area amounts to some $137 billion for the EU-15 or $85 billion for the EU-11 (see Table 11.5). The majority of the remainder are in dollars and some of these would be pooled leaving a net excess supply – the so called 'dollar overhang' – estimated to range between $230 billion (European Commision, 1990) and $50 billion (Masson and Turtelboom, 1997). Not all of this will be offloaded to the markets, however, since the ECB has the right to call upon national central banks to provide further reserves beyond the initial requirements of the Maastricht treaty. If some countries need to borrow to meet these obligations the likely dollar overhang may shrink to $42 billion according to Arrowsmith *et al.* (1998).

The official holdings of non-EU central banks are also likely to be rebalanced to reduce the current holdings of dollars and increase those in euro either for the purpose of foreign exchange diversification or for exchange rate pegging. It is unlikely that these operations will be hurried and the rebalancing will probably take place over a longer period than the market has come to expect but they will enhance the position of the euro as a reserve currency. The fact that the total official reserves worldwide (at some 1.4 trillion US dollars) are small relative to the asset holdings of the private sector is likely to diminish the impact of this rebalancing on

Table 11.5 EU countries' gold and foreign exchange
reserves after EMU (US$ bns, as at end 1996)

	Total FX reserves in 1996	of which		
		in US dollars	in EU currencies	non-EU (total)
Austria	20.6	12.5	7.4	13.2
Belgium	14.7	6.4	7.0	7.8
Denmark	14.1	3.4	9.0	5.2
Finland	6.4	2.0	3.7	2.7
France	15.3	10.3	4.1	11.2
Germany	69.1	62.0	7.0	62.1
Greece	17.6	5.2	10.4	7.2
Ireland	9.8	3.0	5.8	4.1
Italy	43.0	22.6	17.2	25.8
Luxembourg	—	—	—	—
Netherlands	22.1	6.1	13.4	8.7
Portugal	13.7	3.7	8.4	5.3
Spain	50.6	37.9	10.7	39.9
Sweden	23.6	5.4	15.3	8.3
United Kingdom	36.1	14.7	17.6	18.4
EU 15	356.7	195.2	137.0	219.9
EMU 11	265.3	166.5	84.7	180.8
Non-EMU 4	91.4	28.7	52.3	39.1

Source: IMF.

exchange rates and asset prices. The component due to EU-11 currencies in
the official reserves of all countries' central banks was $265 billion at the
end of 1996, and there is a high likelihood that this will increase. The total
effect of all readjustments to international private sector and official portfolios is estimated by Arrowsmith *et al.* (1998) and reported in Table 11.6.
They calculate that if the euro becomes attractive as an official reserve
currency outside the EU-11, to restore the euro share to the present share for
the EU-11 national currencies euro holdings would have to increase by
$66 billion (column 1, line 1). While these figures are large, the time frame
over which the adjustment is likely to take place is unknown: the numbers
give a guide to the extent of the change but provide no indication of the
period of time that would elapse before such changes were complete. As the
euro grows in status as an international currency it is likely that central
banks will readjust their portfolios in a gradual manner and the share of
euros in the official reserves of non-EU central banks is likely to increase.

Table 11.6 Potential increases in international holdings of euro assets: some illustrative figures, US$ bns, end-1996 data

	With an EMU of 11		With an EMU of 15	
	To restore present EMU-11 share	To achieve equal share with dollar	To restore present EMU-15 share	To achieve equal share with dollar
Official currency reserves	66	358	111	364
Foreign currency deposits	250	182	225	138
International debt securities	408	321	397	228
Total	724	861	733	730

Source: Arrowsmith *et al.* (1998).

Will the euro become the dominant international currency, replacing the US dollar? It will take some time for the euro to establish its own credentials as a suitable international currency but it will certainly assume a second place position to the dollar for two reasons. First, the euro is a direct replacement for the second placed international currency, the Deutsche Mark. This means that the domestic markets of Germany and the other EU-11 countries will all adopt the euro as their domestic currency. The euro will have considerable network externalities in their wider export and import markets and this will create incentives for residents of those countries to use the euro as a transaction vehicle for the reasons outlined above. We agree with Gebhard (1998) that the euro will take on the transaction vehicle role of the Deutsche Mark but the euro will also have a significantly wider market, comprising a share of world trade at least as large as that of the United States (a share equal to a quarter of world trade) according to estimates by Hartmann (1996). Second, the ECB has shown that it has no intention of abandoning the low inflation reputation of the Bundesbank but rather, as an institution without a history, intends to reap as much credibility as possible by emulating the Bundesbank's monetary policy stance. This ought to provide a sound footing for the euro as a currency in which to conduct trade. Together these features will create a large demand for the euro as a transactions vehicle outside, as well as inside, the EU-11.

Table 11.6 confirms this intuition. It gives the magnitude of changes required to maintain the share of foreign currency deposits held in EU-11 currencies at the end of 1996 reported by Arrowsmith *et al.* (1998). To achieve the standing of the US dollar the deposits would need to rise by $182 billion and $138 billion for the EU-11 and EU-15 respectively. This is unlikely, and Swoboda's argument suggests that these numbers will be smaller due to the efficiency gains from holding one currency instead of fifteen. The dollar will also probably retain a significant position in financial markets due to inertia. To achieve the standing of the US dollar the euro denominated debt securities would need to rise by $321 billion and $228 billion respectively. Finally, in order to achieve an equal status with the US dollar in official use the euro would need to rise by $358 billion, which entails a switch from the dollar to the euro of $260 billion in 1996 terms. We regard these changes as unlikely to occur within the foreseeable future. Over time we may observe a binary divide in emerging markets between exchanges involving eastern European currencies dominated by the euro and exchanges involving Latin American and Asian currencies conducted through the dollar, but the dollar will dominate overall.

Portes and Rey (1998) argue conversely that the euro will take on some of the international status of the dollar, possibly even replacing its function in certain areas. This result is calculated using recent financial market data and estimates of the transactions costs of using the euro. The size of the Euro-area will be much greater than the dollar area so their assumption of equal transactions costs leads naturally to the conclusion that the euro will take over the dollar's position.

We have argued that history shows that dominant currencies tend to display inertia, and the encroachment of the euro on the US dollar is likely to be much slower, notwithstanding the advantages to the use of the euro, than many commentators suggest. We conclude that the euro will not displace the dollar as the most heavily used international currency.

5 CONCLUSIONS

International moneys are often used as vehicles to conduct trade, foreign exchange operations and official interventions well beyond the realm of the issuing country. A network of users and stability of the currency in terms of its purchasing power have been associated with the post-war currencies – the US dollar, Deutsche Mark and yen – that have fulfilled this role. Theory tells us that lower costs and higher network benefits will confer on a currency an international status; they will therefore be crucial in determining whether a currency is adopted for use as an international currency. We have then considered the likely determinants of these costs and benefits to determine whether the euro is likely take on an international role. We conclude that the euro will take on a prominent role as an international currency even although it is unlikely to overtake the dollar. It has all the necessary characteristics to do so but there is considerable inertia in the system which allows existing international currencies to retain their places even when a strong rival emerges. Nevertheless, we judge that the euro will become a significant international currency, first of all in the extended import and export market of the EU and in the emerging markets of eastern Europe, then in the 'out' countries and later in third party trades of non-European countries as a transactions vehicle.

ACKNOWLEDGEMENTS

I am particularly grateful to Lars Calmfors, Alec Chrystal, Peter Englund, Ron McKinnon, Eric Pentecost, Paul Soderlind, Alan Sutherland and participants in the conferences on Risk Allocation and EMU, Swedish Parliament, December 1998 and From EMU to EMS: 1979 to 1999 and Beyond, London Business School, January 1999 who commented extensively on this paper.

REFERENCES

Arrowsmith, J., Barrell, R. and Taylor, C. (1998) 'Managing the euro in a tri-polar world', paper presented at the 21st colloquium of the Societe Universitaire Européenne de Recherches Financières, Frankfurt, October 1998.

Artis, M. J., Kohler, M. and Mélitz, J. (1998) 'Trade and the number of optimal currencies in the world', CEPR discussion paper No. 1926.

Bessembinder, H. (1994) 'Bid-ask spreads in the interbank foreign exchange markets', *Journal of Financial Economics*, **35**: 317–48.

Black, S. (1990) 'The international use of currencies', in Suzuki, Y., Miyake, J. and Okabe, M. (eds) *The Evolution of the International Monetary System*, Tokyo: University of Tokyo.

Chrystal, K. A. (1977) 'Demand for international media of exchange' *American Economic Review*, **67**: 840–50.

Chrystal, K. A. (1984) 'On the theory of international money', in *Problems of International Finance*, Black and Dorvance (eds), Basingstoke: Macmillan.

Chrystal K. A., Wilson, N. D. and Quinn, P. (1983) 'Demand for international money 1962–77', *European Economic Review*, **21**: 287–98.

Dowd, K. and Greenaway, D. (1993) 'Currency competition, network externalities and switching costs: Towards an alternative theory of optimal currency areas', *Economic Journal*, **103**: 1180–9.

European Commission (1990) *One Market, One Money*, European Economy No. 44.

Gebhard, C. (1998) 'The evolution of the Deutsche Mark as an international currency', in Frowen, S. F. and Pringle, R. (eds) *Inside the Bundesbank*, Basingstoke: Macmillan.

Grassman, S. (1973) 'A fundamental symmetry in international payments patterns', *Journal of International Economics*, **3**: 105–16.

Hartmann, P. (1996) 'The future of the Euro as an international currency', LSE FMG Special Paper No. 91.

Jones, R. (1976) 'The origin and development of media of exchange', *Journal of Political Economy*, **84**: 757–75.

Kiyotaki, N. and Wright, R. (1989) 'A search theoretic approach to monetary economics', *Journal of Political Economy*, **97**: 927–54.

Krugman, P. R. (1980) 'Vehicle currencies and the structure of international exchange', *Journal of Money, Credit, and Banking*, **12**: 513–26.

Lucas, R. E. Jnr (1990) 'Liquidity and interest rates', *Journal of Economic Theory*, **50**: 237–64.

Masson, P. R. and Turtelboom, B. (1997) 'Characteristics of the Euro, the demand for reserves and policy co-ordination under EMU', IMF working paper 97/58.

McCauley, R. (1997) 'The Euro and the dollar', BIS working paper 50.

McKinnon, R. I. (1969) 'Private and official international money: The case for the dollar', *Princeton Essays in International Finance*, 74.

Milner, C. R., Mizen, P. D. and Pentecost, E. J. (1996) 'The impact of intra-European trade on sterling currency substitution', *Weltwirtschaftliches Archiv*.

Milner, C. R., Mizen, P. D. and Pentecost, E. J. (1998) 'Currency substitution and trade: Evidence from cross sectional data', *Economic Inquiry*, forthcoming.

Mizen, P. D. and Pentecost, E. J. (1994) 'Empirical evidence on currency substitution in Europe: a case study of sterling', *Economic Journal*, **104**: 1057–69.

Mizen, P.D. and Pentecost, E.J. (ed.) (1996) *The Macroeconomics of International Currencies*, Cheltenham: Edward Elgar.

Mundell, R. (1998) 'What makes a great currency? *Central Banking*, **9**(1): 35–42.

Page, S. (1977) 'Currency invoicing in merchandise trade', *National Institute Economic Review*, 81/3.

Page, S. (1981) 'The choice of invoicing currency in merchandise trade', *National Institute Economic Review*, 98/4.

Portes, R. and Rey, H. (1998) 'The emergence of the Euro as an international currency', NBER working paper No. 6424.

Rey, H. (1997a) 'International trade and currency exchange', LSE CEP discussion paper No. 322.

Rey, H. (1997b) 'Inflation and moneyness of currencies', *LSE mimeo*.

Swoboda, A. (1969) 'Vehicle currencies and the foreign exchange market: The case of the dollar' in *International Market of Foreign Exchange*, R. Aliber (ed.) New York: Praeger.

Tavlas, G. (1998) 'The international use of the US dollar: an optimal currency area perspective', *World Economy*, **20**: 707–47.

Tavlas, G. and Ozeki, Y. (1992) *The Internationalization of Currencies: An Apraisal of the Japanese Yen,* IMF Occasional Paper.

Thom, J., Patterson, J. and Boustani, L. (1998) 'The foreign exchange and over-the-counter derivatives market in the United Kingdom', *Bank of England Quarterly Bulletin,* **38**: 347–60.

Discussion of Chapter 11

Alan Sutherland

Chapter 11 tackles an interesting and important question for the future of the euro and it summarises some of the central concepts and quantitative issues. But in the end it leaves many open questions. The main conclusions of the chapter amount to little more than an observation that the euro will be an important international currency and that its use will increase through time. This conclusion is almost certainly correct, but it is very limited. The main problem with the chapter is that it fails to use a clear theoretical framework. Such a framework (based on the Krugman, Chrystal or Rey models cited in the chapter) would have added clarity to the chapter's existing conclusions while allowing the author to provide answers to (or at least to shed more light on) many additional questions.

An example of a point which is less clear than it might have been in the chapter, but which would have been clarified by a model, relates to the euro's eventual status relative to the dollar. The author correctly points out that all the major models predict multiple equilibria in the selection of an international vehicle currency. The chosen vehicle currency benefits from network externalities which reinforce its position. These externalities eventually come to dominate the underlying factors (such as trade in goods or financial assets) which caused the incumbent vehicle currency to be selected in the first place. These externalities are crucial to determining the eventual position of the euro. The fact that the euro will be a major currency simply because of the size of the Eurozone will certainly reduce transactions cost for euro trading. But in itself this is highly unlikely to be enough to outweigh the enormous network externalities currently enjoyed by the dollar. Mizen's conclusion that the euro is unlikely to replace the dollar as the most important international currency is therefore reinforced by appeal to the theoretical models.

But this conclusion itself raises a number of other questions which could be analysed within a theoretical model. Even if the euro does not become the main international currency it seems likely that its role as an international currency must increase. But what does this mean and what do the models say about this issue? In terms of the main models it means that a few bilateral markets between the euro and other currencies may develop. Or it may mean that euro financial markets develop a greater international role (while use of the euro in trade transactions remains less developed). But one can envisage other intermediate equilibria. For instance (as is hinted at in the chapter) it is surely possible that the euro will develop a strong regional role in Europe and Africa while the dollar dominates in the rest of the world. In other words there may be equilibria with two vehicle currencies. It would be interesting to develop the theoretical models to investigate what conditions are required to generate different types of intermediate equilibria. This would point the way to empirical work which would provide valuable information about the future role of the euro.

12 Epilogue

David Cobham

My co-editor, George Zis, looked back to the start of the EMS twenty years ago in Chapter 3. In this short epilogue I shall look forward to the prospects for EMU as from its first year of operation, and argue that there are substantial grounds for optimism even though, as always, some things might have been better done differently.

It is worth reflecting first of all on the road that has been travelled to get to this point. European monetary integration is an unprecedented venture, for a number of reasons. One is the lack of a comprehensive political union prior to the creation of a monetary union. A second is the advanced level of monetary/financial technology already in use (by comparison, for example, with the level obtaining at the start of the German or Italian monetary unifications of the nineteenth century), which makes the changeover to a new single currency in the EU context more difficult and more costly. The road to EMU has also been a difficult and sometimes tortuous one, from the first real attention to the issue in the late 1960s through the over-optimistic plans of the Werner Committee to the dark days of fluctuating exchange rates in the mid-1970s; even the establishment of the EMS itself had the explicit aim of creating a zone of monetary stability rather than bringing about monetary union. Moreover, the nature of EMU has changed in some fundamental points along the way, in response to changes in macroeconomic understanding and political perceptions. It is surely inconceivable that any agreement on monetary union made in the 1970s or the early 1980s would have involved quite the institutions (or the timetable) agreed in the Maastricht treaty.

1 THE PROCESS OF MONETARY INTEGRATION

George Zis has clearly shown the extent to which economists (and others) underestimated the likely success of European monetary integration at the start of the EMS. The same failure can be found in later episodes also, notably in the response to the upheavals of 1992–93. At that time many economists reacted by arguing that some major change to the Delors–Maastricht strategy was now needed; in the event no such change was made (other than the acceptance of the wider 15 per cent bands as 'normal'), but EMU still began on the date specified (as the last possible date) in the Treaty. In both cases the underlying reason for so many economists' failure to anticipate success was that they underestimated the political will to bring it about. In part, at least, this must be because the valuation they themselves put on the benefits of wider European integration was low and they assumed that the valuations of others could not be very different. And it must be asked whether some of the criticisms currently directed by economists at EMU – notably those concerning fiscal policy – are not a continuation of the mistakes of the past.

While the story of European monetary integration over the 1980s and 1990s is a story of largely unwavering political commitment by a range of continental European leaders, those leaders have at the same time shown a remarkable ability to make technical adjustments in the light of good technical advice (for example, in the choice of conversion rates which was in the end handled very smoothly). Thus, although economists as a profession repeatedly got the likely overall outcome wrong, they were able to make a major contribution in recommending appropriate arrangements to be adopted both on the way to the intended objective and for the operation of that objective. In addition they played a role in the remarkable changes in public and political perceptions in many countries over the period about key aspects of monetary policy, such as the nature of the long run trade-off between inflation and unemployment and the value of central bank independence, although those changes also took place partly in response to events and experience.

The process of convergence in terms of the Maastricht criteria (which can be seen as the culmination of a sustained earlier period of more broadly defined convergence) is discussed in this book in Chapters 4, 5 and 6 on Germany, France and Italy. In each case the extent of fiscal consolidation has been less than economists would have hoped, and – particularly in the German and French cases – the politicians were left looking weak and incompetent. In particular, the application in these cases of criteria for distinguishing between successful and unsuccessful consolidations developed by Alesina and Perotti (1997) suggest failure rather than success. However, it may be that here too economists have been looking for something more clearcut than can be expected: as Chiorazzo and Spaventa argue for the Italian case, an accumulation of a large number of small changes *can* amount in the end to a substantial structural adjustment.

More importantly for the future of EMU, the Stability and Growth Pact sets out some serious constraints on fiscal policy which – although they have been widely criticised – can be defended as a way of ensuring 'monetary' dominance rather than 'fiscal' dominance, where the latter has 'unpleasant monetarist arithmetic' effects (Artis and Winkler, 1998). It is possible that the constraints will not be applied in a binding way, since they depend on agreements between national governments. But, just as EMU in the end started at the date specified in the Treaty, here too it is important not to underestimate the strength of formal agreements at the EU level: while economists brought up on Coasian analysis often assume that agents will renegotiate any agreements or regulations which are against all their various interests, in the continental European tradition laws and agreements are much less open to such renegotiation (as exemplified by the adherence to the Maastricht Treaty strategy after the upheavals of 1992–93) and there must therefore be an expectation that the Pact will be largely adhered to.

It is also possible that those who are pessimistic about fiscal policies under EMU are systematically misreading Euroland politicians. The Jospin government in France since June 1997, for example, was widely perceived from the UK as 'Old Labour', and indeed much of its rhetoric was of that sort, but its actions have often been much closer to 'New Labour'. Much of the rhetoric of the new German Minister of Finance, Oskar Lafontaine, against the ECB may similarly turn out to be hot air rather than the harbinger of policies which could endanger EMU.

2 MONETARY POLICY UNDER EMU

Chapter 2 by Vítor Gaspar and others provides the most detailed and comprehensive account so far available of the monetary policy strategy of the ECB. In broad terms this can be characterised as a strategy of pragmatic discretion within a framework of rules, or as a combination of monetary and inflation targeting. The evolution of this strategy provides further evidence of the ability of European policymakers to make technical adjustments in response to convincing technical arguments (such as those emphasising the difficulties of operating monetary targets in the face of likely money demand shifts), while cleaving to their original underlying aims. But the ECB now finds itself facing criticism on the issue of accountability and transparency: it does not intend to publish the minutes of its Governing Council meetings until many years later, and the way in which different national central bank governors or ECB Board members voted will not be made public either.

This is an awkward issue, only briefly touched upon in this volume in comments by Goodhart and Haldane. To some extent the concept of accountability was promoted by Bank of England authors such as Briault *et al.* (1996), at a time when the Bank's own independence was strictly limited. These authors constructed a measure of central bank accountability, along similar lines to conventional indices of central bank independence. They found that the Bank of England was the most accountable of their sample of central banks, and the Bundesbank (on which the ECB was largely modelled, in this area as in others) the least accountable. They also argued that the empirical evidence suggested an inverse relationship between independence and accountability, which could be interpreted in terms of less independent CBs trying to compensate for their lack of independence and to strengthen their credibility by making greater efforts to operate in a transparent and accountable way. However, the Briault *et al.* measure of accountability is open to at least as many criticisms as conventional indices of CB independence, and alternative perspectives can be found, for example in Bini Smaghi (1998) which stresses the variety of mechanisms of accountability and also argues that the ECB will be accountable.

A useful way of shedding some light on the issue is to return to the time-inconsistency literature and the rationale for central bank independence. While it is true that the original time-inconsistency arguments of Kydland and Prescott (1977) are in terms of a social planner trying to maximise a social welfare function, much later discussion (for example Cukierman, 1992) emphasises in part the possibility that politicians and governments pursue their own objectives which are different from society's. Such discussion can easily come to view governments' behaviour as devious or even malicious to an extent that is difficult to reconcile both with politicians' own self-images and with the existence of a democratic process in which they can be sanctioned by a discriminating electorate for the exclusive pursuit of their own interests. However, Bean (1998) has offered a more plausible explanation of the inflationary bias, namely that governments:

> are expected to deliver a high level of output through the *whole range* of their policies (monetary, fiscal, structural, and so on), and are rewarded by the electorate if they achieve this, and punished if they do not. The level of economic activity thus becomes a signal of government competence. Furthermore the natural rate is not known with any certainty, and the beneficial output effects of monetary policy expansion typically show through a year or so ahead of their effects on inflation. Thus governments, particularly near election time,

may be prepared to risk a more expansionary monetary policy than is really prudent. (Bean, 1998, p. 1799, italics in the original; also quoted by Goodhart, 1999, p. 110).

Bean then goes on to argue that central bank independence should be modelled, not in terms of a central banker with a more inflation-averse loss function, but in terms of a central banker whose loss function contains a term in the variance of output but no term in its level. Thus in Bean's words, '*it is the act of delegation itself that solves the time-inconsistency problem*' (1998, p. 1799, italics in original).

This conception of central bank independence also has implications for the issue of accountability. In the Briault *et al.* view, accountability is a way of compensating for the lack of credibility due to a lack of independence. Hence, accountability is about central banks being obliged to explain and justify their actions, so as to convince the financial markets that they are not in fact pursuing some ulterior motives at variance with some stated aim of price stability, as in the 'devious politician' view of time-inconsistency. But if the act of delegation has solved the time-inconsistency problem, there is no reason for independent central banks to pursue such motives and no reason for the financial markets to suspect that they are doing so. In that case the accountability which is needed for monetary policy to be efficient, for example in the sense of minimising the unemployment costs of price stability, is about central banks providing good explanations of what they are doing *tout court*.

As Bini Smaghi (1998) and Gaspar in Chapter 2 make clear, the ECB will be accountable through a range of mechanisms which include a precise definition of the objective of price stability, announced reference ranges for monetary growth (set on the basis of publicly stated assumptions about the growth of prices, output and velocity), a substantial monthly bulletin and other publications, and public speeches and parliamentary statements by Executive Board and Governing Council members. While the amount of detail that is forthcoming, and the extent to which public statements and publications will respond to specific criticisms, are yet to be seen, it seems likely that the ECB will be able to claim with some justification that it is indeed highly accountable, in the sense of providing the fullest information possible and minimising the uncertainties faced by the financial markets and the private sector. By contrast many of the recent criticisms made of the ECB's unwillingness to publish its minutes, for example, appear to be driven by the 'devious politician' model which is not appropriate here.

3 THE UK AND EMU

Michael Artis has shown clearly in Chapter 7 that, in terms of standard optimum currency area analyses, the economic case for UK entry into EMU is uncompelling. But it is perhaps worth saying something here about the impact on this question of the allocation of interest rate decisions to the Bank of England and its new Monetary Policy Committee as from May 1997.

Initial evaluations of this fundamental, and at the time surprising, change suggested that it would weaken the case for UK entry: once monetary policy had been taken out of the hands of governments the argument that the UK in particular would benefit from having its monetary policy set by an independent ECB, through a more stable monetary policy and lower interest rates (as the result of a reduced risk premium) disintegrated, and it appeared that the UK would have much less to gain now from adopting the single currency. Experience has shown, however, that this was wrong in two respects.

The first is that, even although monetary policy may have been more stable since May 1997 (and it has surely been more closely focused on the objective of price stability – albeit as defined by the government), the exchange rate has not been. Indeed, the rises in UK interest rates during the rest of 1997 and part of 1998 were accompanied by an appreciation of sterling which put sharp pressure on the tradable goods (mainly manufacturing) sector. Instrument independence for the Bank of England seemed, therefore, if anything to reinforce the case for entry into EMU as a way of permanently stabilising the UK's exchange rate with the bulk of its trading partners.

The second point concerns the question of divergence and convergence between the UK and continental European, or Euroland, business cycles. Analyses of business cycle correlations typically focus on relatively long periods, in which the extent of divergence or convergence appears to be a structural phenomenon incapable of quick or easy change. Since the UK government's 'five economic tests' (much criticised by economists such as Buiter (1998) as well as Artis) include the criterion of business cycle convergence, it would be easy to think that this 'test' might be insuperable if the past was a guide to the future.

Empirical research prompted by New Classical work on business cycles has shown that, although cycles clearly exist, they are less regular than sometimes assumed. In the present context what should be emphasised is both major exogenous shocks and policy decisions. It is well known that

German unification (given the policy response of the German government, as discussed by von Hagen and Strauch in Chapter 4) had the effect of prolonging in Germany over 1990 and 1991 a boom which had already peaked in France and other continental countries (and this divergence then led to difficulties and conflicts over the level of interest rates in the EMS). In the UK, on the other hand, the boom of the mid- to late-1980s started earlier and was allowed to go further, in terms of inflation rather than of time, so that the UK went into recession before and more severely than France. The UK then experienced a recovery (boosted by but not entirely due to the depreciation of 'Black Wednesday' in September 1992) earlier than most continental European countries.

If the UK is to enter EMU in the near or even foreseeable future, it seems obvious that some business cycle convergence is highly desirable, if not essential (the example of Ireland might indicate it is the former rather than the latter). As of 1997, then, what was required was that macroeconomic policy should be strongly tightened, to take the top off the gathering boom and to allow a less exuberant but more prolonged expansion during which Euroland might 'catch up' with the UK. Since the use of fiscal policy was heavily restricted for political and policy reasons, a monetary squeeze was the obvious way in which this could occur.

Recent forecasts from the National Institute (1999) provide some evidence that the UK may indeed have embarked on the scenario required. Growth in the UK is forecast to fall from 3.5 per cent in 1997 and 2.5 per cent in 1998 to 1 per cent in 1999, before recovering to 2.5 and 2.6 per cent in 2000 and 2001 respectively. By contrast, the Euro-area is forecast to grow by 2.2 per cent in 1999, as against 2.7 per cent in 1997 and 2.8 per cent in 1998, and then by 2.4 per cent in each of 2000 and 2001. By 2000, then, the UK and Euroland may be more closely in line. Moreover, if the UK is indeed characterised by a more flexible US-type labour market than Euroland (*pace* the arguments of Bazen and Girardin in Chapter 5), the UK ought to be able to aim for a sustained expansion comparable to the US expansion of the 1990s, so that – although UK expansion started earlier – it can continue to expand for as long as the Euro-area is expanding.

4 PROSPECTS

The arguments set out above imply that there are grounds for substantial optimism about EMU, with respect to the ability of European leaders to make sensible pragmatic adjustments when required, with respect to the kinds of fiscal and monetary policies likely to be operated, and with respect to the likelihood that the largest non-EMU EU country, the UK, may be able to join before too long.

The discussion here has also emphasised the contributions economics and economists have made to EMU. EMU is 'our' project as well as European leaders' project, and economists may come out of the experience better in the long run if they acknowledge that. Moreover, given the shifts of public opinion over the last twenty years on macroeconomic and EMU-related issues, EMU can and should be seen as a project in which the peoples of (continental) Europe have played a positive rather than a merely passive role. It is surely this that underlies the political will of European leaders and at the same time constitutes the ultimate basis on which EMU rests.

REFERENCES

Alesina, A. and Perotti, R. (1997) 'Fiscal adjustment in OECD countries: composition and macroeconomic effects', IMF Staff Papers, **44**: 210–48.

Artis, M. and Winkler, B. (1998) 'The Stability Pact: safeguarding the credibility of the European Central Bank', *National Institute Economic Review*, **163**: 87–98.

Bean, C. (1998) 'The new UK monetary arrangements: a view from the literature', *Economic Journal*, **108**: 1795–1809.

Bini Smaghi, L. (1998) 'The democratic accountability of the European Central Bank', *Banca Nazionale del Lavoro Quarterly Review*, **205**: 119–43.

Briault, C., Haldane, A. and King, M. (1996) 'Independence and accountability', Bank of England working paper, No. 49.

Buiter, W., 'Britain and EMU', mimeo, July 1998 (http://www.econ.cam.ac.uk/faculty/buiter/public.htm).

Cukierman, A. (1992) *Central Bank Strategy, Credibility and Independence: Theory and Evidence*, Cambridge, MA: MIT Press.

Goodhart, C. (1999) 'Central bankers and uncertainty', *Bank of England quarterly Bulletin*, **39**: 102–14.

Kydland, F. and Prescott, E. (1977) 'Rules rather than discretion', *Journal of Political Economy*, **85**: 473–92.

National Institute (1999) 'The world economy: recent developments', *National Institute Economic Review*, **167**: 35–69.

Index